Spanish as an International Language

NEW PERSPECTIVES ON LANGUAGE AND EDUCATION
Series Editor: Professor Viv Edwards, *University of Reading, Reading, Great Britain*
Series Advisor: Professor Allan Luke, *Queensland University of Technology, Brisbane, Australia*

Two decades of research and development in language and literacy education have yielded a broad, multidisciplinary focus. Yet education systems face constant economic and technological change, with attendant issues of identity and power, community and culture. This series will feature critical and interpretive, disciplinary and multidisciplinary perspectives on teaching and learning, language and literacy in new times.

Full details of all the books in this series and of all our other publications can be found on http://www.multilingual-matters.com, or by writing to Multilingual Matters, St Nicholas House, 31–34 High Street, Bristol BS1 2AW, UK.

NEW PERSPECTIVES ON LANGUAGE AND EDUCATION
Series Editor: Professor Viv Edwards, University of Reading, Great Britain

Spanish as an International Language
Implications for Teachers and Learners

Deborah Arteaga and Lucía Llorente

MULTILINGUAL MATTERS
Bristol • Buffalo • Toronto

Library of Congress Cataloging in Publication Data
A catalog record for this book is available from the Library of Congress.
Arteaga-Capen, Deborah.
Spanish as an International Language: Implications for Teachers and Learners
Deborah Arteaga-Capen and Lucia Llorente.
New Perspectives on Language and Education: 14.
Includes bibliographical references and index.
1. Spanish language--Study and teaching--Foreign speakers. 2. Spanish language--
Variation. 3. Second language acquisition. I. Llorente, Lucía I. (Lucía Isabel) II. Title.
PC4127.8.A83 2006
467'.009–dc22 2009017376

British Library Cataloguing in Publication Data
A catalogue entry for this book is available from the British Library.

ISBN-13: 978-1-84769-172-9 (hbk)
ISBN-13: 978-1-84769-171-2 (pbk)

Multilingual Matters
UK: St Nicholas House, 31–34 High Street, Bristol BS1 2AW, UK.
USA: UTP, 2250 Military Road, Tonawanda, NY 14150, USA.
Canada: UTP, 5201 Dufferin Street, North York, Ontario M3H 5T8, Canada.

The policy of Multilingual Matters/Channel View Publications is to use papers
that are natural, renewable and recyclable products, made from wood grown in
sustainable forests. In the manufacturing process of our books, and to further
support our policy, preference is given to printers that have FSC and PEFC Chain
of Custody certification. The FSC and/or PEFC logos will appear on those books
where full certification has been granted to the printer concerned.

Typeset by Techset Composition Ltd., Salisbury, UK.
Printed and bound in Great Britain by Short Run Press Ltd.

Contents

Acknowledgements

While writing this book, we presented our ideas in scores of conferences. Needless to say, we could never have finished this volume if not for the audiences at those scholarly meetings, because they gave us invaluable feedback and more ideas for the text. We wish to particularly thank Linda McManness of Baylor University and Antxon Olarrea, University of Arizona, two wonderful friends and terrific scholars and critics. In addition, our experience coordinating both Spanish Teaching Assistants and Part-time Instructors in Spanish has left us with a clear view of the challenges that first-language (L1) and second-language (L2) speakers, students, and teachers face. We thank both the instructors whom we have overseen throughout the years, as well as our students, for the insight that they have given us.

We must also express our deep gratitude to every one of our professors, including Heles Contreras, the late Victor Hanzeli, Julia Herschensohn, Jürgen Klausenburger, Fritz Newmeyer, Carlos Otero, the late Judith Strozer, and Karen Zagona, to all of whom we owe special gratitude. Deborah's thanks extends to scholars in other fields who have been unswerving in their kindness and understanding, particularly Michael Bowers, Jim Christensen, Diane Donovan-Vaughn, Christopher C. Hudgins, and Shaily Jain. We also send a special acknowledgement to Viv Edwards, Marjukka Grover and Anna Roderick, extraordinary editors at *Multilingual Matters*, as well as to all of their staff, for encouraging us on this book and for publishing it in such a timely matter.

Finally, we dedicate this volume to our family members, who have, in every way possible, helped us see this project to fruition. Our dedication, therefore, is a joint one: Deborah Arteaga wishes to thank Denise Meredith, Mary Meredith, Robert Meredith, Becca, Rachelet, and Yoli for all of their love and support during the writing of this book. Lucía would like to express her deep gratitude and great love to her mother and father, Isabel and the late Ladicio Llorente.

Spanish as an International Language

We are grateful to the following companies for permission to reproduce various figures and tables:

Map on p. 9 and p. 37 has been reprinted from Teschner, Richard, *Camino Oral*, 2nd edition © 2000, p. 186. Reprinted by permission of McGraw-Hill, New York.

Diagram of speech organs on p. 32 has been reprinted from Bergmann, A., Currie Hall, K. and M. Ross, S. *Language Files: Materials for an Introduction to Language and Linguistics*, 9th edition © 2004, p. 51. Reprinted by permission of the Ohio State University Press, Columbus, Ohio.

Tables on pp. 97–98, pp. 100–101 have been reprinted/adapted from Azevedo, Milton, M., *Introducción a la lingüística española*, 1st edition © 1992, pp. 344, 345, 347. Reprinted by permission of Pearson Education, Inc., Upper Saddler River, NJ.

Three definitions (*leg, pay, pelo*) on pp. 157–160 have been reprinted from Styles Carvajal, C. and Horwood, J. (eds), *Oxford English/Spanish Dictionary*, © 1999, pp. 570, 1280, 1388, 1389. Reprinted by permission of Oxford University Press, Oxford, England.

Exercises on pp. 173–176 have been reprinted from Salaberry, Rafael; Barrette, Catherine M., Elliot, Phillip; Fernández-García, Marisol, *Impresiones*, 1st edition © 2004, pp. 32, 144, 214, 322. Reprinted by permission of Pearson Education, Inc., Upper Saddle River, NJ.

Exercises on pp. 176–179 have been reprinted from Hershberger, R., Navey-Davis, S. and Borrás Álvarez, G. *Plazas. Lugar de encuentros*, 3rd edition © 2008, pp. 194, 226, 309. Boston, Thomson-Heinle.

Exercises on p. 176, pp. 181–185 have been reprinted from Knorre, M., Dorwick, T., Pérez-Gironés, M., Glass, W. and Villarreal, H. *Puntos de Partida: An Invitation to Spanish*, 8th edition © New York: McGraw-Hill.

Chapter 1
Linguistics Perspectives on Spanish in a Pluricentric Society: Who Cares How They Speak? *Why Variation in the Spanish Language is Important*

1.1 Introduction

Currently, Spanish enjoys a position of tremendous importance among the world's languages. Indeed, with over 330,000,000 speakers, Spanish is now considered to be the second most widely spoken language in the world (Summer Institute for Linguistics (SIL) Ethnologies Survey, 1999). The perfusion of Spanish is also felt here in the United States. According to the Census of 2000, there are over 28,000,000 Spanish speakers in the United States, a 61.70% increase over the numbers of Spanish speakers reported in the 1990 census. This growth in the Spanish-speaking population in the United States affects all parts of the country, as seen in (1) below, which illustrates the increase in the number of Spanish speakers from 1990 to 2000, by region (U.S. Census Bureau, 2003: 7):

(1) Spanish Spoken at Home by the Population 5 Years and Over: 1990 and 2000.

Area	1990	2000	Percent change
United States	17,345,064	28,101,052	62.0
Region			
Northeast	3,133,043	4,492,168	43.4
Midwest	1,400,651	2,623,391	87.3
South	5,815,486	9,908,653	70.4
West	6,995,884	11,076,840	58.3

How does this nationwide growth of Spanish affect those in the United States? From a cultural perspective, one cannot help but notice the nation-wide dissemination of the Spanish language. All one has to do is call a financial institution or other business to be given the option of pressing 'one' for English or 'two' for Spanish. Spanish is heard daily throughout the United States, in grocery stores, doctors' offices, nail salons, movie theaters, and schools. There are several television channels and radio stations devoted exclusively to programming in Spanish, and Spanish books, magazines, and newspapers are seen in every venue in the United States where their English counterparts are sold. Schools, from grammar school to high school to higher education, have felt the impact of the growth of Spanish as well. According to García *et al.* (2007) approximately 5.5 million school age students are not native speakers of English; 80% of these students speak Spanish at home.

With respect to universities across the United States, the impact of the unprecedented growth in Spanish is reflected in the enrollment patterns in university-level language classes. According to the most recent survey of the Modern Language Association, over 823,035 students were enrolled in Spanish classes in institutions of higher education in the fall of 2006. This number far outweighs the combined enrollment of students in *all* other languages, namely 700,204 students (Furman *et al.*, 2006).[1] Indeed, in the fall of 2006, Spanish enrollment constituted 52.2% of total foreign language enrollment at the university level (Furman *et al.*, 2006: 20). The instruction of Spanish is therefore of extreme importance to many institu-tions of universities and community colleges across the country.

This tremendous growth in Spanish presents several challenges for high-school and university-level instruction for several reasons. One is adminis-trative, in that it is often difficult to schedule enough sections for Spanish language classes. Another is that because of this tremendous increase, many of the introductory Spanish language classes at large institutions are not taught by tenured or tenure-track faculty members. They are instead assigned to adjuncts or Teaching Assistants, whose linguistic preparation may vary widely; there may or may not be any formal coordination of these instructors. For example, at a large public institution in the Southwest United States, of 40 sections of first-year Spanish language offered a few years ago, only one was taught by a full-time faculty member. However, regardless of the instructor in question, we believe that specialized instruc-tor training is needed for Spanish because of its unique characteristics.

In this book we argue that the most important linguistic aspect of Spanish that instructors and students of Spanish need to understand is the notion of variability (regional/sociolinguistic). Crucial to our discussion is the adoption of a descriptive, not prescriptive, view of language.[2] A descriptive view of language makes no value judgment regarding regional or social variation, whereas a prescriptive view holds one variety (typically that of the upper class in a given country) as superior to others. For example, a prescriptive view of language would reject (2a) in favor of (2b), despite the fact that most native speakers say (2a), as they feel that it is gender neutral:

(2) (a) *Everyone has their book.*
    (b) *Everyone has his book.*

A descriptive view of language would accept both (2a) and (2b), in recognition of the fact that the English language has evolved to reflect sociological change. In other words, the pronoun *their* is used to indicate *his* or *her*, whereas (2b) is considered by many to be sexist, in that it is felt to only represent males. An example in Spanish can be found in (3a) and (3b); again, those who hold a prescriptive view of language will reject (3b) even though many native speakers prefer it over (3a):

(3) (a) *¿Qué hora es?* 'What time is it?' (literally, 'What hour is it?')
    (b) *¿Qué horas son?* 'What time is it' (literally, 'What hours are they?')

As is the case for most, if not all, divergences between prescriptive norms, as in (3a), and language as it is used, as in (3b), the former make less sense to the native speaker. This is because only one hour, 1:00 a.m. or 1:00 p.m., uses the singular verb *es* 'is.' All of the others, from 2:00 a.m. to 12:00 p.m. to 12:00 a.m. or 12:00 p.m., use the plural form *son* 'are'.

In the past, a prescriptive view of language was shared by most, if not all, language instructors, at both the high school and college level, as discussed in detail in Chapter 5. Vestiges of prescriptivism can still be seen today in Spanish textbooks; many language teachers continue to embrace this viewpoint. Indeed, our students, particularly our college students, are, in fact, taught to be hyperliterate. However, we believe that such a perspective does not serve our students well, because it does not give them the flexibility that they need to truly communicate with Spanish native speakers of varying nationalities and social classes. As discussed in detail in Chapter 6, we advocate instead the presentation for active knowledge of a standard variety of Spanish, by which we mean a regionally and sociolinguistically neutral variety that cuts across regional and social differences. For the purposes of the L2 classroom, we believe that the term *academic Spanish* is preferable to *standard Spanish*, as it carries with it no negative sociolinguistic judgment, and it is accurate.[3] We next consider regional variability (dialects) in Spanish.

1.2 Regional Variation of Spanish

Dialectal variation, or regional differences in speech, is a feature of natural language. All languages of the world have dialects, that is, varieties of the language that are particular to a group of speakers. Sometimes, the term dialect is tinted negatively, as it is associated with varieties that are considered stigmatized (as we discuss below). When we use this term throughout this book, however, we simply refer to 'any variety of a language spoken by a group of people that is characterized by systematic differences from other varieties of the same language in terms of structural or lexical features' (Bergmann *et al.*, 2007: 301). All speakers of a language speak a dialect; in fact, individual speakers speak an idiolect (individual variation in speech). An example of a dialect in the English spoken in the United States would be the dialect spoken in the Southern United States, compared, for example, to the one spoken in New York City.

It is not always easy to determine whether two or more language varieties are indeed distinct dialects of the same language or, rather, two separate languages. In order to make that distinction, the criterion of mutual intelligibility is often used: if the speakers of two language varieties, which show systematic differences, can understand each other, then we are in the presence of dialects of the same language. This criterion does not always work properly, as we need to consider the situation that is referred to as *dialect continuum*. In such a case, we find a large number of dialects; each of them is closely related to the next, and therefore mutually intelligible. The dialects at both ends of the continuum, however, are so different systematically that speakers cannot, in fact, understand each other. Furthermore, there are also cultural and historical differences that make the distinction between language and language variety (or dialect) difficult.

For example, in China, Cantonese, Fukien, and Mandarin are not considered to be mutually intelligible. Yet even the native speakers of these varieties (who share the same nationality) consider them dialects of the same language, because they use the same writing system, which is intelligible by all literate speakers. This view is the official position of the Chinese government, for political reasons. The Catalan language, on the other hand, which originated in Cataluña, a region in North Eastern Spain, has regional varieties, such as Valenciano (spoken in the Comunidad Valenciana) and Mallorquín (spoken in the Balearic Islands). These varieties of Catalan evince minor yet systematic differences in the areas of the lexicon (vocabulary), morphosyntax (rules of sentence and word formation), and phonology (sound system). They therefore should be considered dialects of the same language. However, again for political reasons, many would argue that they are separate languages. As Posner (1996: 338) points out, in all these arguments 'myths of separate ancestry play more part than linguistic classification'.[4]

It is important to note that, even if dialects may vary, no dialect is structurally superior to another. The popular notion of dialect is that there is only one correct form of a language (generally, the one used by the speaker), but in fact the standard varies from dialect to dialect. Hazen (2001) provides an interesting example. In normal US Southern pronunciation, the words *pin* and *pen* are pronounced the same. Some other US dialects, however, make a distinction between the vowels in these words, when they appear before an /n/. The speakers of these latter dialects may consider the Southern pronunciation incorrect, when in truth it is simply different.

With respect to regional variation, however, the unique nature of Spanish in this regard cannot be overemphasized, because of its pluricentricity, meaning that it has several centers of prestige (e.g. Madrid, Bogotá, Buenos Aires, Caracas, Mexico City, Lima and San José), as noted by Teschner (2000).[5] As a result, in Spanish, there is not one single 'standard' variety across dialects; each dialect has, rather, its own standard variety.[6] The situation of Spanish is therefore in contrast to a monocentric language, like French, in which only one dialect (Parisian French) is considered to be the standard.[7]

This is not to say, however, that there are no prestige dialects in Spanish. This notion is expressed by Lipski (1994: 14–15), who argues that when moving from the written to the spoken language, what is considered standard spoken Spanish allows a good deal of variety in practice, with the existence of competing prestige norms being evident. Indeed, the prestige norm is frequently based on the speech of the educated inhabitants of the capital of a given country. In larger, more complex societies where there is greater fragmentation, however, the norm may be located elsewhere. This is the case in Spain, for example, where the educated, urban speech of Old Castile and principally of the cities of Burgos and Valladolid is more likely to be adopted as a standard than that of Madrid. In the capital city, high inward migration from other parts of Spain and population mobility in general lead to the coexistence of many varieties of Spanish.

As for Latin America, Lipski notes that the speech of the Colombian capital of Bogotá is losing much of its former prestige. Similarly, in Peru, while the prestige norm of the capital Lima is still implicit in news media and education, in reality this norm has ceased to exist and there is a fragmentation into popular varieties. Mexico City and Buenos Aires differ in that they manage to impose their prestige norm over considerable heterogeneity. Once we reach the level of non-standard spoken Spanish, however, divergences may be such that certain varieties are mutually incomprehensible.

The pluricentric nature of Spanish is highly relevant to university-level Spanish language classes in the United States, because Spanish speakers in the United States hail from a variety of Spanish-speaking regions, as seen in the diagram in (4)[8]; Guzmán (2001: 2):

(4)

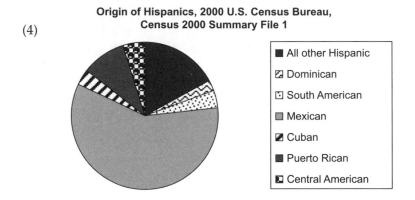

Origin of Hispanics, 2000 U.S. Census Bureau, Census 2000 Summary File 1

■ All other Hispanic

▨ Dominican

▱ South American

▢ Mexican

▨ Cuban

■ Puerto Rican

▨ Central American

Given the range of dialects spoken, Spanish students will therefore inevitably come into contact with markedly different dialects of Spanish. This exposure to different dialects may occur at school, through their instructors or fellow students, during travel or study abroad, through interactions with native speakers, or at work, through Spanish-speaking colleagues. Many Spanish students, known as heritage speakers, also speak Spanish at home, and therefore bring to class familiarity with a specific dialect of Spanish. Valdés (2000: 1) describes how the term *heritage speaker* is used in the United States:

> Within the foreign language teaching profession in the United States, the term 'heritage speaker' is used to refer to a student of language who is raised in a home where a non-English language is spoken, who speaks or merely understands the heritage language, and who is to some degree bilingual in English and the heritage language (...). For the most part, the experiences of these heritage speakers have been

similar. They speak or hear the heritage language spoken at home, but they receive all of their education in the official or majority language of the countries in which they live. What this means is that, in general, such students receive no instruction in the heritage language. They thus become literate only in the majority language.

Despite the similarity of experiences, then, heritage speakers are not a homogeneous group, since their mastery of the heritage language varies in degree. These speakers are also diverse in terms of origin, as discussed in Section 1.2. Many heritage language speakers enroll in our Spanish classes with the objective of learning the standard variety of the language, a mastery of which would offer them valuable opportunities, both social and professional. Their goals can be integrative, in the sense of Gardner and Lambert (1972), in that these students seek greater identification with their family's culture. Conversely, they may study academic Spanish with an instrumental aim, in which case improving their Spanish will help them to meet career goals, or because of other practical motivations. Only a few US universities have Spanish language programs specifically addressed to heritage speakers, programs taught by instructors trained to address the special circumstances of students who speak Spanish at home.

In smaller institutions, where enrollment numbers and economic constraints do not permit separate classes for native and non-native speakers, heritage language students are placed in regular Spanish classes, which serve all types of students. Regardless of the class in which they are enrolled, heritage speakers come into our classrooms with all the characteristics mentioned above: heterogeneity as far as their geographical origin and social background are concerned, multiple degrees of mastery of their heritage language and, quite often, a lack of awareness of the differences between the language spoken in their community and the academic variety.

Another challenge faced by all students is that instructors of Spanish, both native speakers and non-native speakers, will themselves represent various dialects of Spanish. Therefore, all of our students, first language (L1) and second language (L2) speakers of Spanish, alike, may be exposed to strikingly divergent dialects in the classroom from one semester to the next, as their instructor changes. Unfortunately, many instructors lack a background in linguistics. Such instructors may be thus unaware of the existence of dialectal variation in Spanish or may hold a prescriptive view of language. In either case, they may lack knowledge regarding effective ways of addressing the issue of the pluricentricity of Spanish. Indeed, they may believe that one variety (often the one that they speak) is superior to all others.

These instructors, like Spanish speakers who have attended high school in Spanish-speaking countries, oftentimes accept the authority of the *Real Academia Española* (RAE) as the final word in language matters.[9] The RAE is a prestigious, influential scholarly institute based in Spain, with a highly prescriptive viewpoint regarding the Spanish language. Its focus has traditionally been Peninsular Spanish, although it is slowly beginning to recognize other dialects. Instructors and heritage speakers alike are often totally unaware that each Spanish-speaking country has a language academy.[10] As discussed in more detail in Section 1.4, such an attitude can negatively impact students in the Spanish language classroom, particularly in the case of our heritage speakers. It can make them self-conscious about the dialect or sociolect that they speak or, conversely, critical of the dialects spoken by other heritage speakers.[11]

We stress throughout this book that it is important for Spanish instructors to present a descriptive view of dialectal differences, particularly given the pluricentric nature of Spanish. One effective way to do this is to familiarize students with the general dialect areas of Spanish, and to show them that dialects vary in tightly controlled ways. We begin with a presentation of the dialectal division, which we will follow in this book.

1.3 Major Dialect Areas of Spanish

For pedagogical purposes, we advocate a broad, macrodialectal approach to dialect areas, which will differ according to the aspect of language being discussed (e.g. phonology vs. morphology). As discussed in detail in Chapter 2 for phonology, we support presenting an outline focusing on processes, with an emphasis on four broad dialectal regions, as follows (5):

(5) (a) *las tierras altas* 'highlands' (also called *la zona alteña/el español alteño*)[12]
     (b) *las tierras bajas* 'lowlands' (also called *la zona bajeña/el español bajeño*)
     (c) *el Río de la Plata* region 'the River Plate area' (e.g., Argentina, Chile, Paraguay and Uruguay)
     (d) *Castile* (also called *la zona castellana/el español castellano*)

By *tierras altas*, we are referring, following Alonso (1982), to the highlands of Mexico and South America; by *tierras bajas* we mean the coastal areas of Latin America as well as Andalusia (Andalucía). The map below indicates the dialectal division of Latin America and Spain.

(6)   Dialectal regions of Spanish (Teschner 2000: 186)

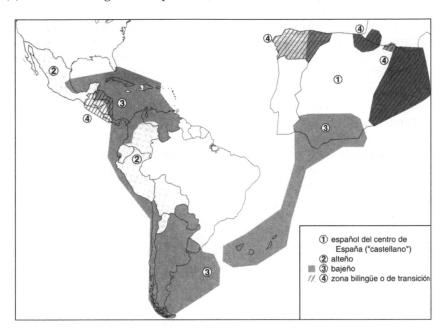

(1) español del centro de
    España ("castellano")
(2) alteño
■ (3) bajeño
// (4) zona bilingüe o de transición

We advocate this division because it allows us to vastly simplify dialectal variation in phonology without sacrificing accuracy. Moreover, while dialects within these macrodialectal divisions are far from uniform in their phonology, they nonetheless share many salient traits. Such characteristics can be presented to students in the form of phonological processes. Finally, because the two groups, *tierras altas/tierras bajas*, span such large geographical areas, a culturally focused presentation will allow for recycling and expansion of information regarding dialectal variation.

With respect to morphosyntax, we propose a simpler dialect division: Latin America and Spain, as discussed in more detail in Chapter 3. We believe that with few exceptions, most morphological and syntactic features can be addressed as a regional variation of one of these two main areas. As discussed in Chapter 4, regional variation in the lexicon is perhaps the most challenging to pigeonhole. We therefore advocate an approach to the lexicon that focuses on the indigenous languages (e.g. Taino, Nahuatl, etc.) of the regions in question (or the lack thereof, as in Spain). We make an exception for Spanish of the Southwest, which we consider to be a different dialectal area due to English influence.

As discussed in Section 1.2, in our view, students will tend to embrace the pluricentricity of Spanish if they are presented with the notion that dialects vary one from another in systematic ways. Indeed, regional variation is manifested in the phonology, the morphosyntax, and the lexicon of a language. Given the nature of dialectal variation in Spanish, we advocate a different approach for each of these subfields of language, which we discuss in more detail below in subsequent chapters. We next turn to a discussion illustrating how dialects can vary regionally, beginning with the phonology of Spanish.

1.3.1 Regional variation in the phonology of Spanish

Variation in phonology is popularly known as *accent*.[13] For example, the speech of a New Yorker is clearly different from the speech of a Texan. The phonological systems of the dialects of Spanish are no less striking. The pluricentric nature of Spanish will be manifested in our classroom in pronunciation, for several reasons. First and foremost, the speech of instructors (including TAs) will reflect certain regional phonological characteristics, which may differ widely. As instructors, we therefore have many decisions to make regarding pronunciation. Assuming that one goal of second language (L2) instruction within a Communicative Approach should be for students to acquire native-like pronunciation (cf. Arteaga, 2000), which regional variety of Spanish pronunciation should be actively taught in our Spanish language classrooms?

Consider the regional variation regarding the pronunciation of *ll*. If we as instructors are from Argentina, for example, do we teach students (or even model), *žeísmo*, as in (7)?

(7) *žeísmo* (River Plate countries)[14]
   calle 'street' [káʒe] or [káʃe]

In this dialectal variant, *ll* and *y* are pronounced as [ʒ] or [ʃ], so that *calle* 'street' is pronounced [káʒe].[15] This pronunciation, which is not found outside the *Río de la Plata* area in South America, contrasts, for example, with the *yeísmo* of most of Mexico, where *calle* is generally pronounced [káje] as in (8)[16]:

(8) *yeísmo* (Andalucía, most of Latin America)
   calle 'street' [káje]

This, in turn, contrasts with the *lleísmo* of the Andes and North Central Spain, in which *ll* represents [λ], so that *calle* is pronounced [káλe]; this is illustrated in (9)[17]:

(9) *calle* 'street' [káλe] (North Central Spain, the Andes)

From the students' perspective, it is easy to see how this variation in pronunciation may seem quite bewildering. They may not understand why one instructor *sounds* different from another or from other Spanish speakers with whom they interact, at work, at home, or while traveling. Even if a new instructor does not insist that students model his or her pronunciation, this sometimes dizzying variety will affect both students' own pronunciation and comprehension of speech. In our view, students need a guidepost for the regional pronunciation that they should adopt in their own speech. They must also be taught to avoid what Arteaga (2000) has referred to as the "cafeteria approach", by which she means adopting salient features from a variety of dialects. It is not uncommon in our first and second year classes to hear students who have adopted the distinción from North Central Spain (in which *z*, *ce* and *ci* are pronounced [θ]) along with the *žeísmo* of the River Plate countries (*y* and *ll* pronounced as [ʒ]), two features that never co-occur naturally in a single dialect![18]

We believe that Spanish instructors must therefore have the linguistic tools to help students make sense of these pronunciation alternates by making good critical use of the information provided to them in textbooks. As argued in detail in Chapter 2, given the pluricentric nature of Spanish in the United States, even as students adopt a stable regional pronunciation, they must be taught to *understand* pronunciations from other dialects areas, if we are to achieve communicative competence through our classes. In other words, students must be taught to understand [káʒe] for *calle* (7) even if they themselves pronounce it as [káje] (8). This is no less important for our heritage speakers, who bring with them to the classroom a regional pronunciation. In the next section, we discuss regional morphosyntactic variation in Spanish.

1.3.2 Regional variation in the morphosyntax of Spanish

As discussed in Section 1.2, the term morphosyntax refers both to word formation (morphology) and to how phrases are combined (syntax). In this way, morphosyntax represents the intersection between morphology and syntax, hence its name. Dialects in Spanish vary a great deal with respect to morphology; this is considered in detail in Chapter 3. Consider a seemingly simple example: *vosotros* 'you-pl-inf'.[19] Used in Spain exclusively, this pronoun is the plural counterpart of the informal second person singular *tú* 'you-sg-inf'. It corresponds to *ustedes* 'you-pl-inf' of Latin America. Examples (10) and (11) illustrate this basic dialectal difference in morphology:

(10) (a) Spain

      ¿Habláis (vosotros) español? 'Do you-pl-inf speak Spanish?'

(b) Latin America
  ¿Hablan (ustedes) español? Do you-pl inf/form speak Spanish?
  (=8a)
(11) Spain and Latin America
  ¿Hablas (tú) español? 'Do you-sg-inf speak Spanish?'

The *vosotros* form, used mainly in Northern/Central Spain, is the plural of *tú*. In Latin America, on the other hand, the *ustedes* form does double duty, as the plural of both *tú* and *usted*. In Spain, the *ustedes* form is only the plural of *usted*.

Both regions concur, however, with respect to the formal second person pronoun (with a third person verb form), using both singular *usted* and plural *ustedes* 'you-pl-inf/form', as illustrated by examples (12) and (13)[20]:

(12) Spain and Latin America
  ¿Habla (Ud). español?
(13) Spain and Latin America
  ¿Hablan (ustedes) español?

The variation in question is not limited to the subject form of address, as *vosotros* also has a corresponding object pronoun, *os* (you-informal-pl, direct and indirect object), as well as a corresponding possessive, *vuestro* (your-informal-pl) as in (14)–(16)[21]:

(14) (a) Spain
      Os veo mañana.
    (b) Latin America
      Los veo mañana.
      (=14a)
(15) (a) Spain
      El perrito tiene miedo de vosotros.
    (b) Latin America
      El perrito tiene miedo de ustedes.
      (=15a)
(16) (a) Spain
      ¿Tenéis vuestro libro?
    (b) Latin America
      ¿Tienen su libro?
      (=16a)

As *vosotros* and its related forms are not used in Latin America, students who do not travel to Europe or otherwise come into contact with Spaniards will never hear these forms. The exception would be perhaps in a Spanish class taught by a speaker of Castilian Spanish. Should *vosotros* then be taught in first-year university-level language classes in the United States? If so, how? These and other related issues are discussed in detail in Chapter 6. University-level textbooks have traditionally skirted the issue by including *vosotros* in all verbal paradigms while noting with a footnote that the form is used exclusively in Spain.[22]

Generally speaking, dialects vary less with respect to syntax (i.e. word order) than to the other subcomponents of language. An example of a syntactic difference between Caribbean Spanish (especially the Spanish spoken in Puerto Rico) and other dialects of that geographical area is that given in (17)[23]:

(17) (a) *¿Qué tú quieres?* 'What do you want?'
      (b) *¿Qué quieres (tú)?* 'What do you want?'

Caribbean dialects lack inversion, so that the expression of subject pronouns is compulsory as illustrated in (17a). The canonical (i.e. typical) word order of most other Spanish dialects is that illustrated in (17b), namely WH word (question word), verb and optional subject pronoun, not usually expressed except in cases of emphasis.[24] We next consider regional variation in the lexicon of Spanish.

1.3.3 Regional variation in the lexicon of Spanish

As discussed in Chapter 4, lexical variation is also highly pertinent in Spanish; indeed, the main difference among Spanish dialects is lexical (De Stefano & Rentel, 1975). In the Spanish of Latin America, this variation is in part due to the high number of terms from indigenous languages that have been incorporated into Spanish (Carreira, 2000; Cotton & Sharp, 1988; Hidalgo, 1990). As discussed in more detail in Chapter 4, these languages include Mapuche (spoken in Chile), Maya (spoken by the Mayans in Southern Mexico and Central America), Nahuatl (spoken by the Aztecs in Mexico), Quechua (used by the Incas), Guarani (spoken in Paraguay) and Taino (originally spoken in the Caribbean).

The examples below illustrate how variation is manifested in the lexicon of Spanish. For example, note the indigenous terms in (18) for *pavo* 'turkey' found in use locally in Latin American Spanish (Cotton & Sharp, 1988):

(18) (a) *cócono* from Náhuatl (Mexico)
      (b) *guajolote* from Náhuatl (Mexico)
      (c) *cutz* from Mayan (Mexico)
      (d) *chompipe* from Quechua (Central America)

Lexical variability is no less important for Peninsular Spanish, which evinces different terms according to the geographical area. For example, consider the following:

(19) (a) *vainas* 'green beans' Northen Spain
      (b) *judías verdes* 'green beans,' Other areas
(20) (a) *lavar los platos* 'wash the dishes' Northern Spain
      (b) *lavar la loza* 'wash the dishes' Other areas

Another source of lexical variation in Spain are other languages, such as Basque, English and French. We return in detail to variation in the lexicon of Spanish, both in Latin America and in Peninsular Spanish, in Chapter 4. We next turn to bilingual students and dialectal variation.

1.4   Heritage Speakers and Regional Variation

As noted in Section 1.2, heritage speakers come to our classes already speaking a Spanish dialect. However, they may or may not have awareness of other regional varieties of Spanish. Moreover, they may hold a prescriptive view of their own dialect (in the case of Spanish of the Southwest, for example) or the dialect of others. In our view, it is even more important for heritage speakers than for our beginning students to gain an understanding of regional variation in Spanish. In a study of 26 university-educated Spanish speakers, eight of whom are heritage speakers, Figueroa (2004) notes that they generally hold a descriptive view of Spanish, viewing variety as a normal function of the evolution of the language. In turn, those born and educated in Spanish-speaking countries hold a negative view of Anglicisms and the dialect of Spanish of the Southwest. They may even go so far as to claim that this variety is not a dialect of Spanish. Indeed, this last group of speakers use the term 'Spanglish' for Spanish of the Southwest, which has very negative connotations. Further, they place great stock in the publications of the RAE, considering the organization to be the ultimate resource on 'correct' Spanish.[25] We next present an introduction of sociolinguistic variation in Spanish.

1.5   Sociolinguistic Variation in Spanish

Another way in which human language exhibits variability is in pragmatic usage, or the use of language in context. Pragmatic usage, unlike phonological or morphosyntactic, requires that the speaker understand certain facts about the world (Cook, 2001; Fromkin *et al.*, 2007). For example, the use of metaphor in language, as in (21), presupposes on the part of the hearer an understanding of society (Fromkin *et al.*, 2007: 183).[26]

(21) (a) *The walls have ears.*
      (b) *Entre el pecho y el hecho, hay mucho trecho.*[27]

In (19a), the hearer must understand that people tend to eavesdrop on conversations, historically by pressing their ear to the wall or door. In (19b), the hearer needs to understand that people do not always follow through on promises. In their L1, children's pragmatic linguistic development lags behind their grammatical development, typically developing after the age of four. Their grammatical development is essentially complete by then (cf. Fromkin *et al.*, 2007).

Another example of pragmatic usage is the reference of deictic pronouns (pronouns whose reference depends on context). For example, consider the first and second person pronouns, as in (22) and (23):

(22) (a) *I will finish it.*
      (b) *(Yo) lo voy a acabar.*
(23) (a) *Will you help me?*
      (b) *¿Me ayuda (Ud)?*

The identity of *I* (*yo*) in (22a) and (22b), as well as the identity of *you* (*Ud*) in (23a) and (23b), depends on the context of the utterances. In other words, the speaker in (22a) and (22b) is co-referential (referring to the same noun phrase) with the person who utters the phrase; in (23a) and (23b), *you* (Ud) refers to the hearer being addressed. If a different speaker utters (22) or if (23) is directed at a different hearer, the identities of the pronouns *I* (yo) and *you* (usted) change.

Another aspect of pragmatics is how speakers perform certain speech acts, such as requesting (or demanding) an action, apologizing for an action and conveying politeness. Pragmatic variation is studied by sociolinguists, who research language use within society. Several recent studies on Spanish (cf. Ahern & Leonetti, 2004; Chodorowska-Pilch, 2004; Hernández-Flores, 2004; Murillo, 2002; Márquez Reiter & Placencia, 2004) have focused on these aspects of pragmatics in Spanish. Hernández-Flores, for instance, argues that the chief function of politeness is to mitigate what would potentially otherwise be a loss of face. For example, when a speaker praises another, this would be construed as an attempt to maintain positive face.

Other pragmatic studies contrast the conveyance of speech acts between one dialect of Spanish and another (e.g. Garcia, 2004; Murillo, 2002; Márquez Reiter & Placencia, 2004; Schrader Knissi, 2004).[28] As an example, consider Márquez Reiter and Placencia (2004), who discuss a salesperson's interactions with customers. In their study, they consider data from Montevideo and Quiteño. They conclude that the former are more direct, less formal (i.e. they use *tú/vos* instead of *usted*) and give a great deal more information to the client. The Quiteño speakers are far more formal and establish a much greater distance between the salesperson and the client, proffering relatively little information. For example, consider the following offers of help (Márquez Reiter & Placencia, 2004: 144):

(24) Montevideo[29]
       Salesperson: *Acá está el 8 para que tú te lo pruebes*
(25) Quiteño
       Salesperson: *No: para hacerla a la medida*

In Reiter and Placencia's analysis, the speaker from Montevideo gives more information to the client than the speaker from Quito. In their view, the fact that the speech of the salesperson from Montevideo includes a subordinate clause in the subjunctive *para que tú te lo pruebes* 'so that you (can) try it on' means that the speaker is using a less formal register. The use of the informal pronoun *tú* further underscores the informality of the exchange. In contrast, the clerk from Quito makes an impersonal offer, hence the use of the infinitive *hacer* 'to do/make.'

García (2004) looks at Argentinean reprimands and responses thereto in the male and female populations. She argues that when Argentineans, both male and female, play the roll of boss, they use warnings and threats, as in (26):

(26) *No estoy de acuerdo en que haya llegado tan tarde*[30]

García argues that gender differences among the speakers are seen when the employee gives an explanation. In her view, males tend to reject the explanation, whereas females often accept it.

Another aspect of pragmatics is register (levels of formality of speech) variation, or changes in linguistic forms based on *situational contexts* (cf. Biber, 1995: 7). Mesthrie *et al.* (2000) note that register and traditional dialect study have, to a large extent, been overtaken by interactional sociolinguistics, a field examining how speakers from various backgrounds linguistically interact. They argue, in fact, that the term *register* is potentially problematic as it refers at once to stylistic variation and levels of formality of speech.

In our L1, we frequently engage in style shifting, or the process of adapting our speech to the appropriate level of formality (Bergmann *et al.*, 2007: 410). Style shifting can be a function of phonological variation, as in (27a) and (27b)[31]:

(27) (a) *What's up?* [wʌtsʌp] (formal register)
           [sʌp] (informal register)

(b) *¿Qué hubo?* [kéúβo] (formal register; 3 syllables)[32]
(=27a) [kjúβo] (informal register; 2 syllables)

By eliminating the first syllable in (27a), native speakers are indicating that the register is informal. Similarly, by transforming [kéú] into [kjú] in (27b), the speech is understood to be familiar. Similarly, style shifting can be manifested through morphological variation, as in (28) and (29):

(28) (a) *I have seen* (formal register)
      (b) *I seen* (informal register)
(29) (a) *Dijiste* (*tú* form, formal register)
      (b) *Dijistes* (*tú* form, informal register)

In (28a), the auxiliary *have* is omitted, which is understood by native speakers to signal informal speech. The verb form in the example in (29b) ends in *s*, which indicates that the speech is familiar. Finally, register variation can be expressed through the lexicon. For example, consider the case of a student who comes into contact with Spanish-speaking individuals while working in the medical field. He or she must be aware of a wide variety of lexical choices for medical conditions and even anatomy. This is illustrated by (30) below:

(30) (a) *estómago* 'stomach' (formal, neutral register)
      (b) *panza, barriga, tripa, tampache* 'stomach' (informal register)

Instead of using the register-neutral term for 'stomach' in Spanish, *estómago*, given in (30a), a patient might use one of the other terms given in (30b).[33] The same kind of register variation is found in all fields. We therefore argue in Chapter 4 that it is essential for both L1 and L2 speakers of Spanish to have a grasp of how register can be reflected in the lexicon.

As seen in (27)–(29), within dialects, speakers have access to a range of forms, which they use to adapt their speech to the context. According to Biber (1995: 7), register variation is distinct from dialectal variation in that the former refers to 'situationally defined varieties,' whereas the latter refers to varieties associated with different groups of speakers. A key difference between the two, in his view, is that speakers switch registers as a function of social context; dialectal differences, on the other hand, are regional. Another way of viewing the difference is to consider that registers are defined, in the words of Halliday *et al.* (1964), 'according to use,' whereas dialects are defined 'according to user'.

The goal of this section has been to provide a general overview of register variation in Spanish. We next address the importance of sociolinguistic variation for heritage speakers, arguing that it is especially relevant for such students.

1.6   Sociolinguistics and Heritage Speakers

Another reason why an understanding of register variation is essential for our students is due to the large number of heritage speakers in the United States. According to many researchers, including Valdés (1997), heritage speakers of Spanish lack the ability to switch between registers; indeed, she lists 'Expansion of Bilingual Range' as one of the key goals of Spanish for Native Speakers (SNS) courses. Similarly, Dressler (1982, 1991) argues that non-dominant languages typically become monostylistic as they are only used in a very informal context, while conversing with very well-known conversational partners regarding a very limited range of topics.[34]

Other recent studies yield contradictory results. For example, Sánchez-Muñoz (2007a) considers register variation in the use of the discourse markers shown in (29) by heritage language speakers of Spanish:

(31)   Discourse particles (Sánchez-Muñoz, 2007a: 2)

Spanish	English
Como	*'like'*
así que	*'so'*
entonces	*'so,' 'then'*

She finds that bilingual college students in Los Angeles vary their use of the discourse markers according to register. For example, consider the case of 'quotative *como*,' which is parallel in use to "quotative *like*" in English, as illustrated in (30) (cf. Ferrara & Bell, 1995; Mathis & Yule, 1994; Romaine & Lange, 1991 for a discussion of English *like*):

(32)   *She said, "what are you doing here?" And I'm **like**, "nothing much...."*

Sánchez-Muñoz reports similar data in the informal discourse of heritage language speakers, as in (33)[35]:

(33)   (a) *¿Has visto tú rivalidad entre los negros y los latinos?*
       (b) *Sí, **como**, "oh no hables con ellos."*
       (c) *Me dijo que preguntó, y preguntó algo y ellos **como** "de qué estás hablando."*

Interestingly, Sánchez-Muñoz found that the use of 'quotative *como*' disappeared completely when the heritage language speakers were engaging in a more formal register, in this case, class presentations. She reports similar findings for the discourse markers *así que* 'so', and *entonces* 'so' or 'then.'

However, with respect to lexical variation, Sánchez-Muñoz (2007b) finds that heritage language speakers have few options at their disposal and are therefore unable to adapt their lexical choices in many cases to a more formal register. This inability of many heritage speakers to engage in style shifting may be compounded by the fact that typically, in classrooms as well as in the workforce, the focus may be on the academic register of Spanish. This is particularly the case at levels requiring advanced speech. To meet these students' needs, we must present to them for passive knowledge the notion of register difference, and examples thereof in Spanish. This is discussed in greater detail in Chapter 6. We next discuss an overview of the chapters of this book.

1.7 Preview of Subsequent Chapters

Assuming no prior training in linguistics, we discuss in this volume topics ranging from pronunciation to vocabulary to the importance of diachronic (evolution of a language) information about Spanish, all through a linguistic lens that helps us to bring into sharper focus the most important aspects of the Spanish language in all its variety. In our discussion, we also take into account the unique needs of bilingual speakers who speak Spanish at home. In the chapters that follow, we show how linguistic information will allow Spanish instructors, both native and non-native, to address many of the challenges that they may face in Spanish language classrooms. Both L1 and L2 learners of Spanish, as we will show, benefit from linguistic information.

Chapter 2: *¿Pescado o pehscao?* The Sounds of Spanish in All Their Variety

Phonology, or the study of the sound system of a language, is the focus of this chapter. We begin with a general linguistic introduction to Spanish phonology (and articulatory phonetics). We then turn to dialectal and sociolinguistic variation in Spanish phonology, emphasizing its relevance for both L1 (first language) and L2 (second language) speakers of Spanish residing in the United States. Furthermore, we take into account heritage speakers, whose pronunciation may well manifest some of these variable features. We conclude with an overview of L2 acquisition of phonology, in order for both Spanish L2 learners and instructors to understand the process of phonological acquisition and to know what is and is not reasonable to expect from students.

Chapter 3: *¿Dicen o decís?* Variation in the Forms of Spanish

After an introduction to basic linguistic notions of morphosyntax, this chapter provides an overview of morphosyntactical variation in Spanish, emphasizing its relevance for both beginning and advanced Spanish speakers, as well as for the heritage speakers in our classroom. We consider both regional variation in Spanish morphosyntax (including forms of address, object pronouns and verbal agreement) and sociolinguistic variation (including analogical formation and gender variation). We conclude the chapter by presenting an introduction to the process of L2 acquisition of morphology, with the goal of helping instructors and students alike to better appreciate the difficulty that L2 learners (L1 English or Spanish) may face in effectively acquiring L2 morphosyntax.

Chapter 4: *¿Frijol o habichuela?* Spanish Lexical Variety: Potential and Pitfalls

In this chapter, we consider the Spanish lexicon. After a general introduction, we turn to the extensive regional and social variation with respect to the vocabulary of Spanish. We next discuss the extensive lexical regional variety found in Spanish, not only between Spain and Latin America, but also within dialects of both Peninsular and Latin American Spanish. Following Cotton and Sharp (1988), among others, we note that Latin American vocabulary is characterized by indigenisms and archaisms. We then give specific examples of where language contact has been the source of new words in Peninsular Spanish. Sociolinguistic lexical variation is the next topic that we address, including taboo words, euphemisms and idiomatic expressions (idioms). We end the chapter with a summary of L2 acquisition of vocabulary, noting that the knowledge of words is crucial to comprehension and production of speech.

Chapter 5: They Said *haiga* in *El Mío Cid?* The History of Spanish as a Window to Variation

In this chapter, we consider diachronic linguistics, arguing that an understanding of basic historical facts about Spanish is essential for both instructors and students of Spanish. We begin with a discussion of the importance (or lack thereof) of diachronic linguistics throughout the decades, from its heyday before World War II (WWII) to a topic rarely addressed within the Communicative Approach common today. As we show, much of the variation found in Spanish today, both dialectal and sociolinguistic, can be traced back to earlier stages of the Spanish language. This kind of insight has many benefits, we argue, as it can legitimize linguistic variation in Spanish in the minds of Spanish L1 and L2 instructors and students, including our heritage speakers. Moreover, an understanding of archaic forms as variation can give all speakers of Spanish a sense that evolution is a natural part of human language.

Chapter 6: Textbooks and Tips: How to Use and Enhance Available Resources in the University-level Class

This chapter is highly relevant for (current and future) L2 instructors and students, both native and non-native. It presents highly concrete and specific suggestions regarding the integration of essential information about Spanish dialectal and register variation into university-level classes of all levels. In the case of the lexicon, we also consider Spanish language dictionaries, and how Spanish speakers can be taught to use them. We then turn to a review of three first-year textbooks, *Impresiones*, *Plazas* and *Puntos de partida*, which we believe capture variation in Spanish (dialectal and sociolinguistic). We show that these three books do not present a jumbled or inaccurate picture of variation. Instead, they accurately present many major linguistic aspects related to dialectal and sociolinguistic variety in Spanish.

Chapter 7: Putting it All Together: Linguistics and Variation in the Spanish Language

This chapter ties together the presentation in the preceding six chapters. It begins by revisiting the book's main theme, which is the importance of pluricentricity with regard to Spanish, as reflected in both the regional and sociolinguistic variation of the language. It then turns to a synthesis of the major points presented in Chapters 2, 3 and 4, including phonological, morphosyntactic and lexical variation in the Spanish language. We also summarize the arguments presented in Chapter 5 in favor of integrating diachronic information into the Spanish language classroom, as it makes students aware of the source, and the legitimacy, of much of synchronic variation. We next present a synopsis of Chapter 6, which addresses the topic of integrating variation into the Spanish language classroom, and provides a review of three popular first-year textbooks that we feel best incorporate the notion of variation. We conclude by suggesting sources for further reading.

Chapter 2

¿Pescado o pehscao? *The Sounds of Spanish in All Their Variety*

2.1 Introduction

This chapter focuses on the phonology of Spanish. We begin with a presentation of the International Phonetic Alphabet (IPA; a set of linguistic symbols used to represent speech sounds cross-linguistically), followed by a discussion of articulatory phonetics (production of speech sounds) and a brief introduction to the basic concepts of phonology. We then turn to a discussion of regional variation in the Spanish sound system in keeping with our central theme of variety, followed by an overview of how sociocultural variation is manifested in the phonology of Spanish.[36] In both cases, we take into account the special needs of heritage speakers, followed by a presentation of the current state of the research in the acquisition of L2 phonology. We next address L1 English transfer effects in L2 Spanish. Finally, we conclude by discussing heritage speakers and Spanish phonology.

2.2 The International Phonetic Alphabet

To represent speech sounds, linguists use the IPA instead of orthography. Although there is reasonably good correspondence in Spanish between spelling and pronunciation, certainly less opaque than that found in English, orthography is nonetheless woefully inadequate to represent speech sounds in Spanish for several reasons.[37] First, one letter may represent more than one sound, as in (1)[38]:

(1)   *excelente* 'excellent'

Example (1) illustrates this fact, as the *x* in *excelente* represents the sounds [ks]. Another problem with using orthography to represent speech sounds is that more than one letter can represent a single speech sound, as in (2):

(2)   *silla* 'chair'

In (2), the sound represented by *ll* is a single speech sound, which we represent here somewhat arbitrarily as [j].[39] Spellings for which there is no corresponding sound pose another difficulty for orthography, for example, the *h* in (3):

(3) *hubo* 'there were'

In modern Spanish, the letter *h* is mute, or silent, in most dialects.

As a final problem with the use of orthography in place of the IPA, consider the fact that the same letter can represent more than one sound. For example, consider the spelling *d*. This letter can represent a stop (closure of two articulatory organs; in this instance the tongue touches the back of the upper teeth). However, it can also be pronounced as a fricative (two articulatory organs almost, but not quite, touch). Compare (4) and (5) below:

(4) *¿Cuándo?* 'when?'
(5) *lado* 'side'

Clearly the sounds represented by the *d* in (4) and (5) are not the same. The *d* in (4) is a stop, similar, but not identical, to the *d* sound in *dog*, whereas the *d* in (5) is a fricative, close to the *th* in the English word *this*.[40] To hear the difference, it is only necessary to substitute one sound for the other, which will produce speech with a foreign accent. In summary, given these limitations of orthography, it is clear that another system is needed to represent speech sounds in Spanish.[41] The system that we will use in this book is therefore the IPA.

In the IPA, the five vowels of Spanish are represented as they are spelled, as in (6)[42]:

(6) *mamá* 'mom' [a]
     té 'tea' [e]
     ti 'you' [i]
     no 'no' [o]
     su 'his/her/your' [u]

Spanish has both diphthongs and triphthongs; the former are a combination of a glide followed or preceded by a vowel, as in (7):

(7) *auto* 'car' [aw]
     aislar 'isolate' [aj]
     deuda 'debt' [ew]
     peine 'comb' [ej]
     hoy 'today' [oj]
     ¡Uy! 'yuck!' [uj]

agua 'water' [wa]
huevo 'egg' [we]
ruido 'noise' [wi]
duodécimo 'duodecimal' [wo]
tiara 'tiara' [ja]
tienes 'you have' [je]
murió 'died' [jo]
diurno 'diurnal' [ju]

In dialects of Latin American Spanish, there is only one triphthong (the combination where a strong vowel appears between two glides), found in the word buey 'ox,' [wej], (8a).[43] On the other hand, Peninsular Spanish has quite a few more triphthongs, as illustrated by (8b) and (8c), due to the use of vosotros forms (discussed in Section 3.6.1) in ar verbs whose stem ends in a weak vowel (that is, [i] or [u])[44]:

(8)　(a) buey 'ox' [bwej] Latin American and Peninsular Spanish
　　　(b) continuáis 'you-pl-inf' [kontinwájs] Peninsular Spanish
　　　(c) cambiéis 'you-pl-inf' [kambjéjs] Peninsular Spanish

Transcription of Spanish consonants does not pose much of a problem, as their phonetic representation is transparent (9):

(9)　teléfono 'telephone' [f]
　　　lado 'side' [l]
　　　mi 'my' [m]
　　　papá 'papa' [p]
　　　tú 'you' [t]

The transcription of r, on the other hand, is a function of its position in a word. In word initial position, after l or n, or where it is spelled rr, the sound is a trill (more than three taps of the tongue against the alveolar ridge, which is located directly behind the upper teeth). The trill is represented by the symbol [r̄]. Consider (10) below, in which both r and rr correspond to [r̄]:

(10)　carro 'car' [r̄]
　　　Rodolfo 'Rodolfo' [r̄]
　　　alrededor 'around' [r̄]

The other phonetic manifestation of the spelling r can be the tap or flap (only one tap of the tongue against the alveolar ridge). The flap is represented as [r] in Spanish, as illustrated by (11):

(11)　caro 'expensive' [r]

Another letter whose articulation, and therefore transcription, depends on the sound's position in a word is *b*, as in English *boy*. In absolute initial position (i.e., a word pronounced in isolation or the first sound a speaker makes in an utterance) or after a nasal consonant (*n* or *m*), the sound is a stop. This means that the two articulatory organs, in this case, the speaker's two lips, actually touch. It is transcribed as [b] in (12) and (13)[45]:

(12)   *Baño al perro.* 'I bathe the dog.' [b]
(13)   *invierno* 'winter' [b][46]

When 'b' is intervocalic (between vowels) or follows a liquid consonant, the sound is a fricative, meaning that the articulatory organs get close to each other, but do not touch. In such cases, the sound produced (and transcribed) is [β], as in (14) below:

(14)   *nube* 'cloud' [β]
       alba 'dawn' [β]

A similar distribution can be seen for the sounds represented by the spelling *g*. The sound [g], as in English *gate*, is transcribed as a stop when it is in absolute initial position. Elsewhere it is transcribed as the fricative [ɣ], a sound similar to the *g* in *sugar* (Dalbor, 1996: 209). The examples below illustrate this distribution:

(15)   *gato* 'cat' [g]
       un gusano 'a worm' [ɡ]
(16)   *agua* 'water' [ɣ]
       algo 'something' [ɣ]

The distribution of the stop [d], as in English *dark* and the fricative [ð], similar to the initial sound of English *there*, is slightly different. The stop [d] is not only seen in absolute initial position, following *n* (17), but also following *l*. The fricative is found elsewhere, as illustrated by (18):

(17)   *¡Dámelo!* 'give it to me' [d]
       falda 'skirt' [d]
       andar 'go around' [d]
(18)   *moda* 'style' [ð]
       fardo 'burden [ð]
       ciudad 'city' [ð]

Although there is some dialectal variation, typically the nasals *m* and *n* are homorganic, which means that they match the following sounds with respect to the place of articulation (see Section 2.3.1 below). In other words, sometimes *n* is pronounced [m] or [ŋ] (as in English *thing*) [ɱ]

(as in English *emphasis*) or even [ɲ] (close to the sound in *onion*) or [n̪]
(pronounced with the tip of the tongue against the back of the upper
teeth). Therefore the phonetic symbols used in the transcription for *m* and
n are somewhat more complicated. They are given below (19)[47]:

(19)   (a) *un amigo* 'a friend' [n]
       (b) *un diente* 'a tooth' [n̪]
       (c) *un ganso* 'a goose' [ŋ]
       (d) *invierno* 'winter' [m]
       (e) *un hielo* 'an ice cube' [ɲ]
       (f) *un foro* 'a forum' [ɱ]

The grapheme *m* has fewer manifestations, [n] in word-final position (20a)
and [m] in all other contexts (20b):

(20)   (a) *álbum* 'album' [n]
       (b) *imposible* 'impossible' [m]

As is the case with *n*, the sounds represented by the spelling *l* are also
homorganic, as in (21).

(21)   (a) *lámpara* 'lamp' [l]
       (b) *el chico* 'the boy' [ʎ]
       (c) *alto* 'tall' [l̪]

In (21a), the sound is alveolar. In (21b), it is a palatal sound (blade of the
tongue against the hard palate). A dental sound (tip of the tongue
against the upper teeth) is found in (21c).

Some sounds are represented differently depending on the dialect, a
phenomenon we discuss below in detail in Section 2.5. Such sounds
include those represented orthographically by the following: *ll* and *y*,
ge/gi and *j*, *ce/ci*, *z* and *n*. For now, we will present the sounds as articulated in most dialects of Latin American Spanish, beginning with *ll* and *y*,
pronounced commonly [j], and similar to the first sound in the English
word *yes* in (22):

(22)   *lloro* 'I cry' [j]

The articulation of *g* depends on the following vowel. When it is followed by an *o* or *u*, it is articulated [g] or [ɣ], as we have seen above.
However, when *g* is followed by *e* or *i*, it is commonly articulated as [ç], a
palatal fricative similar to the initial sound in the English word *cute*, or
as [x]. Similarly, the grapheme *j* is also transcribed by [x]. This velar sound
is produced when the back of the tongue raises (but does not touch) the

soft palate. Some native speakers of English produce it automatically in the German word *Bach*. Consider (23) below:

(23) *gente* 'people' [x] or [ç]
     jamón 'ham' [x]

Finally, let us consider the sound represented by the spellings *s*, *z*, *ce* and *ci*. In the dialects of Latin American Spanish, these sounds are transcribed as [s], as illustrated by (24):

(24) *salsa* 'salsa' [s]
     cinco 'five' [s]
     cerca 'near' [s]
     zapato 'shoe' [s]

We have now presented all the phonetic symbols necessary to represent Spanish speech sounds. Let us consider some examples of fully transcribed words instead of isolated sounds (25):

(25) (a) *trabajaba* 'he was working' [traβaxáβa]
     (b) *angustiado* 'anguished' [aŋgustjáðo]
     (c) *llegaría* 'he would arrive' [jeɣaría]
     (d) *ahumado* 'smoked' [awmáðo]
     (e) *infame* 'infamous' [iɱfáme]
     (f) *sociedad* 'society' [sosjeðáð]
     (g) *Jalisco* 'Jalisco' [xalísko]
     (h) *húngaro* 'Hungarian' [úŋgaro]
     (i) *llovió* 'it rained' [joβjó]
     (j) *guitarra* 'guitar' [gitár̄a]

We next consider some phonological processes that affect the spoken stream in Spanish. These include syllabification, synalephy (fusion of two identical vowels), syneresis (vowel linking within a word), as well as suprasegmentals or rhythm, stress and intonation.

2.3 Phonological Processes and Suprasegmentals in Spanish

The most important phonological process needed for transcription is correct syllabification. Wherever possible, Spanish prefers a CV (consonant–vowel) syllable, also known as an open syllable, as in (26):

(26) *un amigo* 'a friend' [ú na mí ɣo]

When two consonants are adjacent, they are divided unless they are the group stop + liquid (*l* or *r*): *gl, gr, bl, br* and *dr*. Examples (27) and (28) illustrate both kinds of syllabic division[48]:

(27)   *examen* 'exam' [ek sá men]
(28)   *hablar* 'to speak' [a βlár]

The process of syneresis refers to the formation of diphthongs or triphthongs within a single nominal utterance.[49] This process, when word internal, is obligatory. This means that like proper syllabification, discussed above, the L1 Spanish speaker invariably applies the rules of syneresis, which the L2 speaker must follow. Let us consider two examples of syneresis[50]:

(29)   *miel* 'honey' [mjél]
(30)   *seudo* 'pseudo' [séw ðo]

In both examples, the formation of a diphthong is obligatory, not optional. L2 speakers of Spanish (L1 English speakers) are often surprised when they encounter the process of syneresis, as their first inclination is to pronounce the diphthongs in (29) and (30) as two separate syllables (e.g. *[mi él], *[se ú ðo]).

One difference between English and Spanish rhythm is that the latter is very even. One way to perceive the difference between Spanish rhythm and English rhythm is to tap out syllables as you speak. In Spanish, rhythm is syllable-timed, meaning that rhythm is a function of the number of syllables in an utterance. English rhythm is stress-timed, which means that rhythm is choppy, because stressed syllables are both longer and louder. They have more phonological prominence, as seen in (31)[51]:

(31)   (a) *Pablo es mi buen amigo y vecino.* (= 31b)
        (b) Paul is my close friend and neighbor.

In (31a), every syllable has roughly the same length. However, in (31b), the syllables *Paul*, *friend,* and *neighbor* must receive phonological prominence.

One problem with transferring English stress to Spanish is that English L1 speakers tend to reduce (i.e. not articulate clearly) vowels, substituting [ə] for unstressed vowels, as can be seen in the following[52]:

(32)   *Alabama* 'Alabama' [æl ə bǽm ə] English

In (32), the stressed vowel is the penultimate (next to the last) *a*. The unstressed vowels are reduced to [ə]. Compare (32) with Spanish (33):

(33)   *Alabama* [a la βá ma] Spanish

In (33), no vowel is reduced; they are all produced with the same articulatory clarity, although the penultimate *a* is slightly longer (but not louder) than the others. As we have seen, rhythm is closely linked to stress in English, which is not the case in Spanish.

A final note regarding stress in Spanish: it is phonemic, meaning that it can change the meaning of a word. Consider (34) and (35)[53]:

(34)   *hablo* 'I speak'
(35)   *habló* 'He spoke'

The example in (34) has penultimate stress on the *a*, whereas (35) has word final stress. The difference in meaning is dramatic, as (34) is the first person indicative of the present tense of the verb to speak (*hablo* 'I speak'), and (35) is the third person indicative of the preterit tense of the same verb (*habló* 'he spoke'). Generally speaking, words in Spanish carry stress according to their endings. Words ending with a vowel have penultimate (next to the last syllable) stress. Conversely, words ending in a consonant have word final stress, with the exception of words ending with *n* or *s*, which also have penultimate stress.

One way of understanding the exception of *n* or *s* is to compare singular and plural forms. Students will recall that an *n* can make a verb plural, whereas an *s* makes nouns plural:

(36)   *habla* 'he speaks'
(37)   *hablan* 'they speak'
(38)   *mesa* 'table'
(39)   *mesas* 'tables'

All of the words from (36) to (39) have penultimate stress. Therefore, the rule regarding *n* or *s* can be understood as one to keep the stress of a word the same, be it singular or plural. Where words do not follow the typical stress patterns, a written accent word is used to indicate this fact, as in (40) and (41):

(40)   *árbol* 'tree'
(41)   *cómelo* 'eat it' (*tú*)

If (40) followed the normal rules of stress, it would be stressed as *[arβól] instead of [árβol]. Similarly, if (41) were stressed regularly, the [e] in *cómelo* would receive stress instead of the [ó]. Therefore, these words, which do not follow the normal stress patterns of Spanish, must have written accent marks. Both L1 and L2 speakers, then, need to understand that orthographic accent marks are only needed when a given word does not follow the stress rules of Spanish.

The final suprasegmental (stress, rhythm, pitch) that we will briefly discuss is intonation, or the rising and falling of pitch. Pitch, in turn, is a function of how quickly the vocal cords vibrate. In Spanish, which is not a tone language (i.e. a language where differences in tone can affect meaning at the word level like Chinese), three major intonation patterns can be observed, as indicated by the numbers in (42)–(44)[54]:

(42)   *¿Qué quieres?* 'What do you want?'
       1   2   1
(43)   *¿Está Pablo?* 'Is Pablo there?'
       1   2   3
(44)   *María vive en Guatemala.* 'María lives in Guatemala.'
       1   2   1

Intonation is not typically represented in transcription, although L2 speakers should take care to use proper intonation, as it can affect sentence meaning, as illustrated by (45) and (46):

(45)   *Tú trabajas para Pedro.* 'You work for Peter.'
       1   2   1
(46)   *¿Tú trabajas para Pedro?* 'Do you work for Peter?'
       2   3   1

Example (45) is a declarative sentence, whereas (46) is a yes/no question, at least in informal speech in Spanish. Now we have enough information to transcribe actual utterances, as in (47) and (48) below:

(47)   *Quiero que lo sepas.* 'I want you to know.' [kjé ro ke lo sé pas]
(48)   *¿Compraste el perro negro?* 'Did you buy the black dog?'
       [com prás tel pé r̄o né ɣro]

We next turn to the articulation of Spanish sounds.

2.4 Articulatory Phonetics

In this section, we discuss articulatory phonetics, a branch of phonetics that is concerned with how sounds are articulated (pronounced). Before beginning our discussion, it is necessary to present an anatomical model of the speech organs:

(49)   Diagram of Speech organs (Bergmann *et al.*, 2004: 51)

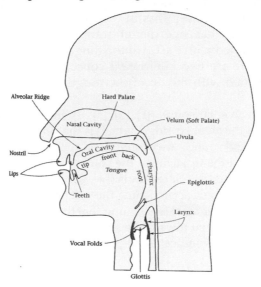

We begin our discussion by the articulatory description of consonants, followed by the articulatory description of vowels.

2.4.1 Articulatory description of consonants

Consonants are described by the following parameters: voicing, place of articulation and manner of articulation.[56] Voicing refers to the vibration (or lack thereof) of the vocal cords. As an example, consider the sounds [s] and [z], which vary in voicing. The sound [s] is a voiceless consonant, whereas [z] is voiced. This difference in voicing can best be illustrated by elongating the [s] or [z] while touching the larynx (i.e. Adam's apple). Vibration will be felt with the articulation of [z] but not [s]. The following table lists all consonants of Spanish according to voicing:

(50)

Table 2.1 Voicing of Spanish Consonants

	p	b	β	t	θ	d	ð	č	k	g	ɣ	x	f	m	n	ŋ	ɲ	ʋ	ɱ	l	ḷ	ʎ	r	r̄	s	w	j
Voiced		x	x			x	x			x	x			x	x	x	x	x	x	x	x	x	x	x		x	x
Voiceless	x			x	x			x	x			x	x												x		

The next parameter, place of articulation, refers to the articulatory organs used to produce a sound. Spanish has four bilabial sounds ([p], [b], [β], [m]); bilabial sounds are pronounced using both lips. The sound [f] is a labiodental sound, pronounced with the upper teeth touching the lower lip. The nasal sound [ɱ], as in the English word *emphasis*, is also labiodental. Spanish has five dental sounds ([d], [t], [n̪], [l̪]). These sounds are articulated with the tip of the tongue touching the back of the upper teeth. There are two interdental consonants in Spanish, [θ], [ð]. They are articulated with the tip of the tongue between the upper and lower teeth.

To produce an alveolar sound ([r], [r̄], [s], [l]) the tip of the tongue must be placed against the alveolar ridge, which is the ridge directly behind the upper teeth.[57] Palatal sounds are pronounced with the blade of the tongue (the part just behind the tip) against the soft palate. Spanish has four such sounds, [č], [ɲ], [ʎ] and [j]. Velar sounds ([k], [g], [ɣ], [x], [ŋ]) are articulated with the back of the tongue approaching the soft palate. Finally, Spanish has one sound ([w]) that is labiovelar, meaning that the lips are rounded and the back of the tongue is raised toward the soft palate.

The table given below indicates the place of articulation with respect to Spanish consonants:

(51)

Table 2.2   Place of Articulation of Spanish Consonants

	p	b	β	t	θ	d	ð	č	k	g	ɣ	x	f	m	n	n̪	ɲ	ŋ	ɱ	l	l̪	ʎ	r	r̄	s	w	j
Bilabial	x	x	x											x													
Dental				x		x										x					x						
Interdental					x		x																				
Labiodental													x						x								
Alveolar															x					x			x	x	x		
Palatal								x									x					x					x
Velar									x	x	x	x						x									
Labiovelar																										x	

With respect to *manner of articulation*, stops refer to the complete closure of two articulatory organs. In other words, two organs touch. Stops (also referred to as plosives) in Spanish include [p], [b], [d], [k] and [g]. For the articulation of fricatives, the articulatory organs get very close to each other, but do not touch; fricatives in Spanish are [β], [θ] [ð], [f], [ɣ], [x] and [s]. An affricate is a sequence of a stop followed by a fricative. Spanish has [č], spelled *ch*, as in *cheque* 'check.' This affricate is a combination of the stop [t] followed by the fricative [š] (English *sh* as in *shoe*). In the articulation of a nasal consonant, there is closure of two articulatory organs in the vocal tract, yet the velum (the end of the soft palate; see (51) above) is lowered, allowing air passage through the nasal tract. Despite the fact that air flows freely in the nasal cavity, because the articulatory organs touch, the consonant articulated is called a nasal stop. The nasal stops in Spanish are [m], [n], [n̥], [ɲ], [ɳ] and [ŋ]. For the articulation of a lateral ([l], [ḷ], [ʎ]), the center of the tip of the tongue makes contact with another articulatory organ, but the sides do not, allowing air to flow freely over them. Glides (approximants) are very vowel-like sounds. There is virtually no obstruction of the vocal tract in their articulation. In Spanish, the glide sounds are [j] and [w].

The table given below indicates the articulatory description of Spanish with respect to manner of articulation:

(52)

Table 2.3   Manner of Articulation of Spanish Consonants

	p	b	β	t	θ	d	ð	č	k	g	ɣ	x	f	m	n	n̥	ɲ	ɳ	ŋ	l	ḷ	ʎ	r	r̄	s	w	j
Stops	x	x		x		x			x	x																	
Nasal stop														x	x	x	x	x	x								
Affricate								x																			
Fricatives			x		x		x				x	x	x												x		
Trill																								x			
Tap																							x				
Lateral																				x	x	x					
Glide																										x	x

Now we have all the terminology needed to give an articulatory description of a consonant. Below we describe a few consonants of Spanish[58]:

(53)   (a) voiced dental stop [d]
        (b) voiceless labiodental fricative [f]

(c) voiced velar nasal stop [ŋ]
(d) voiceless alveolar fricative [s]

A summary table of the table of consonants in Spanish with respect to these parameters is given below:

(54)

Table 2.4   Complete Articulatory Description of Spanish Consonants

	p	b	β	t	θ	d	ð	č	k	g	ɣ	x	f	m	n	ņ	ɲ	ŋ	ɱ	l	ḷ	ʎ	r	r̄	s	w	j
Voiced		x	x			x	x		x	x	x			x	x	x	x	x	x	x	x	x	x	x		x	x
Voiceless	x			x	x			x	x			x	x												x		
Bilabial	x	x	x											x													
Dental				x		x										x					x						
Interdental					x		x																				
Labiodental													x						x								
Alveolar															x					x			x	x	x		
Palatal								x									x					x					x
Velar									x	x	x	x						x									
Labiovelar																										x	
Stop	x	x		x		x			x	x																	
Nasal stop														x	x	x	x	x	x								
Affricate								x																			
Fricative			x		x		x				x	x	x												x		
Trill																								x			
Tap																							x				
Lateral																				x	x	x					
Glide																										x	x

We next consider the articulation of Spanish vowels.

2.4.2   Articulatory description of vowels

The articulatory description of vowels differs from that of consonants; in many ways it appears less concrete. As all vowels are voiced, and in their articulation there is no obstruction of the vocal tract, they are described according to the following three parameters: tongue height (high, mid or low), place of articulation (front, central, back) and tongue rounding or lack thereof (rounded, unrounded). The table in (55) gives the articulatory description of the five vowels in Spanish[59]:

(55)

Table 2.5   Articulatory characteristics of Spanish vowels

	a	e	i	o	u
High			x		x
Mid		x		x	
Low	x				
Front		x	x		
Back				x	x
Central	x				
Rounded				x	x
Unrounded	x	x	x		

The examples in (56) give the articulatory description of Spanish vowels:

(56)   [a] a low central unrounded vowel
       [e] a mid front unrounded vowel
       [i] a high front unrounded vowel
       [o] a mid back rounded vowel
       [u] a high back rounded vowel

Key terms in phonology are presented in the next section.

2.5   Spanish Phonology

Two concepts that are particularly useful for the purposes of our discussion are those of phoneme and allophone. In Section 2.2 above, we addressed the distribution of [b] and [β]; the former sound is found after a nasal and in absolute initial position, the latter elsewhere. For the native speaker, however, the sounds are represented abstractly in his or her mental phonology as /b/ (note the slashes in lieu of brackets). In other words, Spanish native speakers are typically unaware of the distribution of [b] and [β] even though they invariably pronounce the sounds correctly.

In our example, [b] and [β] are allophones of the same phoneme, /b/. Another way of viewing the allophone vs. phoneme dichotomy is that the former is what is actually pronounced and the latter is the abstract mental representation of a sound. Moreover, if a speaker substitutes [b] for [β] in a word, the meaning does not vary, even though the resultant pronunciation will be non-native, as illustrated by (57):

(57)   *la ballena* 'the whale' [la ba jé na] (non-native) vs. [la → a jé na] (native)

When deciding whether sounds are allophones of the same phoneme or of two different phonemes, one needs to decide if substitution of one sound for another changes the meaning of a word. The sounds [r] and [r̄] are clearly allophones of different phonemes because substitution of [r] for [r̄] will be understood by native speakers as a different word (58):

(58)   *caro* *[ká r̄o] for [káro] 'expensive,' pronounced as *carro* 'cart/car'

The words *caro* and *carro* are not homophones (i.e. pronounced the same), nor do they have the same meaning. Pairs of words like *caro* and *carro* that vary in only one sound (given in the same order) are known as minimal pairs. Minimal pairs, in turn, allow us to identify all of the phonemes of a language. We next turn to how regional variation is manifested in the sound system of Spanish.

2.6   Dialectal Variation in Spanish Phonology

Dialects in Spanish vary widely with respect to the sound system. Indeed, a native speaker will be able to recognize that a given pronunciation is typical of a certain region and will characterize this difference with the non-linguistic, popular term 'accent'. While not all of these dialectal details need be presented to beginning Spanish students, in our view, it is nonetheless necessary for instructors and advanced students to be familiar with this dialectal phonological variation. We remind readers that for phonology, we have argued in Chapter 1 that the following dialectal divisions are needed (cf. (17) in Chapter 1 repeated as (59) below):

(59)   (a) the so-called *tierras altas* 'highlands' (also called the *zona alteña*)[60]
       (b) the *tierras bajas* 'lowlands' (also called *the zona bajeña*)
       (c) the *Río de la Plata* region 'the River Plate area (e.g., Chile, Paraguay, Uruguay)
       (d) *Castile* (also called *the zona castellana*)

The maps in (60) illustrate these dialectal areas (cf. (6) in Chapter 1 above), repeated below as (60):

(60)   Main dialectal regions of Spanish (Teschner 2000: 186)

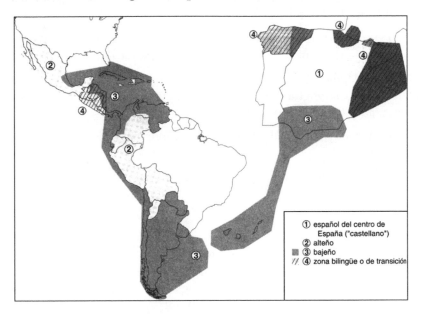

① español del centro de
España ("castellano")
② alteño
③ bajeño
// ④ zona bilingüe o de transición

With respect to the *tierras altas*, there is a marked consonantism. In certain dialects in Latin America, this can be at the expense of the articulation of vowels. We begin therefore by presenting the phonological variations in the *tierras altas*, all of which show the overriding consonantism of this dialect. As an example of the consonantism in this dialect, we first consider *debilitamiento vocálico* (vocalic reduction).[61] In the speech characterizing the *tierras altas*, only the vowels [o] and [e] undergo reduction; the vowel [a] is especially resistant. Finally, the context for the *debilitamiento* is very limited: it is typically found in posttonic vowels preceded by a sibilant (generally [s]). Consider (61) and (62) below (Teschner, 2000: 219):

(61)   *De todos los clientes importantes de los pueblos eran ... los más apreciados.*
       'Of all the important clients of the towns, they were the most estimed.'
(62)   [de tó ð°s l°s kljén̩ t°s im por tán̩ t°s ðe l°s pwé β l° sé ran l°s má sa pre sjá ð°s]

The *reducción vocálica* characteristic of the *tierras altas* is indicated by superscripts on the vowels in (62). These vowels have the same quality as non-reduced vowels, but they are articulated with a shorter duration than other vowels. It is not necessary, in our view, to actively teach or learn *reducción vocálica*, but it is necessary to stress the consonantism of this dialect, which is manifested in other ways. For example, consonant clusters are not simplified in the dialect zone of the *tierras altas* (or in Castile):

(63)   extraordinario 'extraordinary' [eks tra or ði ná rjo]
        cf. or [e tra or ði ná rjo] *tierras bajas* and the *Río de la Plata* zone

There is devoicing of consonants in syllable-final position, which should be viewed as a strengthening mechanism, in the dialect region of *the tierras altas* and also the dialect of Castile (64):

(64)   *ciudad* 'city' [sju ðáθ] (cf. [sju ðá] of the *tierras bajas* and the *Río de la Plata* zone)

In this dialect, the sound represented by the spelling 'j' is manifested by a voiceless velar fricative, whose friction in articulation is heard clearly (65)[62]:

(65)   *jamón* 'ham' [xa món]

As discussed in Section 2.4.1, there is some alternation where the spelling is *ge* or *gi*. Some speakers, mostly in *the tierras altas*, continue to articulate a velar fricative, (66), producing a great deal of friction, but may instead articulate a palatal fricative, similar to the second sound in the English word *cute* (66):

(66)   *gente* 'people' [xéṇ te] tierras altas
(67)   *gente* 'people' [çéṇ te] = (74)

The graphemes *ll* and *y* are also pronounced differently according to dialect. Generally speaking, within the *tierras altas*, the graphemes *ll* and *y* are homophonous, both realized as [j] (68) and (69):

(68)   *llama* 'he calls' [já ma]
(69)   *yo* 'I' [jó]

However, within the dialect area of the Andes (as well as *Castile*), the grapheme 'll' is pronounced as a palatal lateral [ʎ] (70), a process known as lleísmo. The sound produced is similar, but not identical, to the medial sound in *million* in English:

(70)   *llanta* 'tire' [ʎaṇ ta]

Conversely, in the *tierras bajas*, there is an emphasis on retaining vowel quality, at the expense of consonants. This tendency is also seen in the *Río de la Plata* zone. One process found in this dialect is syncope of intervocalic (between vowels) [ð], as in (71):

(71)　*cocido* [ko sí o] 'cooked'
　　　(cf. [ko sí ðo] of the *tierras altas* and *Castile*)

Another process prevalent in both the *tierras altas* and the *Río de la Plata* area is the aspiration or deletion of syllable-final consonants. Consider (72) and (73)[63]:

(72)　*las mujeres* 'the women,'
　　　[lah mu hé reh] or [la mu hé re] (cf. [las mu xé res] in the *tierras altas*)
(73)　*obstrucción* 'obstruction' [o tru sjón] (cf. [oβs trúk sjón] or [op strúk sjón] of the *tierras altas* and *Castile*).[64]

In (72) it is the syllable-final [s] that is aspirated to [h] or deleted entirely; in (73) it is the syllable-final [β] and [k], respectively, that are deleted. The sequence 'ge,' 'gi' and 'j' is articulated as [h] in the dialect of the *tierras bajas*, as seen in (74):

(74)　(a) *jamón* [ha món] or [ha móŋ] (cf. [xamón] in the *tierras altas*)
　　　(b) *gente* [héṇ te] (cf. (66)–(67))

Velarization of word-final nasals ([n] to [ŋ]) is common throughout the *tierras bajas*, as in (75):

(75)　*pan* 'bread' [páŋ]

As discussed in Section 2.2, this phenomenon is obligatory in all dialects of Spanish word internally before velar consonants, such as [k], [g] or [x], as in (76):

(76)　*Inca* 'Inca' [íŋ ka]

However, in the Caribbean, particularly in Cuba, syllable-final nasals velarize as well, so that there is no homorganic co-articulation of nasal consonants, as illustrated by (77):

(77)　*donde* 'where' [dóŋ de] (cf. [dóṇ de])

Another process typical of the *tierras bajas*, or at least the Caribbean subregion of that dialectal zone, as well as Andalusia, is lambdacism, whereby the syllable-final [r] is realized as [l] (78)[65]:

(78)　*arte* 'art' [ál̩ te] (cf. [ár te] of the remaining dialect areas)[66]

The *Río de la Plata* region has the vocalism of the *tierras bajas*, combined with one characteristic that is only found in that zone, namely *žeísmo*.

Speakers of the *Rio de la Plata* region would pronounce the grapheme 'll' or 'y' as [ʒ] or [ʃ], as in (79) below:

(79)   *lloro* 'I cry' [ʒó ro] or [ʃó ro][67]

Castile, in turn, shares the consonantism of the *tierras altas*, but has important dialectal characteristics, as well. For example, this dialect has distinción. In most dialects of Spanish, including Southern Spain and Latin America, the spellings *z*, *ce*, *ci* and *s* represent the phoneme /s/, a phenomenon known as seseo. However, in North Central Spain there is a phonemic distinction (known as *distinción*) between /θ/, represented orthographically as *z*, *ce* or *ci*, and /s/, spelled *s*. The sound [θ] is a voiceless interdental fricative, similar to the initial sound in the English word *think*. We believe that students should be exposed to both pronunciations, but should be encouraged to adopt the pronunciation typical of native speakers in their area. The examples in (80)–(82) illustrate *distinción* and *seseo*[68]:

(80)   *azar* 'fate' [a θar] vs. *asar* 'to roast' [a sár], *distinción*, Castile
(81)   *azar* 'fate' [a sár] vs. *asar* 'to roast' [a sár], *seseo*, the remaining dialect areas
(82)   *sin* [sín] 'without,' *distinción*, Castile, *sin* [sín] *seseo*, the remaining dialect areas

In this section, we have provided an overview of the main phonological dialectal characteristics of Spanish. We next consider phonological variation that indicates a difference in register.

2.7   Register Variation in Spanish Phonology

Phonological differences among registers are quite extensive in Spanish. As an example of a phonological process found in informal speech consider (83). This example reflects another aspect of the process syneresis, in this case the formation of diphthongs within a word of the vowels [e] and [o] plus another vowel (cf. Barrutia & Schwegler, 1994; Dalbor, 1996):

(83)   (a) *teatro* 'theater'
             Formal register: [te á tro]
             Informal register: [tjá tro]
         (b) *poeta* 'poet'
             Formal register: [po é ta]
             Informal register: [pwé ta]

Although syneresis is not obligatory, it is quite common within a word, in all but the most formal registers. Similarly, the process of synalephy, or vowel linking across word boundaries, also characterizes natural, informal speech between words:

(84)   *Me imagino* 'I imagine'
       Informal register: [me**j** ma xí no]
       Formal register: [me i ma xí no]

Also found in informal speech is a process known as elision, the deletion of one of two identical vowels, a process that occurs not within a word but rather across word boundaries. In very slow, careful speech, characteristic of the formal register, it does not occur. However, in informal speech, if there are two identical vowels, one stressed and one unstressed, only one is retained. The resultant vowel may be longer, particularly if one of the vowels is stressed (two stressed vowels do not undergo synalephy in Spanish).[69] Consider the example given in (85) below.

(85)   *Va a hablar* 'He/She/You (formal) is going to speak [baβlár]

In example (85) above, the vowels in the verb *va*, the preposition *a* and the initial vowel in *hablar* have all merged to create one vowel, [a].

Oftentimes when discussing phonological variation among registers of Spanish, it is necessary to take into consideration regional variation as well. We discussed, in Section 2.6, the aspiration or deletion of syllable-final [s], common to the *tierras bajas*. However, this process is not register neutral. For example, Barrutia and Schwegler (1994: 219) give three possibilities for the pronunciation of the underlying syllable-final [s] in Cartagena (Colombia), such as in *niños* 'boys' [ní ɲos], (86):

(86)   (a) *niños* [ní ɲos] Formal
       (b) *niños* [ní ɲoh] Informal
       (c) *niños* [ní ɲo] Very informal

In (86a), the final /s/ is pronounced as such, whereas in (86b) aspiration of the /s/ occurs, so that the resulting sound is not unlike /h/ in English. In (86c), we see the most informal pronunciation, in which syllable-final /s/ is completely elided or deleted.

Barrutia and Schwegler argue that even in the *tierras bajas* certain formal social contexts, such as university settings, job interviews, news broadcasts or reading aloud, favor the retention of /s/, while less formal contexts, such as conversation, cartoons or comedies, favor its elision.

One interesting feature, according to Barrutia and Schwegler, is that /s/ is retained when speaking to a long-distance operator, but not when speaking to a local one. In other words, salient dialectal features are neutralized when speaking with someone from another dialect region. This example of the variable rule of /s/ elision or aspiration illustrates the intersection between dialectal features and registers. It is well documented that certain dialectal processes are more likely to be present in informal speech than in formal speech. We next consider heritage speakers and phonological variation.

2.8 Heritage Speakers and Dialectal and Register Phonological Variation

As we have noted earlier in Chapter 1, heritage speakers come to our classrooms already speaking a dialect of Spanish. It has long been accepted that the focus of SNS courses should be morphosyntactic variation (Hidalgo, 1990; Valdés, 1991). Little, if any, emphasis is placed on phonology, for as Hidalgo (1990) states, regional differences in pronunciation are rarely stigmatized.[70] However, it is nonetheless important for heritage speakers to be open-minded with respect to the pronunciation of their classmates or of other native speakers of dialects different from their own. For this reason, we recommend that the notion of dialectal phonological variation be presented to students as the first semester progresses, in order to raise their language awareness, in the sense of Cook (2001: 87). We give specific suggestions on how to do this in Chapter 6.

One problem that heritage speakers may face, as discussed above in Chapter 1, is exposure to, and acquisition of, only one register. In their speech, therefore, they may invariably manifest phonological and phonetic traits of informal speech. It does not serve such students well if we fail to address this issue, without, of course, being judgmental on their lack of mastery of the formal register. Again, the goal is not to supplant the heritage speaker's pronunciation. It is to let him or her know that there is an appropriate social context for such speech (e.g. with family and close friends), but that the pronunciation of academic Spanish has different features. We present specific tips for addressing register variation and heritage speakers in Chapter 6. In the next section, we turn to a general discussion of L2 acquisition of phonology.

2.9 L2 Acquisition of Phonology

L2 acquisition of phonology has been the subject of much recent research. The main question posed by researchers is whether or not ultimate attainment (i.e. accent that can be taken for native) is possible after the Critical Period has passed. An early seminal study, Asher and García (1969), investigated the Age of Onset of English L2 for Cuban immigrants, finding that those most likely to have acquired a native-like accent arrived in the United States by the age of four. Oyama (1982a, 1982b) replicated these findings for L1 speakers of Italian (English L2).

Arteaga (2000) argues that phonetics is important for the Spanish language classroom for a plethora of reasons: first, explicit phonetic training improves student pronunciation, as noted by Bongaerts (1999) and others. Second, accented speech is typically not neutrally received by the listener (Oyama, 1982a). Third, learners themselves care about pronunciation (Oyama, 1982a). Fourth, accurate speech production improves comprehension (Meador *et al.*, 1997; Oyama, 1973, 1982a, 1982b).

Fifth, intelligibility with all conversational partners must entail reasonably accurate pronunciation, which needs to be the goal. This is because to produce speech understood by a wide range of native speakers, the accent of the L2 speakers needs to be at least comprehensible (Elliot, 1997). A sixth reason as to why pronunciation in the L2 Spanish classroom is important is that students must be able to understand native speech, which will reflect a range of optional and obligatory native phonological processes (cf. Zampini, 1994). Seventh, short-term memory, which is generally impaired in the L2 (Gathercore & Baddeley, 1993; Papagno & Vallar, 1992; Service, 1992), improves with accuracy of pronunciation. Finally, if students are expected to understand a wide range of native speech, they must be exposed to common dialectal differences.

Some studies argue that an additional factor in L2 pronunciation is the learner's attitude toward the language, while other findings contradict this assertion. Elliot (1997) and Suter (1976) argue in favor of the notion that student interest plays an important role in ultimate attainment of pronunciation. Hammond and Flege (1989) claim the opposite, namely that speakers with the least empathy toward a language group (indeed, those with a hostile attitude) are the most adept at imitating native pronunciation.

Sometimes, the relevant factor is students' attitude toward a non-native pronunciation. Hammond (1991), in a study of 282 English as a Second Language (ESL) students, found that there is a strong correlation among students with excellent or good English pronunciation between disapproval of a foreign (in this case, Spanish) accent in English and their pronunciation proficiency. However, non-proficient students also showed a marked disapproval of a Spanish accent in English, so that attitude alone is no guarantee of success.

Many studies argue for the need for teaching suprasegmentals in a communicative-based methodology.[71] When non-native speakers have not mastered suprasegmentals, communication may be affected, as noted by Wong (1985). In her study of L2 English (Wong, 1985: 228), examples included improper stress in English (e.g. *two more* for *tumor*) and non-native (i.e. too even) rhythm, which she characterizes as 'disruptive.' In Section 2.3 above, we have argued that suprasegmentals are also essential for the mastery of Spanish pronunciation, particularly for the *comprehension* of native speech.

Chen (1982) also notes the communicative importance of pitch, rhythm and intonation, emphasizing phonemic contrasts. Pennington (1989: 20), in turn, represents a study that preferred a top-down approach (i.e. global processing of utterances rather than a "bottom up" approach, which focuses on the segments themselves). It is an approach that stresses "prosody, phonological fluency, voice quality and gestures."

Indeed, the importance of suprasegmentals cannot be underestimated in a Communicative Approach because of their discourse function. As we have seen above (expressions (47) and (48)), intonation can determine the difference between a question and a statement (or an exclamation), and therefore should be explicitly taught. In Spanish, again as discussed in Section 2.3 above, stress is phonemic, as illustrated by pairs like *papá* [pa pá] 'dad' and *papa* [pá pa] 'potato,' and therefore should be emphasized in a communicative/proficiency-oriented classroom.

Finally, we turn to the topic of fluency. How is one to define it? Rate of speech cannot be the defining characteristic, because rapid, non-native speech can be completely unintelligible. A better alternative can be found in Simões (1996: 87), who provided the following definition of fluency: 'the number of accurately pronounced syllable nuclei in sequences of words found acceptable in Spanish discourse.' Echoing Delattre (1965), Simões defines 'acceptable vocalic nuclei' as those articulated 'within the field of vowel dispersion.'[72] In our view, we do not want to take the goals of intelligibility and fluency too far, because it would only emphasize phonological contrasts (e.g. the substitution of [g] for [k], *vaca* 'cow' vs. *vaga* 'lazy') and not phonetic ones (e.g. the substitution of [d] for [ð], incorrect *hablado* 'spoken' [ha βlá do] for *hablado* [ha βlá ðo]).

The crucial point here is that if a student produces incorrect *[ha βlá do] for [ha βlá ðo], he or she would be most likely understood. The pronunciation of *vaca* for *vaga*, on the other hand, would potentially lead to communication difficulties. However, some phonetic variants (such as [ə]) would also be deemed unacceptable because the resultant vowels would fall outside the stated 'field of dispersion.' Focusing only on fluency, Simões concludes by recommending that phonetics be covered in language curricula.

While Simões fails to discuss the articulation of consonants, his study is nonetheless an attempt to find the degree of accuracy required from students, a controversial topic. Dansereau (1995) makes the point that oral ACFTL interviewers, despite their stated objectives, fail to take student pronunciation into account. She has therefore proposed a phonetics program for first-year French students, which emphasizes the notion of intelligibility, which is typically linked to the accuracy of pronunciation.

Turning now to heritage speakers, the reason for differences in phonological acquisition among bilinguals is a subject of debate. These may be largely subsumed under two hypotheses: the unfolding hypothesis and the interaction hypothesis. Proponents of the former include Oyama (1979), Elman (1993), Marchman (1993), Best (1995) and Yeni-Komshian *et al.* (1997). This hypothesis has much in common with the Critical Period Hypothesis (CPH), in that it claims that the more established the phonological system of the L1, the more likely this system will affect the phonology of the L2.

One study supporting the unfolding hypothesis is that by Yeni-Komshian *et al.* (1997), who studied 240 Korean–English bilinguals living in the United States. Like Asher and García (1992), her research found a direct link between their proficiency in pronouncing either Korean or English and their age of arrival in this country, with the youngest (1.5–8.5 years, 16 out of 240 total subjects) having the greatest likelihood of pronouncing English like monolingual speakers. Those speakers arriving between 8.5 and 22 years (46%) tended to achieve a rating similar to monolingual Korean speakers. In her study, only one speaker out of the 240 achieved a rating of native-like pronunciation in both English and Korean. These findings show the inadvisability of expecting or requiring native-like pronunciation from bilinguals in both Spanish and English, as they will very likely show some phonetic interference in both their L1 and their L2.

The interaction hypothesis, conversely, recognizes the mutual influence of the two phonological systems on each other (cf. Weinrich, 1953). In this view, divergences from the monolingual norms are inevitable, although not necessarily negative in nature (Cook, 2001 vs. Selinker, 1972). This mutual influence, in turn, is a result of the bilinguals' inability to fully separate the L1 system from the L2 system, and will vary according to language use and language dominance.

The interaction hypothesis receives support from a study of Italian/English bilinguals by Flege *et al.* (1997), who found a correlation not only between degree of foreign accent and age of arrival, but also between the amount of the other language's use and divergence from native pronunciation norms. Of the speakers in their study who spoke Italian extensively, a higher percentage were found to have a non-native accent in English than those in the low use group. These findings suggest that factors other than age of acquisition affect bilingual phonology.

Other researchers have argued that explicit phonetics training can, in some cases, offset the age of acquisition. Birdsong (1999) reports three studies, two of Dutch L1 English L2 speakers and one of Dutch L1 French L2 speakers. In the three studies, the subjects read aloud words and/or sentences, which were rated by a panel of native speaker judges. Interestingly, there were a few L2 learners, particularly in the highly proficient group, who passed for native English speakers, receiving similar scores (in some cases even higher) on their pronunciation *vis-à-vis* L1 English speakers. All of these speakers had studied English phonetics. In the next section, we take into consideration how L1 transfer of English sounds may affect the L2 pronunciation of Spanish.

2.10   L1 English Transfer to L2 Spanish

As mentioned in Section 2.9 above, in L2 acquisition of phonology, a great deal of L1 transfer typically occurs, particularly if the L2 is learned after puberty. Arteaga (2000), as discussed in detail in Chapter 6, recommends that a learner's dialect be presented to Spanish language students from the beginning, which focuses on the following sounds and processes: [r] vs. [r̄], alveolar [l], vowel tension, absence of vowel reduction, spirantization of stops and nasal assimilation. We will take each of these in turn in the discussion that follows.

No dialect of Spanish pronounces the [r] or [r̄] as [ɹ] as in English. The English [ɹ] is a retroflex sound, which means that the tongue curves back during its articulation. One reason why use of the English [ɹ] gives such a marked accent in Spanish is that it affects the articulation of the adjacent vowels; this is known as producing 'r-colored' vowels. Consider examples (87) and (88) below:

(87)   *rural* 'rural' [r̄u rál] Spanish L1
(88)   *rural* 'rural' [rɑ́ rəl] English L1 Spanish L2

In (87), the vowels have the same articulation, as in *tuna* 'spiny fruit found in Central America.' In (88), on the other hand, the vowels differ sharply from those found in *something* (articulated as *somethin'*). The sound [r] is not difficult for L1 speakers of English, as it exists in English, equivalent to the pronunciation of *t* in the English expression *pot a tea* = loosely *para ti* 'for you' or *d* as in the English expression *moo dough* = loosely *muro* 'wall' (examples from Dalbor, 1996: 263).

The trill [r̄], however, is much more challenging for L2 speakers of Spanish (L1 speakers of English), as there is no equivalent sound in English. It may help students to know that in order to articulate [r̄], the tongue must be fairly lax, and there must be sufficient air flow. Moreover, the tongue should be near, but not touching, the alveolar ridge. Many speakers find that the sound [r̄] is more easily articulated between vowels, at least at first. Regardless of the student's ability to articulate [r̄] from the beginning, the retroflex English [ɹ] should be avoided, and [r] substituted instead.

There is not a dialect of Spanish that evinces a syllable-final velar lateral [ɫ], a common pronunciation error in the speech of English L2 speakers.[73] The velar lateral exists in English in syllable-final position. Compare (89) with (90):

(89) *all* [áɫ]
(90) *light* [lájt]

In (89), the sound pronounced is a velar sound. As we have seen, in the articulation of velar sounds, the back of the tongue raises toward the soft palate. In (90), in contrast, the sound is alveolar, pronounced with the center part of the tip of the tongue against the alveolar ridge.

The alveolar lateral [l] should be the target sound, as it exists in all positions in Spanish. Students must take care to produce [l] both in syllable-initial and syllable-final position as in (91) and (92):

(91) *lámpara* 'lamp' [lám pa ra]
(92) *algo* 'something' [ál ɣo]

The five vowels of Spanish are pronounced with a great deal of articulatory tension. In other words, the speaker's jaw does not change place during their articulation. In English, however, speakers diphthongize the vowels [o] and [e], articulating instead [ow] and [ej] as in [*ków mej] *come* 'he/she eats' (cf. L1 Spanish [kó me]). In Section 2.2 above, we discussed the interrelationship between stress and vowel reduction in English. In short, unstressed vowels, particularly the vowel [a], reduce to [ə] in English, but not in Spanish, as in the following:

(93) (a) *Ana está sentada en la mesa.* 'Ana is seated on the table.'
        (b) * *[á nə es tá seņ tá ðə en la mé sə]* L1 English speech
        (c) *[á na es tá seņ tá ða en la mé sa]* L1 Spanish speech

L1 English speakers learning Spanish also have difficulty with the stop/fricative alternation, discussed in Section 2.4 above. In other words, they substitute the stops [b], [d] and [g] for the fricatives [β], [ð] and [ɣ], as in the following:

(94)   (a) *He dedicado el libro a Olga.* 'I have dedicated the book to Olga.'
       *[e **de di** ká **do** el lí bro a ól **ga**] L1 English speech
       (b) [e ðe ði ká ðo el lí βro a ól ɣa] L1 Spanish

Two of these fricatives exist in English [ð] (spelled *th* as in *there*) and [ɣ] (spelled *g* as in *sugar*). There is no equivalent in English to the fricative [β], although it can be explained to students that the lips do not touch in its articulation, as opposed to [b]. In our view, the instructor should present this stop/fricative alternation, particularly emphasizing that the stops are rarely pronounced in the speech stream.

Finally, nasal assimilation poses another challenge for L1 English speakers. Nasal assimilation is found in English, but only word internally, such as in (95):

(95)   [íŋ ki] 'inky'
       [ín kí] inn key (*[íŋ ki])[74]

In our experience, if nasal assimilation is explicitly taught to students, they will, in most cases, correct their non-native speech accordingly. We next turn to the sounds system of bilingual students.

2.11   Heritage Speakers and Spanish Phonology

The issue of phonology and heritage speakers is a complex one. As discussed in Section 2.9, their pronunciation may have overtones of English depending on their age of acquisition and dominance of Spanish. In such cases, the instructor will need to tread carefully, for a number of reasons. First, the heritage speaker may already be self-conscious about his or her 'accent' in Spanish. Perhaps family members or others have ridiculed the heritage speaker's speech, and it may therefore be a sensitive issue. Moreover, out of fairness, the instructor must compare the speech of the heritage speaker, not to native speakers, but to the Anglophone speakers in the classroom. If the speech of the heritage speaker in question does indeed reflect transfer of English phonology, he or she will benefit from the remedial exercises in Spanish phonetics that we recommend for Anglophone learners of Spanish.

As discussed in Section 2.9, while findings are contradictory, there is nonetheless research that supports the notion that bilinguals are not fully able to separate the phonology of both of their languages, particularly those speakers who learned their second language after puberty. In such cases, we should therefore expect the students to show evidence of at least some phonetic interference in both their L1 and their L2. Indeed, far from being unnecessary in the SNS classroom, instruction in Spanish phonetics should therefore be an integral part of the curriculum, particularly since heritage learners care about pronunciation and want overt correction, as noted by Arteaga (1999). After getting to know his or her students, the teacher will be able to gauge the readiness on the part of the heritage speaker to address English overtones in his or her speech.

Moreover, overt instruction in phonetics is beneficial even for those heritage students with native-like pronunciation, as it will assist them in mastering the orthographic system of Spanish and will improve their skills in reading aloud (Hudelson, 1981; Nash, 1973). For Nash (1973: 134), phonology should be used to counteract orthographic interference in bilinguals. She recommends that when teaching orthography 'We need to design better materials for teaching pronunciation that deal with problems of spelling contrasts as well as problems of sound contrasts.' Therefore, a complete description of phonological performance recognizes the equal partnership of phonology and orthography in the representation of language.

In an attempt to measure heritage students' impressions regarding pronunciation as well as student interest in learning about phonetics, Arteaga (1999) gave a written survey to students of a second semester SNS class, which is a second year course. The university students in question will, after completing this sequence, be prepared to enter junior-level grammar and literature courses.[75] The table in (96) provides the results of Arteaga's survey (Arteaga, 1999: 10):

(96)

Table 2.6   A questionnaire given to students in an SNS class

Questionnaire	Strongly agree (%)	Agree (%)	Neutral (%)	Disagree (%)	Strongly disagree (%)
It's important to be able to pronounce Spanish correctly.	92	8			
When I speak Spanish, I sound American.	8		50	17	25
I would like to practice Spanish pronunciation more.	50	33	17	8	

(*Continued*)

Table 2.6 *Continued*

Questionnaire	Strongly agree (%)	Agree (%)	Neutral (%)	Disagree (%)	Strongly disagree (%)
I feel comfortable speaking Spanish to people from Spanish speaking countries.	34	25	33	8	
I am happy with my accent in Spanish.	25	17	50	8	
My friends and family tease me sometimes about my accent when I speak Spanish.	9	33		33	25
I can speak at least as fast in Spanish as I speak in English.	34	8	8	42	8
I would like to speak Spanish faster than I do.	8	33	25	17	17
I have trouble with the Spanish 'rr' sound.				42	58
I would feel more comfortable speaking Spanish if my accent were better.	33	25	9	25	8

As seen in Table 2.3, students in Arteaga's survey unanimously agreed that it was important to pronounce Spanish correctly, and they expressed a strong desire for additional pronunciation practice (83%). Almost half (42%) of the students cited a common experience of peer/family ridicule of their accent in Spanish. Similarly, about half (41%) of the students felt that their fluency rate in spoken Spanish was lower than in English. These students expressed a desire to increase their fluency rate in spoken Spanish. Importantly, a majority of the students surveyed saw a clear link between their self-confidence in Spanish and pronunciation, stating that their confidence in spoken Spanish would be greater if their pronunciation were to improve.

As part of her survey, Arteaga recorded students' oral reports and performed a phonetic analysis. The L1 learners' Spanish pronunciation varied widely, but her analysis revealed nonetheless that one-third of the class showed transfer, in some cases highly marked, of English phonetic characteristics. These results are in keeping with those reported by Yeni-Komshian *et al.* (1997) and Flege *et al.* (1997) for L2 speakers cited in Section 2.9. The most problematic sequences for these students were [r̄], non-diphthongization of vowels and homorganic nasal assimilation, which are problems also found in L1 English speech (cf. Section 2.10). Arteaga's survey provided empirical support for the integration of phonetics in the SNS classroom, as well as affective responses indicating student interest for such a program.

2.12 Conclusion

In this chapter, we began by presenting an overview of the IPA. We explained to the reader the pitfalls of using orthography to represent speech sounds. We then turned to a general presentation of Spanish articulatory phonetics, in which we gave the articulatory description for Spanish consonants and vowels, followed by a brief introduction to the phonological processes found in the Spanish speech stream. We next discussed dialectal and sociolinguistic variation, the focus of this book, as present in Spanish phonology. We then considered the phonology of heritage speakers. We then gave an overview of L2 phonological acquisition, followed by a discussion of how L1 English transfer may affect the pronunciation of our L2 Spanish speakers. We concluded by discussing heritage speakers and Spanish phonology. In the following chapter, we turn to the morphosyntax of Spanish in all its variety.

Chapter 3

¿Dicen o decís? *Variation in the Forms of Spanish*

3.1   Introduction to Spanish Morphosyntax

What is the difference between *mesa* 'table' and *mesita* 'little table'? These two words are both singular, feminine nouns, referring to a piece of furniture. However, they do not have the same meaning, as *mesa* refers to a table, while *mesita* refers to a little table or a night stand. Part of our knowledge of language includes an understanding of word forms, or morphology. A morpheme is the smallest unit of meaning; therefore, our example *mesa* can be divided into the following two morphemes, as indicated by the hyphen (-), in (1):

(1)   *mes-a* 'table-f'

The morpheme *mes* is the noun stem, meaning 'table'; the final morpheme, *a*, indicates gender (in this case, feminine). The word *mesita* contains an additional morpheme, which corresponds to the diminutive *it* (a morpheme meaning 'little'):

(2)   *mes-it-a* 'table-little-f'

As seen by our examples (1) and (2), in nominal (relating to nouns) morphology in Spanish, gender (here feminine) and number (here singular) are typically indicated. Indeed, we could make *mesa* and *mesita* plural, by adding the plural morpheme *s*: *mes-a-s, mes-it-a-s*).

What about verbs? Consider the difference between *hablaron* 'they spoke' and *hablan* 'they speak'. In both verb forms, the theme vowel *a* follows the stem, indicating that the verb belongs to the first conjugation (i.e. it is an *ar* verb). The final *n* indicates that both these verb forms are third person plural (corresponding to a subject *ellos* 'they'). Yet, despite these similarities, the verbs *hablaron* and *hablan* are not identical, as they vary in terms of tense (past vs. present). Indeed, the preterit tense of *hablaron* is indicated by the morpheme *ro*, which *hablan*, the present tense, lacks.

52

Both verb forms can be divided into morphemes, as illustrated by the hyphens in (3) and (4):

(3)   *habl-a-ro-n*
      speak-thematic vowel-PRET-3pl
      'They spoke'
(4)   *habl-a-n*
      speak-thematic vowel-3pl
      'They speak'

In this brief introduction to nominal and verbal morphology, we have seen examples of the so-called bound morphemes (i.e. those that cannot stand alone). They are, therefore, always attached to other morphemes. Some morphemes, on the other hand, are free, as in the monomorphemic (one morpheme) example in (5):

(5)   *examen* 'test'

In (5) the word *examen* is a free monomorphemic word, which cannot be analyzed into further morphemes. The example in (6), on the other hand, contains the morphemes *examen* and the plural (bound) morpheme *-es*:

(6)   *exámen-es* 'tests'

Most bound morphemes in Spanish take the form of prefixes (i.e. they precede the noun or the verb stem) or suffixes (i.e. those that follow the noun or verb stem). Consider the following:

(7)   *tocó* 's/he/you touched'
      toc-ó
(8)   *retocó* 's/he/you retouched'
      re-toc-ó

The verb *tocó* has no prefix, although it has a suffix (*ó*), which indicates both the tense and the verb conjugation class (i.e. an *-ar* verb). In (6), there is syncretism (i.e., one form has more than one function, in this case, the suffix *-ó*, which indicates both the thematic vowel and the preterit tense). *Retocó*, on the other hand, has both the suffix *-ó* and the prefix *re-*, meaning 'again.'

     To summarize our discussion this far, note that the examples in (1)–(8) above also illustrate bound morphemes which have other morphemes attached to them. The basic morpheme in a word is the root or stem (as exemplified by *mes, habl* or *toc*); affixes (suffixes or prefixes) are attached to it in order to make up the word. Examples of these affixes are *it*, the diminutive marker in *mesita*; the plural markers *s* or *es*, in *mesitas* and *exámenes*;

ro, the preterit marker in *hablaron*; *a*, the thematic vowel in *hablaron*; *n*, the person marker in both verb forms *hablan* and *hablaron*; or *re*, the prefix indicating 'again'. With the exception of '*it*,' the affixes that we have used as examples do not change the basic meaning of the word (i.e. in the verbs *toca* 's/he/you touch' and *tocó* 'she/he/you touched,' the meaning of 'touch' remains constant), because they are considered to be inflectional. In Spanish, inflectional affixes typically express the notions of grammatical gender and plurality, for example, in noun morphology, and the notions of tense and aspect in verb morphology.

In addition to inflectional morphemes, however, we also find derivational morphemes. Derivation, in this context, makes reference to the process of creating words out of other words. Both *mes-a* and *mes-it-a* in examples (1) and (2) above contain the root *mes*, and the inflectional morpheme *a* indicating feminine gender. *Mesita*, nevertheless, has an additional circumfix, *-it*, indicating 'little'. By circumfix or infix we mean a morpheme that occurs between two other morphemes. We can tell that *it* is an infix rather than a suffix from examples like *Marcos-Marquitos* 'Marcus, little/dear Marcus', where the infix *-it* has been inserted directly into the monophomorphemic *Marcos*. In other words, the diminutive form is not **Marquisitos*.[76] Another example, from Bermúdez-Otero and Borjars (2006: 19), is *azuquítar* 'little sugar.' It is clear that the morpheme *-it* is inserted into the monomorphemic *azúcar* 'sugar.'

As discussed above, the morpheme *it*, the diminutive morpheme, is clearly a derivational morpheme, as it has changed the basic meaning of the word *mesa*, creating a word with a different meaning (e.g. 'little table' as opposed to 'table'). Regularly, derivation works with the phonological form of a word, as is, and, by adding affixes to it, creates (possible) new words. The list of derivational affixes in Spanish, as in many other languages, is very long, but we will provide some examples. In a word such as *imposible*, in number (9) below, we find an example with a prefix (an affix that precedes the stem) *in*, which adds a negative content to the basic adjective *posible*[77]:

(9)   *im-posible*
      not-possible
      'impossible'

As number (10) below shows, a word such as *juventud* 'youth' contains a suffix (an affix that follows the stem). The stem itself, *juven* (with a slight phonetic variation in comparison with the regular shape of the adjective *joven*), expresses the meaning 'young', whereas the suffix *tud* indicates 'characteristic of being'.

(10)   *juven-tud*
       young-characteristic of
       'youth'

In this particular example, not only has -*tud* added new meaning, but it has also changed the grammatical category of the word (from an adjective, *joven*, we have arrived at a feminine noun *juventud*).

In Spanish, as in many other languages, we can also find words where both prefixes and suffixes are present. If we consider the word *antidemo-crático* 'undemocratic/against democracy', for example, in (11) below, we find that it contains the prefix *anti*, indicating the idea of 'against', the stem *democrat*, carrying the meaning of 'democracy,' the suffix *c*, indicating that the word in question is an adjective, and an inflectional affix *o*, indicating masculine gender:

(11)   *anti-democrát-i-c-o* 'antidemocratic'

Another aspect of morphosyntax is the fact that in addition to word forms, utterances may differ with respect to their word order, or syntax. This is illustrated by (12) and (13) below:

(12)   *Tú vas al cine.* 'You go to the movies.'
(13)   *¿Vas tú al cine?* 'Do you go to the movies?'

In (13), the subject *tú* is postposed, meaning that it follows the verb. The utterance is therefore interpreted as a question. In addition to the syntax, intonation, as discussed in Chapter 2, or changes in pitch, also indicates that (13) is a question.

Syntactic differences do not always obviously result in meaning differences, as in (14) and (15):

(14)   *Voy a hacerlo* 'I am going to do it'
(15)   *Lo voy a hacer* (= 14)

In (14), the **clitic** (or object pronoun attached to the verb) *lo* follows the infinitive *hacer*, whereas in (15) it precedes the conjugated verb *voy*. Nonetheless, the meaning of the two utterances is the same. The syntactic phenomenon illustrated by (14) and (15), known as **clitic climbing**, is not possible with all verbs taking infinitives (see Strozer, 1976, for discussion). Note that in (14) and (15), the subject pronoun is not expressed, as is typical in Spanish, except in cases of special emphasis; Spanish, like Italian but unlike English, therefore, is referred to as a **null subject language**. We next address dialectal variation with respect to Spanish morphosyntax.

3.2   Regional Variation in Spanish Morphosyntax

According to De Stefano and Rentel (1975: 330), regional variation in syntax and morphology, while fewer in number than those of phonology or the lexicon, might be the most stable aspects of regional variation. Generally speaking, dialects of a language vary more in terms of morphology than in terms of syntax. Spanish follows this general pattern. While there is a great deal of regional variation in Spanish with respect to word forms, word order is similar across most dialectal areas, although there are exceptions, as we will see below. We begin our discussion by considering Spanish nouns, and how they vary across dialects.

3.2.1   Spanish nouns and gender variation

Following the loss of the neuter gender in the development from Latin to Spanish, discussed in more detail in Chapter 5, nouns are either masculine or feminine. In other words, Latin had three genders, masculine, feminine and neuter, whereas Spanish has two, masculine and feminine. For the most part, the gender of a noun in Spanish can be identified from its form: a final morpheme *a* indicates a feminine noun, and a final morpheme *o* indicates a masculine one. However, words ending in *e* or a consonant are not transparent in terms of gender.

Azevedo (1992: 338) provides some examples of gender variation in Spanish, but dismisses its relevance, arguing that the morphological category of gender is arbitrary. Stewart (1999: 111), however, following Fontanella de Weinberg (1999), states that there is considerable gender variation, both in Latin America and in Spain. Many of the cases in gender variation across dialects include the idea of analogy, for they are due to a desire to regularize or systematize forms that do not follow the basic guidelines of the language. We use the term *analogy* to refer to a process of regularization (i.e. making an irregular form regular, such as *rompido* for *roto* 'broken') that reduces the suppletive (irregular) forms in the grammar of a given language (Crystal, 1980: 17). We discuss analogy in detail in the next section.

3.2.2   Variation and change based on form

Some nouns ending in *o*, such as *moto* ('motorcycle'), *radio* ('radio') or *foto* ('photograph'), happen to be feminine because of their origin (i.e. they are shortened forms of feminine nouns: *motocicleta*, *radiotelegrafía* and *fotografía*, respectively). Given their form, however, there seems to be a contradiction in using feminine determiners with these nouns, as they end in *o*, and in many areas of Latin America and Spain, the masculine form is preferred (e.g. *el moto, el radio, el foto*).

The same occurs with nouns ending in *a*, which, because of their etymological origin, Greek, are masculine (*problema* 'problem', *poema* 'poem' and *reúma* 'rheum'). They are sometimes made feminine, in order to match their gender with their form. This procedure is quite frequent in the Spanish of the Southwest, as González Pino and Pino (2000: 13) point out: 'In the Southwest we have sometimes changed the gender of vocabulary items. It is not uncommon to hear *la problema, la sistema, la mapa, el canción, la papá.*'

A similar case, in the reverse direction, can be observed in terms such as *la modista* 'seamstress,' a feminine profession traditionally, with a masculine form *el modisto*, or the pair *la maquinista/el maquinisto* 'the machininist.' In the former pair, the connotations of both words are not exactly the same. However, the masculine version, at least in Peninsular Spanish, implies not just the ability to sew, but rather the more creative part of the profession, such as designing clothes.

As mentioned above, some nouns ending in *e* or a consonant are not transparent as far as gender is concerned, and may also vary (e.g. *el/la estudiante, el/la calor* 'heat', *el/la mar* 'sea', *el/la color* 'color'). According to the *Real Academia* in their *Esbozo* (1973: 179), the preference for one gender or another can be attributed to a variety of reasons, including pragmatics. For example, the authors mention that *la mar* is an expression used by seagoing people, whereas *la calor* and *la color* are non-educated forms, or found in the language used by peasants in different regions.

Finally, words such as *el alma* 'soul' and *el área* 'area' (where the traditional explanation for the clashing article has been related to the fact that they begin with a stressed [á]) also reflect great variation. We provide a diachronic explanation for this in Chapter 5, but synchronically (the language at a given point in time, here Modern Spanish), many speakers associate *el* with the masculine gender. Some native speakers produce (the prescriptively correct) phrases *el agua negra* 'the black water' or *las bellas aguas* 'the beautiful waters'. In Argentinean and Chilean Spanish, by analogy, the gender of these words has been reassigned, so that whatever modifier that appears with them takes the masculine form, such as *el agua negro*. In the next section, we consider neologisms (i.e. new word formations) which reflect a change in society.

3.2.3 Politically correct variation and change

Changes in society have allowed women to enter the workplace in areas that were traditionally reserved for men. These changes have also had an impact on the Spanish language, and in response the feminine forms of some professions have been created, for example, *el médico/la médica* 'doctor,' *el juez/la jueza* 'judge,' *el jefe/lajefa* 'boss' and *la azafata/el azafato* 'flight attendant.' The acceptance of these new feminine or new masculine forms, however, is not uniform in all areas of the Spanish-speaking world. Peninsular Spanish has historically been more conservative in this regard. As Zamora Vicente (1960: 341) points out, 'el español americano tiende a hacer más notoria que el peninsular la innovación de hacer adjetivos o nombres femeninos a voces que no tienen distinción genérica.'[78]

In the same vein, Fontanella de Weinberg (1999: 158) states that these feminine forms are commonly used in some Latin American countries by all society members. Such use, however, is not universally accepted, as seen by the use of the words *los miembros y las miembras* 'members,' which turned by the Spanish Minister for Equality, Bibiana Aído, in one of her first speeches. This happened in June 2008, shortly after her nomination, and received a great deal of attention in the Spanish media, who rejected this neologism. We next turn to variation in possessive forms, according to dialect.

3.3 Regional Variation in Possessive Forms

Possessive forms are directly related to personal pronouns, and refer to the three grammatical persons, both because of their origin and because of their meaning. Spanish uses possessive adjectives less frequently than some other languages, say English, preferring to use the definite article in constructions where an indirect object pronoun is used, indicating who or what is affected (what in traditional grammar is called the *dative of interest*). Thus, in Spanish, we do not use the possessive adjective, as in (16), but rather the definite article, as in (17), to express the same idea:

(16)   (*) *Voy a cortarme **mi** pelo.* 'I am going to get a haircut' (literally, 'I am going to cut me **my** hair').

(17)   *Voy a cortarme **el** pelo.* 'I am going to get a haircut' (literally, 'I am going to cut me **the** hair').[79]

Third person possessive adjectives (*su(s)*) are extremely ambiguous, for they may refer to a female or male possessor, either singular or plural, and also to somebody with whom we have a formal relationship (i.e. to whom we refer as *usted* or *ustedes*). The sentences in (18)–(23) illustrate this ambiguity:

(18)   *María tiene un perro. Es **su** perro.* 'Mary has a dog. It is her dog.'

(19)   *Juan tiene un gato. Es **su** gato.* 'Juan has a cat. It is his cat.'

(20) **Usted** *tiene un apartamento. Es* **su** *apartamento.* 'You (singular, formal) have an apartment. It is your apartment.'

(21) **María y Elena** *tienen abuelos. Son* **sus** *abuelos.* 'María and Elena have grandparents. They are their grandparents.'

(22) **Juan y Pablo** *tienen hermanos. Son* **sus** *hermanos.* 'Juan and Pablo have siblings. They are their siblings.'

(23) **Ustedes** *tienen una casa. Es* **su** *casa.* 'You (plural, formal) have a house. It is your house.'

In order to avoid this ambiguity, a prepositional phrase introduced by *de* ('of') and followed by the subject pronoun can be added. Thus, we can modify the sentences listed above, in the following manner:

(24) **María** *tiene un perro. Es* **su** *perro* **de ella.** 'Mary has a dog. It is her dog.'

(25) **Juan** *tiene un gato. Es* **su** *gato* **de él.** 'Juan has a cat. It is his cat.'

(26) **Usted** *tiene un apartamento. Es* **su** *apartamento* **de usted.** 'You (singular, formal) have an apartment. It is your apartment.'

(27) **María y Elena** *tienen abuelos. Son* **sus** *abuelos* **de ellas.** 'María and Elena have grandparents. They are their grandparents.'

(28) **Juan y Pablo** *tienen hermanos. Son* **sus** *hermanos* **de ellos.** 'Juan and Pablo have siblings. They are their siblings.'

(29) **Ustedes** *tienen una casa. Es* **su** *casa* **de ustedes.** 'You (plural, formal) have a house. It is your house.'

The constructions illustrated in (24)–(29) have the benefit of clarifying who the possessor is. Across dialect areas, as noted by the *Esbozo* (1973: 428), the general tendency is to limit the clarification phrase to *usted* and *ustedes*, as in (26) and (29), both in Spain and in Latin America. However, in some countries, such as Mexico, the presence of the prepositional phrase, without limitations, is a fact in daily usage. In Spain, on the other hand, its use is definitely limited to *usted* and *ustedes*, and it has a very old fashioned tone (the *Esbozo* (1973: 429) provides literary examples from the turn of the century). We next consider regional variation with respect to diminutives.

3.4 Diminutives and Regional Variation

In Section 3.1 above, we made reference to the process of derivation (the formation of new words, on the basis of existing ones by means of affixes). One important subset of derivational morphology in Spanish is what some scholars term 'affective derivation,' where the affix used serves to express the attitude, positive or negative, that the speaker has with respect to the idea denoted by the stem or base.[80] In this section we will discuss the main suffixes that Spanish L1 users utilize to express an opinion about the noun, as well as how different dialects differ as to the choices they make. We also touch upon how the affective values that are sometimes associated with this kind of derivation vary from one dialect to another.

It is generally agreed that the affective content (positive or negative) of the infix is prevalent over the objective meaning they might carry (for example, the ideas of 'little', 'large', etc.).[81] We begin by discussing the main diminutive infixes in Spanish: *it*, *ic* and *ill*. The first one, *it*, is the most common, and is used in all dialects. As Penny (1991: 246) states, *it* denotes approval or affection, and is diminutive in value.[82] In other words, the infix indicates affection on the speaker's part, coupled with an understanding that the object in question is smaller somehow, in stature or in age, as in the following:

(30) *Tuvo una **niñita**.* 'She had (i.e. gave birth to) a little baby girl.'
(31) *Deja ver **tu manito/manita**.* 'Let me see your (little) hand.'
(32) *Compré un **regalito** para tu **hijita**.* 'I bought a gift for your (little) daughter.'

Expressions (30)–(32) contain the diminutive *it* (**ito**, **ita**). In (30) above, the example indicates both affection and age of *niñita*, whereas the example in (31) indicates the small size of the child's hand. With respect to the object (*regalito*) bought in (32), the speaker talks about it positively, because of the affection holds for the addressee's *hijita*. In the same vein, when we refer to a family member using the diminutive form, it does not necessarily mean that the person is small in size (e.g. *mi sobrinita* 'my little niece' may or may not be young or small in size) but it might well refer to someone about whom we especially care.

Diminutives used to describe affection are just one instance of this affective derivation. For example, compare the sentences in (33) and (34):

(33) *Estoy leyendo una novela.* 'I am reading a novel.'
(34) *Estoy leyendo una novelita.* 'I am reading a novel that is not scholarly.'

Native speakers of Spanish intuitively understand that the book that is being read in (34), *una novelita*, as opposed to *una novela* in (33), is light, not very serious, reading. It is not necessarily a small book. Another infix, *ic*, as in (35), also has an affective value, added to its diminutive value:

(35) *Compraron **una casica**.* 'They bought a little house.'

Use of *casica*, however, is not as general as the use of *casita*. In Spain, it is used in certain areas (such as Navarre, Aragon, Murcia and Eastern

Andalusia), and it is also used in some areas of Latin America, particularly in Central America (Penny, 1991).

The suffix *ill* has evolved throughout history, given that it used to have both an affectionate and diminutive value, as still is the case in Andalusia where *ill* continues to be the preferred infix expressing affective emotion. However, in other parts of the Spanish-speaking world, the meaning of *ill* has changed to describe a more despective or pejorative interpretation; consider (36) below:

(36)   *Llevaba **un vestidillo** de algodón.* 'He wore a simple cotton garment/ garment of poor quality.'

The word *vestidillo* can mean 'little garment' or 'garment regarded positively' in Andalusia. Many other dialects, however, would interpret *vestidillo* negatively, due to its infix (e.g. a simple garment/garment of poor quality).

Another diminutive suffix found within the Spanish-speaking world is *ín*. It is similar to *it* and *ic*, in the sense that it is both affectionate and diminutive, as illustrated by (37):

(37)   *un gatín* 'a little cat'/'A cat that I view favorably.'

This infix is mostly used in certain areas of Spain (such as León and Extremadura), but not in Latin America, where it is rarely found. It is important to note that *ín* cannot be applied to just any stem. In other words, it is not a productive suffix.

The suffix *ej* also has a diminutive sense, but the value that is predominant is a pejorative one; consider (38):

(38)   *Pasamos por una **calleja**.* 'We passed through a narrow, not well paved or lit street.'

The speaker views *calleja* in (38) in a negative manner, as indicated by the gloss. The pejorative value of the suffix *ej* was already present in the initial stages of the language. In turn, *uel*, which originated in Latin *ŏld(us)* originally kept the diminutive and affective value, but in present-day Spanish it is also pejorative in most dialects. Compare, for example, (39) and (40):

(39)   *Es un **actor**.* 'He is an actor.'
(40)   *Es un **actorzuelo**.* 'He is a poor actor.'

Both *actor* and *actorzuelo* refer to 'an actor,' but the latter calls into question the professional skills of that person, so that it is a rather insulting term. Because we are dealing with affective values, however, nothing can be written in stone, since things might vary from individual to individual, according to their idiolect. For some speakers, *pollito* and *polluelo* (on the basis of *pollo* 'chicken') might be equally affectionate ways of referring to a recently hatched chicken.

The suffix *uc* is not very common in the standard language, but where it is found it has both a diminutive and a pejorative value. It is used mostly in Northern Spain (in Cantabria), where it actually is the most widespread suffix used to indicate affection. Consider (41):

(41)   *Le invité a mi casuca.* 'I invited him to my little house/house to which I am attached/house I view negatively.'

If a speaker talks about *mi casuca* (on the basis of *casa* 'little house'), two interpretations are possible: an affective one and a pejorative one.

We must also point out that it is possible to attach these infixes, particularly *it*, to adverbial bases. Indeed, adverbs such as *ahorita* (derived from *ahora* 'now'), *prontito* (derived from *pronto* 'soon'), *tempranito* (derived from *temprano* 'early'), *cerquita* (derived from *cerca* 'close by'), *lejitos* (derived from *lejos* 'far away'), *despacito* (derived from *despacio* 'slowly') or *rapidito* (derived from *rápido* 'quickly') are very common in daily life. Some speakers accept infixes such as *ill* (e.g. *tempranillo, lejillos*) with adverbial bases. Whatever the infix attached, the notion expressed in these cases is familiarity, as they are found in colloquial speech.

It is generally agreed that diminutives are used much more in Mexico, Central America and South America than they are in Spain. Hualde *et al.* (2002: 169) point out that in the Andes and in Mexico diminutives are particularly frequent, and that its use even affects numbers (such as *dosito*, on the basis of *dos* 'two'), some pronouns (e.g., *ellita*, on the basis of *ella* 'she') or even some verb forms (for instance, *callandito* 'quietly', on the basis of *callando*, the gerund of *callar* 'to keep quiet'). As these examples illustrate, diminutives are an intrinsic part of Spanish language use at present, and speakers apply them across many word categories, not just the traditional ones. In the next section, we discuss how Spanish verb forms may vary dialectally.

3.5   Variation in the Verb Forms

The verb system is very homogeneous across Spanish-speaking countries. Emphasizing this idea, Stewart (1999: 96) points out that even the non-standard and often stigmatized forms that have appeared [such as the use of *stes* as second person singular preterit ending, for example *dijistes* instead of standard *dijiste* ('you said')] seem to be common to all dialects. Regarding this particular instance, the *Real Academia* also states in its *Esbozo* (1973: 252) that its use 'se halla bastante extendido' 'it has spread to several areas,' but considers it a characteristic of careless and vulgar speech. In this section, we will explore areas of dialectal variation concerning the verbal group, such as agreement, tense, mood choice and analogical formations. We begin by considering verbal agreement.

3.5.1 Regional variation in verbal agreement

Generally speaking, in Spanish, the conjugated verb agrees in person and number with the subject, whether or not it is expressed, as in (42a), and whether or not it is postposed, as in (42b):[83]

(42) (a) *(Yo)* **hablo** *ruso* '(I) speak Russian.'
      (b) **Llega** *Juan hoy* 'Juan arrives today.'

However, there is a class of verbs, the so-called impersonal verbs, which are typically conjugated in the third person singular, regardless of accompanying noun phrases; this has been analyzed syntactically as agreement with a null third person impersonal pronoun (cf. English *it, there*). Examples of these kinds of verbal constructions are given in (43):[84]

(43) (a) **Está lloviendo** *mucho.* '(It) is raining a lot.'
      (b) **Ha hecho** *una helada terrible esta noche.* '(There) was a strong freeze last night.'
      (c) **Hay** *muchas personas en la fiesta.* '(There) are many people at the party.'
      (d) *Hubo tres accidentes de carro en aquella esquina.* '(There) were three car accidents at that corner.'

In such cases, the subject pronoun is not expressed in any dialect of Spanish.[85] However, in impersonal expressions, dialects of Spanish show variation with respect to verbal agreement, particularly where there is a plural noun phrase that is postposed, as is the case in (43d) above. For some speakers, the verbal agreement in (44) is found:

(44) (a) **Hacen grandes heladas** *esta temporada* (cf. 43b). 'There are strong freezes this season.'
      (b) **Hubieron tres accidentes** *de carro en aquella esquina ayer* (cf. 43d). 'There were three car accidents at that corner yesterday.'

Although in standard Peninsular Spanish, and in the prescriptive written language across the Spanish-speaking world, these verbs only appear in third person singular, as in (43) above, there are many dialects where pluralization of the verb from third person singular to third person plural, as in (44), is common.

Why is this variation found with impersonal verbs across Spanish dialects? As the *Esbozo* (1973: 384–5) points out, the verbs *hacer* 'to do/to make' and *haber* 'to be' may express the idea of existence or presence, and are equivalent to the verbs *ser* and *estar* 'to be.' This undetermined meaning gives rise to variation. Moreover, according to the *Esbozo* this pluralization is due to the interpretation, on the part of the speakers, of these verbs as personal verbs. It is suggested that in sentences like the ones listed in (44), the verb agrees with its complement, because the latter is felt to be its subject.

In the present day, the stigmatization of these structures varies. Stewart (1999: 97) points out that the plural of impersonal verbs is common in the Catalan-speaking parts of Spain, as well as the Canary Islands, and large parts of Latin America, among both educated and non-educated speakers, especially in urban areas. However, in parts of Spain, such as Navarre and Aragon, plural verbs in impersonal expressions rarely occur, and are considered to reflect uneducated speech. In the next section, we take up the topic of the usage of verb tenses across geographical areas.

3.5.2 Tense use

3.5.2.1 Past tense and verbal aspect

Verbal aspect in Spanish can best be exemplified by the contrast between the preterit and the imperfect, as in (45):

(45)   (a) *Iba a la playa.* 'I used to go to the beach.'
       (b) *Fui a la playa.* 'I went to the beach.'

Both verbs, *iba* and *fui*, are in the past tense; yet, in the case of (45a), the action is perceived to be habitual (cf. 'I used to go to the beach'), whereas in (45b) we understand that the reference is to a single moment in time (cf. 'I went to the beach'). This difference in telicity (indicating a completed action) between the imperfect and the preterit is one example of the verbal aspectual system in Spanish. As another example, consider (46)–(47):

(46)   *He ido a la playa* (present perfect). 'I have gone to the beach.'

(47)   *Fui a la playa* (preterit). 'I went to the beach.'

In (46), the present perfect *he ido* indicates that the action is anchored to the present, not to a specific point in time (e.g. recently), whereas in (47) we understand that the temporal reference is to a specific point in time in the past (e.g. yesterday). This difference in telicity between the present perfect and the preterit is not found in all dialects of Spanish.

Speakers in the northern part of Spain (particularly those of Galicia, León, Asturias and Cantabria), on the other hand, rarely use the present perfect tense tense. Penny (2000: 159), based on the examples provided by other scholars, such as Lapesa (1980) and Zamora Vicente (1960), concludes that 'in these areas the preterit is used to refer to past situations which occur in periods of time still current at the moment of speaking,' a usage that is also typical of Latin American Spanish, with the Canary Islands as the geographical link. The example in (48) below illustrates this usage:

(48)   *Esta semana **hablé** dos veces con ella.*
       'This week I spoke twice with her.'

In (48) above, the preterit is used despite the fact that the action is directly connected to the present (i.e. this week).

However, generally speaking, in most areas of Spain, this fusion of the present perfect and the preterit does not occur. As Alarcos (1947) pointed out, in the main contrast between these forms in terms of aspect in regions other than the northern varieties has to do with the speaker's perception of how the past situation described relates to the moment of speaking: in other words, whether it is perceived to be current (in which case the perfect tense is used) or not (in which case the preterit would be used). The examples in (49)–(50) illustrate this contrast:

(49)   *La semana pasada **hablé** dos veces con ella.* 'Last week I spoke twice with her.'
(50)   *Esta semana **he hablado** dos veces con ella.* 'This week I have spoken twice with her.'

Stewart (1999: 100) states that in some Latin American varieties, such as Mexican Spanish, the difference between these two tenses is aspectual (perfective vs. imperfective), meaning that the use of the perfect tense implies that the past situation continues to be valid at the time of speaking, and might be continued or repeated in the future (Penny, 1991: 160).[86]

An additional difference of Mexican Spanish concerns the frequent use of present indicative with the adverbs *aún* 'still' and *todavía* 'yet' where other varieties would use the present perfect, as in (51)–(52):

(51)   *Todavía no **hablo** con ella.* 'I have not spoken to her yet (literally, 'I do not speak with her yet')
(52)   *Todavía no **he hablado** con ella.* 'I have not spoken with her yet.'

We next turn to a discussion of how the future tense in Spanish varies across dialectal regions.

3.5.2.2 Future tense

According to Zamora Vicente (1960: 434), Latin American Spanish uses the future tense less frequently than Peninsular Spanish, preferring periphrastic or analytic constructions (structures in which grammatical functions are expressed by free morphemes) to synthetic constructions (a structure in which grammatical functions are expressed by bound morphemes). Latin American dialects especially prefer periphrastic *ir a* 'go to' + infinitive (53a) to the synthetic future (53b):

(53)   (a) *Voy a trabajar.* 'I am going to work.'
       (b) *Trabajaré.* 'I will work.'

While dialects of Latin American Spanish show a preference for periphrastic constructions, the specific forms used may vary from one regional variety to another. For example, in Central America and Colombia, the idea of future is expressed by means of *va y* + present tense, as in (54a), as noted by Zamora Vicente (1960: 434), which is equivalent to standard (54b):

(54)   (a) *Va y se cae.* 'S/he/you will fall' (literally, 'S/he/you goes and falls').
       (b) *Se caerá.* 'S/he/you will fall.'

Interestingly, the replacement of the synthetic form (54b) with the periphrastic form (54a) does not affect the so-called future of probability, as in (55), where the syncretic (= synthetic) future tense form is generally found across dialects:

(55)   *¿Dónde **estará**?* 'Where might/can s/he/you be?'

In all dialects of Spanish, future time can also be expressed by means of the present tense, as in (56):

(56)   *Mañana **llego**.* 'I arrive tomorrow.'

Stewart (1999: 101) adds that in Peru, it is common to use the present progressive for this purpose, as in (57):

(57)   ***Estoy llegando** mañana.* 'I am arriving tomorrow.'

This use of the present progressive to indicate futurity, although found in English (cf. 'I am arriving tomorrow'), is not seen in other dialects of Spanish. Across dialect areas, on the other hand, progressive forms can be used in order to express actions in progress in either the past or future, as in (58)–(62):

(58) **Estoy escribiendo** *en este momento* (present). 'I am writing at this moment.'

(59) **Estaba escribiendo** cuando sonó el teléfono (imperfect). 'I was writing when the phone rang.'

(60) **Estuve escribiendo** *tres horas* (preterit). 'I was writing for three hours.'

(61) **Estaré escribiendo** mañana (future). 'I will be writing tomorrow.'

(62) **Estaría escribiendo** *si tuviera tiempo* (conditional). 'I would be writing if I had time.'

Despite this fact, present and imperfect progressive forms ((58) and (59) above) are the most common ones. In particular, *estuve escribiendo* 'I was writing', but with perfect telicity, is rarely found, but when it occurs, it reflects the same aspectual difference as *estaba* and *estuve* (imperfective vs. perfective).

Additionally, we should bear in mind that *estar* is not the only auxiliary (e.g. helping verb) used with the gerund. Indeed, we also find progressive forms with verbs such as *andar* (literally, 'to walk'), *continuar* 'to continue,' *ir* 'to go,' *seguir* 'to continue,' 'to follow,' and *venir* 'to come,' as expressions (63)–(67) show:

(63) **Anda escribiendo** *un cuento*. 'S/he/you is writing a short story.' (literally, 'She is going around writing a short story').

(64) **Continuamos trabajando** *en el mismo lugar*. 'We continue working in the same place.'

(65) *El curso ya* **va terminando**. 'The course is coming to an end' (literally, 'The course is already goes finishing').

(66) **Seguimos pensando** *lo mismo*. 'We continue thinking the same.'

(67) **Vienes repitiendo** *la misma historia desde hace años*. 'You have been telling the same story for years' (literally, 'You come repeating the same story for years').

Generally speaking, such continuous forms seem to be less frequent in Peninsular Spanish than in Latin American Spanish. Stewart (1999) indicates that this is a rather recent development (over the last 50 years or so), and points to the idea of languages in contact as the source for this change: in this view, where Spanish is in close contact with English, the increased use of progressive forms has occurred. However, such a view cannot be an explanation for the spread of such forms in Latin America, given that there are several dialects, such as those in South America, which have little contact with

English, yet use progressive forms and other periphrastic forms with greater frequency than Spain. We next discuss analogical formation in Spanish.

3.5.3 Analogical formation

Azevedo (1992: 334–335) lists some processes of analogical regulariza-tion as morphological characteristics of various dialects, especially, but not limited to, Andalusian. These processes affect mostly irregular verbs, including forms such as some irregular future, preterit and past participle radicals (stems). For example, on the basis of future forms such as *podré* ('I will be able to') or *vendré* ('I will come'), future forms such as *hadré* ('I will do/make') or *quedré* ('I will want') appear (vs. standard *haré*, *querré*). Galmés de Fuentes (1983: 252) document similar forms, not only in Andalusia but in other Peninsular and American varieties as well.

Similarly, irregular preterit roots, such as *anduv-* for *andar* ('to walk'), can become regularized, so that the past tense for this verb becomes *andé, andaste, andó, andamos, andasteis, andaron* 'I walked, you walked, he walked, we walked, you all walked, they walked' (cf. standard *anduve, anduviste, anduvo, anduvimos, anduvisteis, anduvieron*). In addition, irregular past participles such as *escrito* 'written,' *puesto* 'put,' *cubierto* 'covered' and *muerto* 'dead' can become regularized: *escribido, ponido, cubrido* and *morido*. Zamora Vicente (1960: 331), in turn, goes a step further, and provides the following examples of their analogical forms: *escribío, ponío, cubrío, morío* 'written', 'put', 'covered', 'dead'.

The dialect of Spanish of the Southwest creates analogical formations systematically. As González Pino and Pino (2000: 13) state, "[in the Southwest] we change past participles, sometimes to regularize them, and do not use the irregular forms common elsewhere. We say *murido* 'dead', *escribido* 'written', *abrido*, 'opened', *cubrido* 'covered', instead of *muerto, escrito, abierto, cubierto.*" Menéndez Pidal (1940: 322) refers to this regularizing tendency, and hypothesizes that formations will end up replacing the irregular forms. Note that Menéndez Pidal does not focus on Andalusia here; rather, he considers this tendency a characteristic of the dialects of Spanish in general.

Another analogical regularization is the change in stress pattern in the present subjunctive. In this mood, the stress regularly falls on the stem in the first, second and third person singular, and third person plural, as is regular. This stress pattern is also generalized to the first and second per-son plural, so that all verb forms receive stress on the stem (Zamora Vicente, 1960: 330). Using *tener* ('to have') to illustrate this process, we would find: *tenga* 'I have', *tengas* 'you have', *tenga* 'she/he has', *tengamos* 'we have', *tengais* 'you pl. have', *tengan* 'they have', 'I have' (vs. standard *tenga, tengas, tenga, tengamos, tengais, tengan*). We next turn to variation in the terms of address in the pronominal system of Spanish.

3.6 Dialectal Variation in the Pronominal System

Spanish evinces a great deal of regional variation in its pronominal system. This great variety is seen in both subject pronouns and object pronouns. Some of this variation is a result of historical developments, which we discuss in detail in Chapter 5. In this section, we discuss how the dialects of Spanish vary in their pronoun usage, beginning with a discussion of Spanish terms of address.

3.6.1 Terms of address

Dialectal variation can be seen in Spanish in both the second person singular and second person plural pronouns, although not within the same dialect. Consider the following (67a), (67b) and (67c):

(68) (a) *Tú hablas con tu primo.* 'You talk to your cousin.'
(b) *Vosotros habláis con vuestros primos.* 'You all talk to your cousins.'
(c) *Ustedes hablan con sus primos.* 'You all talk to your cousins.'

As discussed in Chapter 1, dialects vary according to which form, *vosotros habláis* (68b) or *ustedes hablan* (67c), is the plural of *tú hablas* (68a). As is the case for subject pronouns (*vosotros/ustedes*) and possessive adjectives (*vuestro(s)/su(s)*), this regional variation is also manifested in object pronouns. In other words, if a dialect of Spanish uses (68b) as the plural of (68a), it also uses (69b) as the plural of (69a):

(69) (a) (*Yo*) *te veo* '(I) speak to *you*.'
(b) (*Yo*) *os veo* '(I) speak to *you-all*.'
(c) (*Yo*) *los veo* '(I) see *them / you-all*.'

In this way, differences in forms of address are systematic across Spanish dialects.

Vosotros is used as the plural of *tú* within Spain. It is the informal form of address for the second person plural, *ustedes* being the formal form of address for the second person plural. The corresponding verbal endings are distinct, as are the corresponding object pronouns and possessive adjectives and pronouns (as seen above). However, throughout Latin America and some parts of Andalusia, a single form, *ustedes*, does double duty: it represents both the formal and informal second person plural, as the plural form for both *tú* and *usted*. These regional differences are illustrated by the table in (70):

(70)   Forms of address in Spanish: informal second person plural

Spain *Informal second person plural*	*Latin America* *Informal second person plural*
Subject pronoun: *vosotros*	Subject pronoun: *ustedes*
(Regular) verb endings: *-ais, -eis, -ís*	(Regular) verb endings: *-an, -en, -en*
Possessive: *vuestro(a)(s)*	Possessive: *su(s)*
Object pronoun: *os*	Object pronoun: *los/las/les*

For native speakers of Latin American Spanish unfamiliar with *vosotros*, the pronoun and its accompanying verb forms may sound archaic or even odd. However, it is important to note that for most speakers of Peninsular Spanish, *vosotros* is obligatory in informal plural contexts, as *ustedes* indicates formality. For these speakers, in other words, *ustedes* is anomalous as the plural of informal *tú*.

The difference illustrated in (70) disappears in the formal form of address, as both Peninsular and Latin American Spanish use *ustedes* as the plural counterpart of *usted*. This is summarized by the table in (71).

(71)   Forms of address in Spanish: formal second person plural

Spain and Latin America formal second person plural
Subject pronoun: *ustedes*
(Regular) verb endings: *-an, -en, -en*
Possessive: *su(s)*
Object pronoun: *los/las/les*

Although all dialects within Latin America use *ustedes* instead of *vosotros* to indicate the informal second person plural, dialectal variation exists nonetheless with respect to the informal second person singular. Indeed, much of Latin American Spanish, unlike Peninsular Spanish, exhibits *voseo*, in which *vos* is used as an informal second person singular. The use of *vos* illustrated by (72b), is, for many Latin Americans, the preferred form for (72a)[87]:

(72)   (a) **Tú hablas** *español* 'You speak Spanish.'
         (b) **Vos hablá(i)s** *español* 'You speak Spanish.'

There is variation, however, with respect to Latin America. For example, Mexico (except for the state of Chiapas, adjacent to Guatemala), Peru, Bolivia, the Caribbean Islands (Cuba, Dominican Republic and Puerto Rico) and most of Venezuela favor *tú*. That is, these areas have preferred *tuteo* (i.e. exclusive use of *tú* for the second person informal singular).

In Argentina, Uruguay, Paraguay, and Central America (areas considered to be culturally distant from the metropolis), *vos* tends to prevail. Finally, in other areas (Chile, Ecuador, Colombia), the two systems (e.g. *tuteo* and *voseo*) are still in competition, giving way to complex sociolinguistic relationships that we will discuss below. It is also important to note that even when *vos* is used as a subject pronoun for informal address, the object pronoun forms that are used are those based on *tú*, that is, *te*, and the corresponding possessive pronouns are *tu* and *tuyo*, as Cotton and Sharp (1988: 147) note.

Unlike *vosotros*, which has clearly delineated verbal endings across dialects in Spain, there is a great deal of regional variation with respect to verb forms used with *vos*, most likely because the verb form is not formally taught in schools in Latin America. For example, three different endings can be used with *vos* with the present tense of regular *ar* verbs just in Chile: *áis*, *ás* and *á* (cf. Azevedo, 1992: 340).[88] Indeed, Fontanella de Weinberg (1999: 1409–1411) presents five different verb patterns for *vos*, with an outline of the most common conjugations for the present, future and imperative. Further, she summarizes the geographical distribution thereof. It is a complex system, which is made even more so by the fact that there are multiple combinations between pronouns (*tú*/*vos*) and verb forms (i.e. those belonging specifically to *tú*, and the different derivations of the *vosotros* verb forms). Consider, for example, the following excerpt, published in the Argentinean newspaper *La Nación*, and gathered by Fontanella de Weinberg (1999: 1407):

(73) *Aquí no estamos para despedirte.* **Vos** no **te** *has ido; no querés irte, no* **te** *irás nunca.* 'We are not here to say goodbye to you. You haven't left, you don't want to go, you won't ever leave.'

In (73), *vos* is used with the reflexive and direct object pronoun corresponding to *tú*. Two of the verb forms, *has ido* and *irás*, also have *tú* endings; *querés*, however, is a derivation of the *vosotros* form *queréis*, the ending of which has become a monophthong. As shown by the examples discussed above, the use of *voseo* is definitely not uniform, nor are its verb endings. Its widespread variants are linked to its origin, because it is a consequence of the fusion of different paradigms, as we have seen. Moreover, in most areas where it is used it was never regularized, since it was not considered a feature of standard speech. In Section 3.8.3.2 below we will discuss further the phenomenon of *voseo* considering the sociolinguistic implications that are involved in its use. We next address dialectal variation with respect to direct and indirect object pronouns.

3.6.2 Direct and indirect object pronouns

Dialects of Spanish show a great deal of variation with respect to third person direct and indirect object pronouns. In Spanish classes in the United States, the system taught is that of etymological usage, the *uso etimológico* 'etymological usage' of pronouns, which differentiates between direct and indirect object pronouns, as shown in (74a) and (74b):

(74)   (a) *Lo vi [a Juan] y le hablé* 'I saw him (John) and I talked to him.'
       (b) *La vi [a María] y le hablé* 'I saw her (Mary) and I talked to her.'

In (74a), *lo* is the direct object of the verb *ver*, whereas *le* is the indirect object of the verb *hablar*. Similarly, in (74b), *la* represents the direct object of *ver*, whereas *le* is the indirect object of the verb *hablar*. In this system, gender is indicated in the direct object pronoun, but not in the indirect object pronoun. There is a clear difference in the grammatical function (case). This usage is summarized in the table in (75) below:

(75)   Table. System 1: Etymological use of third person object pronouns in Spanish

Direct object	*Indirect object*
Singular: *lo/la* 'him/her/it/you'	Singular: *le* 'to him/her/you'
Plural: *los/las* 'them/you'	Plural: *les* 'to them/you'

The regional variation that exists with respect to object pronouns is a form of syncretism, as discussed in detail in Chapter 5. What is found synchronically in dialects is an overgeneralization of the indirect object (*le/les*) or of the direct object (*lo/la/los/las*). In the first alternative, known as *leísmo*, *le* does double duty as both the direct (masculine) and indirect object pronoun. Compare (76) below with (74a) above:

(76)   *Le vi [a Juan] y le hablé* 'I saw him (John) and I spoke to him.'

In such a system, illustrated by the table in (77), in the masculine, neither case nor gender is indicated by the object pronoun, although number remains (*le* vs. *les*); *la* is kept as the direct feminine object pronoun.

(77)   Table. System 2: *leísmo* (with masculine, animate nouns)

Direct object	Indirect object
Singular: *le, la*	Singular: *le*
Plural: *les, las*	Plural: *les*

It is important to note that the system given above functions solely with animate nouns (e.g., people). With inanimate nouns (e.g., things), *leísmo* is not found in any dialect of Spanish. In other words, both (78a) and (78b), but not (78c), are possible in a *leísta* dialect:

(78)   (a) *Lo vi* 'I saw it' (e.g., the car).
          (b) *Le vi* 'I saw him.'
          (c) **Le vi* 'I saw it.'

El uso etimológico and *leísmo* do not lend themselves easily to geographical limits, in that both variants are found throughout Latin America and Spain. Although typically in the United States only the *uso etimológico* is presented to students in beginning Spanish classes, it is interesting to note that both systems are considered standard by the *Real Academia* when the referent is a person, as stated in the *Esbozo* (1973: 424–425). In other words, both (74a) and (76) would be considered grammatically correct both from a descriptive and from a prescriptive point of view.

The reason for the development of *leísmo* is commonly thought to originate in the use of *a* personal 'personal *a*' vs. dative *a*. The former is used when the direct object is a person or a personalized object, as in *Vi a María* 'I saw María' and *Vi a mi perrito 'I saw my dog.'* The a personal can also precede a plural noun, as in *Quiero a mis papás* 'I love my parents.' A homophonous free morpheme introduces an indirect object: *Le hablé a María.* 'I spoke to María.' For a child, there could be a fusion of personal/dative a, which would explain the development of *leísmo*. In other words, if a native speaker interprets the a in both cases to have the same function, it would be a natural development to replace both by the same pronoun, in this case *le les*.

In Spain, a third variant exists, *loísmo/laísmo*, in which *lo/la*, *los/las*, the accusative (direct object) pronouns, are used as both direct and indirect object pronouns. An example of *laísmo* can be seen in (79) below:

(79)   *La vi y la hablé.* 'I saw her/you and I spoke to her/you.'

This system, in which syncretism has favored the accusative over the dative (indirect object), as summarized in the table in (80), is considered by linguistics to be marked, or atypical for the language:

(80)   System 3: *loísmo/laísmo*

Direct object	Indirect object
Singular: *lo, la*	Singular: *lo, la*
Plural: *los, las*	Plural: *los, las*

In this system, *lo* and *la* are used for the indirect and the direct object pronouns. For example, this variant allows *La hablo*, (Literally 'I speak her') for *Le hablo* 'I speak to her/him/you.' This variation most likely has the same source as leísmo. In other words, if a child interprets both *Le hablo a María* and *Veo a María* as personal 'a' s/he will replace both forms with the direct object pronoun.

Another interesting aspect of regional variation concerning third person indirect and direct object pronouns has to do with constructions in which both pronouns are used together, and therefore the indirect object pronoun becomes *se* as in (81b) below:

(81)   (a) **Les** *conté* **el problema** *a mis amigos*. 'I told my friends the problem.'
        (b) **Se lo** *conté*. 'I told it to them.'

Se in these constructions is very ambiguous, because it may make reference to a singular or plural, feminine or masculine, indirect object. The example in (82) shows the myriad sources of *se* in the expression *se lo conté*:

(82)   (a) *Le conté el problema a María.* 'I told María the problem.'
        (b) *Le conté el problema a Juan.* 'I told Juan the problem.'
        (c) *Le conté el problema a usted.* 'I told you (sing. formal) the problem.'
        (d) *Les conté el problema a mis hermanas.* 'I told my sisters the problem.'
        (e) *Les conté el problema a mis amigos.* 'I told my friends the problem.'
        (f) *Les conté el problema a ustedes.* 'I told you (pl. formal) the problem.'

In (82), then, *se* can be the replacement of *le* referring to a feminine singular indirect object, *a María*, in (82a) or to a masculine singular indirect object, *a Juan*, in (82b). *Se* can further replace plural indirect object forms; in other words, in our examples above, *se* can replace *les* (which refers to a feminine plural indirect object), in *a mis hermanas* 'my sisters,' in (82d), and when referring to a masculine plural indirect object, *a mis amigos* 'my friends,' in (82e).

As the sentences in (82) further show, Spanish allows for a prepositional phrase to reduplicate the information in the pronoun *le*, which is obligatory. In our examples, *le* refers to *a María* 'to Mary' in (82a), *a Juan* 'to John' in (82b), *a usted* 'you (formal)' in (82c), *a mis hermanas* 'to my sisters' in (82d), *a mis amigos* 'to my friends' in (82e) and *a ustedes* 'to you all' in (82e). The pronoun *se* is even more ambiguous than *le*, as it does not have a plural form. The use of the clarification phrase with *se* is the common way to make the sentence less ambiguous, both in Peninsular Spanish and in cultured Mexican Spanish, as noted by Cotton and Sharp (1988: 159). Consider the examples in (83):

(83)   (a) *Se lo conté **a ustedes**.* 'I told it to you all.'
     (b) *Se lo conté **a mi(s) hermana(s)**.* 'I told it to my sister(s).'
     (c) *Se lo conté **a mis amigos**.* 'I told it to my friend(s).'

In these examples, the clarification phrase counteracts the ambiguity of *se*.

Popular Mexican Spanish has a different way of addressing the ambiguity of *se*. Specifically, this dialect indicates the plurality of *se* (where it is replacing *les*) by adding an *s* to the direct object pronoun *lo/la*.

(84)   *Se los dije.* 'I told it to them/you-all.'

In other words, in (84) *los* could be a synthesis of the direct object pronoun corresponding to *el problema*, and the *s* reflecting the plurality of *mis hermanas*, *mis amigos* or *ustedes*; see (82) above. We next consider the regional variety in the syntax of Spanish.

3.7   Syntactic Phenomena

Generally speaking, dialects of a language evince fewer syntactic differences than they do phonological, morphological or lexical ones. Spanish is no exception to this general rule. In this section, we consider question formation in Caribbean Spanish, conditional sentences, *dequeísmo*, and *queísmo*.

3.7.1   Questions in Caribbean Spanish

In Spanish, as in most languages, there are two basic types of questions: those that require a yes/no answer and those that look for specific information and therefore contain a specific question word.[89] Yes/no questions may not require inversion of the subject pronoun (86), because the rising intonation is enough to turn a declarative sentence into a question.

However, in the case of information questions, inversion of the subject pronoun, if expressed, is obligatory (87) in most dialects of Spanish. Compare the following examples:

(85)   *Hablas español.* 'You speak Spanish' (declarative sentence).
(86)   *¿Hablas español?* 'Do you speak Spanish?'
(87)   *¿Qué necesitas (tú)?* 'What do you need?'

Should (87) above lack inversion of the subject pronoun, it would be considered grammatically incorrect or odd in most dialects of Spanish. However, this word order is, in fact, a common feature of colloquial Caribbean Spanish (that of Cuba and the Dominican Republic, for example; see Rivero (1980), among others, for discussion). That is, (88) below would be a perfectly acceptable utterance in this area of the Spanish-speaking world (see Ordóñez & Olarrea, 2001, and references cited therein, among others):

(88)   *¿Qué **tú** necesitas?* 'What do you need?'

Further, in this dialect, the expression of subject pronouns is far more common than in other varieties (see Flynn & O'Neil, 1988, among others). In other words, in Caribbean Spanish, the expression of *tú* in (88) would be typical and would not have the emphatic overtones that it would have in other dialectal regions (see Contreras, 1991; Toribio, 2000). We next discuss the regional variety in conditional sentences in Spanish.

3.7.2 Conditional sentences

According to traditional grammar, conditional sentences are made of two clauses; the main clause is the protasis (Spanish *prótasis*), whereas the conditional sentence proper, the one introduced by *if* (*si* in Spanish), is the apodosis *apódosis*. The prescriptive rule requires the use of past or pluperfect subjunctive in the *si* clause, whereas the conditional or conditional perfect must be used in the *prótasis*. This is exemplified by (89) and (90) below:

(89)   *Si **ganara** la lotería, **viajaría** por todo el mundo.* 'If I **won** the lottery, I **would travel** around the world.'

(90)   *Si **hubiera tenido** dinero, **habría viajado** por todo el mundo.* '**If I had had money, I would have traveled** around the world.'

In example (89), the verb following *si*, *ganara*, is in the imperfect subjunctive. The main verb *viajaría* is in the conditional. In (90), on the other hand, the *si* clause takes a verb in the pluperfect subjunctive, followed by the conditional perfect in the main clause (e.g. *habría visitado*). Actual usage in

Spanish, however, is not so straightforward. Stewart (1999: 103) acknowledges the fact that in the colloquial language, the conditional has been commonly replaced by the subjunctive form. That is, in an effort to simplify the structure, the same tense/mood is used in both *prótasis* and *apódosis*. In this way, (91) and (92) below could very well be used in much of the Spanish-speaking world instead of (89) and (90) above, respectively, with the same meaning[90]:

(91)   Si **ganara** la lotería, **viajara** por todo el mundo (= (88)).
(92)   Si **hubiera tenido** dinero, **hubiera viajado** por todo el mundo (= (89)).

The *Esbozo* (1973: 473, 474) of the *Real Academia* prescriptively allows the replacement in the case of the simple tense, but not in the case of the compound one. That is, (91) above would be admissible, but not (92). Indeed, the replacement of the conditional present and past by the imperfect and the pluperfect tenses seems to be a more common phenomenon in Latin America than in Spain, where the *Real Academia* has greater influence. However, there are areas (Northern Spain in particular) where the replacement has gone in the opposite direction. In other words, conditional forms are used in both the *protasis* and the *apodosis*. This usage is considered marked (*Esbozo*, 1973: 473). In these areas, (93) below would be the equivalent of (89) above:

(93)   Si ganaría la lotería, viajaría por todo el mundo.

We next turn to another morphosyntactic process that varies across dialects, namely *dequeísmo*.

3.7.3 *Dequeísmo*

Dequeísmo is widespread in Spanish on both sides of the Atlantic. In this structure, the preposition *de* ('of') is used before *que* ('that', a linking conjunction) that introduces subordinate noun clauses. The prescriptively correct usage is illustrated in (94a). An illustration of the use of the preposition *de* where none is needed, is seen in (94b).

(94)   (a) *Pienso* **que** *estás equivocado.* 'I think that you are wrong.'
         (b) **Pienso* **de** *que estás equivocado* (= 94a).

Another source of *dequeísmo* is the generalization of *de* when another preposition would be required. Consider (95a) and (95b) below:

(95)   (a) *Confío* **en que** *te mejores pronto.* 'I hope you will get better soon.'
         (b) **Confío* **de** *que te mejores pronto* = (95a).

In the example (95a), the prescriptively correct preposition en is used following *confiar* (e.g. *confiar* en 'to trust'). In example (95b), the preposition
de has been substituted for *en*. If one adopts a prescriptive approach
regarding *dequeísmo*, it would be considered a mistake, because it is stigmatized, both in Spain and in Latin America (see Gómez Molina, 1995, or
Fontanella de Weinberg, 1999). In the *Diccionario panhispánico de dudas*
(2005: 214–215), also written by the *Real Academia*, this scholarly organization does not leave any doubt about its position in this regard. In fact, it
provides a lengthy list of examples of this phenomenon, as well as a possible test to determine whether it is appropriate to use *de* or not, by asking
the question corresponding to the subordinate clause, as in (96).[91]

(96) (a) *Pienso de que te pondrás bien.* 'I think (of) that you will get better.'
      (b) **¿De qué piensas?* *Of what do you think?
      (c) *¿Qué piensas?* What do you think?

In other words, for speakers to arrive at the (prescriptively) correct form,
they are directed to ask the question corresponding to (96a). Native speakers, even those who naturally produce (96a), will not accept (96b). It is
interesting to note, that even in dialects where *dequeísmo* is common,
speakers will not accept (96b). One possible explanation for this is that de
is considered by speakers favoring dequeísmo as the marker of a subordinate clause.

Queísmo is the opposite variant, that is, the deletion of *de* (or another
preposition) preceding *que* in cases where it would be prescriptively obligatory. Like *dequeísmo*, it is found both in Spain and in Latin America. For
example, the expression *estar seguro de que* ('to be positive about') frequently becomes *estar seguro que*. The expression in (97) illustrates this
phenomenon, commonly considered a hypercorrection, or an incorrect
form that is produced by analogy with a prescriptive one, in this case an
overgeneralized correction of *dequeísmo*:

(97) *Estoy seguro que vas a mejorar pronto.* 'I am positive that you are going
      to get better soon.'

In summary, both *dequeísmo* and *queísmo* are widespread in the Spanish-
speaking world, although they are not prescriptively accepted. We next
turn to sociolinguistic aspects of morphosyntactic variation.

3.8   Sociolinguistic Aspects of Morphosyntactic Variation

There are cases in Spanish in which variations in morphosyntax reflect
not (only) a regional difference, but also a difference in register. In other

words, the choice of one form over another has sociolinguistic consequences. This means that the listener will interpret the speaker's speech as formal or informal, depending on whether or not he or she modifies the morphosyntax. We begin in this section by discussing how morphosyntactic variation in Spanish nouns can affect register.

3.8.1 Gender of nouns

In Section 3.3 above, we discussed some instances of gender modification in the case of feminine nouns that start with a stressed vowel *á*, particularly in popular speech. For example, instead of the normative (prescriptive) form *el área* ('the area'), *la área* would be commonly used in colloquial speech in certain parts of the Spanish-speaking world. In his discussion on articles, Leonetti (1999: 790) states that hesitancy between both forms is very frequent in present-day use, as speakers alternate between the analogical and prescriptive forms.

In other words, the language is in flux with respect to the gender of articles used in these cases. Leonetti discusses the alternation not only in the case of nouns that actually could take both genders (such as *azúcar* 'sugar'), but also in the case of nouns that are clearly feminine, as well as nouns derived from them (e.g., the diminutive form). The examples that he provides are *el agüita/la agüita* ('the water,' diminutive form) and *el aguamarina/la aguamarina* ('the aquamarine'). In these pairs of words, the first element is the normative one.

According to Leonetti's interpretation, speakers associate *el* with the masculine gender, and this is the source of the analogical tendency that we discussed previously, which manifests in two important phenomena. On the one hand, when adjectives precede one of these nouns, they tend to appear in the masculine form, in agreement with *el*. For example, *el extenso área* ('the extense area') would coexist with normative *la extensa área*. On the other hand, not only articles, but also other determiners and quantifiers, would take the masculine form with these nouns. For instance, *este área* ('this area') would be used instead of prescriptive *esta área*. As we have seen above, these are common replacements in colloquial speech in many parts of the Spanish-speaking world.

Álvarez de Miranda (1993) and Janda and Varela-García (1991) have studied this phenomenon extensively, and point out that this substitution, where, for example, the adjective agrees in masculine gender with the article, is much more common when the adjective precedes the noun, but less frequent when it is postposed. Leonetti, however, offers instances of this latter situation as well (continuing with our example, *el área extenso* 'the extense area'). As mentioned above, this was initially a common phenomenon in colloquial Spanish, but for some speakers, it is currently spreading to the written language, evidence that for them the language is in a state of change with regard to the use of determiners with nouns beginning with stressed *á*. We next turn to a construction in which the definite article precedes names.

3.8.2 Use of the definite article with names

Names are considered to be definite noun phrases, and therefore are not, as a general rule, preceded by articles. However, there are some instances in which they do appear accompanied by a definite article, especially in familiar varieties of speech. Compare the utterances in (98) and (99):

(98)   *Carmen vino a visitarte.* 'Carmen came to see you.'
(99)   *La Carmen vino a visitarte.* '(The) Carmen came to see you.'

The example in (98) corresponds to standard usage, whereas (99) represents familiar/popular use. Dialects vary with respect to the use of the definite article before a name. In some dialects, this usage is associated with speakers without formal education, and may have pejorative overtones.

There are other dialect areas, however, that generally accept the usage of a definite article with a proper noun. For example, in both Catalán and Portuguese, definite articles can accompany a personal first name, and in those regional varieties that are in contact with these two languages, the use of articles with names is frequently found even among more educated speakers. Further, the use of the definite article with a name is also common in the Andean regions of Latin America (see Cotton & Sharp, 1988).

Finally, there is one instance in which all varieties of Spanish admit the use of articles with proper personal names. In informal speech, proper names are frequently shortened (for example, *el Fede* for *Federico* 'Fredick', literally 'the Frederick', or *la Luci* for *Lucía*, literally 'the Lucy'). We next consider the sociolinguistic aspects of the terms of address.

3.8.3 Terms (forms) of address

D'Ambrosio (2004) argues that part of communicative competence in Spanish is knowing the correct form of address. This is a complex issue, because the use of forms of address varies according to the norms of courtesy, interpersonal distance, and social and cultural differences. In addressing this issue, we will be concerned with the opposition formal–informal. The formal and informal ways of address have been studied extensively, following the seminal study by Brown and Gilman (1960) who make the distinction between two main concepts, power and solidarity, as the governing factors for usage. In Spanish, power can be shown in asymmetric ways of address (one of the speakers is addressed as *usted*, whereas the other one is addressed as *tú* or *vos*). The differences in status that exist between both interlocutors (e.g. related to age, family or work relationship, social background, gender) are manifested in this way.

In Brown and Gilman's framework, the other concept, where solidarity (or perceived equality in social distance) exists, the relationship is symmetric, that is, the terms of address that the speakers exchange are the same. In other words, if they are addressed formally as *usted*, they mirror the use of *usted* in their answer, and if they are addressed informally with *tú/vos*, they themselves use the same terms. Present-day usage varies across the Spanish-speaking world; the most conservative communities (especially in rural areas) still predominantly have asymmetric relations, whereas in most metropolises symmetric relationships are more common. In the following sections we will consider, briefly, the most common patterns.[92]

3.8.3.1 Tú and vosotros(as) *vs.* usted and ustedes

In Spain, *tú* is the familiar second person singular term of address, with *vosotros(as)* as its plural counterpart. The subject pronouns *usted* and *ustedes* are the corresponding formal ways of address due to their origin, as discussed in detail in Section 3.6.1. That is to say that both agree with a third person, singular or plural, verb form. Social changes in Spain since the death of Franco have favored more symmetric relationships, and the use of *tú/vosotros* is widespread. Schwenter (1993: 73), for example, reports the following dialogue between a customer and a shop assistant, in which the salesperson addresses the client (whom s/he does not know), with *tú*:

(100) Clienta: *Hola.* 'Client: Hi.'

Dependiente: *Hola. ¿Qué quieres?* 'Clerk: Hi. What do you-sg-inf want?'

In some parts of Spain, however, *usted* is still commonly used when the parties do not have a close relationship; the opposition is therefore between *tú* and *usted* for the singular forms. The plural form is *ustedes* for both formal and informal ways of address. This is the case in the Canary Islands and some areas of Andalusia. This is exemplified by (101), (102) and (103):

(101) *¿Qué quieres (tú)?* 'What do you want?'
(102) *¿Qué quiere (Ud)?* 'What do you want?'
(103) *¿Qué quieren (Uds.)?* 'What do you want?'

In other words, as is the case in Latin America, (103) in these regional varieties represents the plural form of both (101) and (102), as opposed to the usage within the rest of Spain, where (103) is the only plural of (102). In the Canary Islands and some areas of Andalusia, we can also find a hybrid combination of verbal endings, exemplified in (104), where the formal, plural pronoun *ustedes* is used with the informal, second person plural, verb form (the one corresponding to *vosotros*):

(104) *¿Qué queréis ustedes?* 'What do you want?'

This usage is considered stigmatized prescriptively. See Green (1990) and Criado Costa and Criado Costa (1992) for further discussion.

The system that we have described as predominant in the Canary Islands and Andalusia is referred to as *tuteo* (the use of *tú* for the informal singular and *ustedes* in the plural) and it is the system that predominates in Mexico and most of the Caribbean. In *tuteo*, *tú* and *usted* are the singular forms of address, informal and formal, respectively. In the plural, however, there is a single form, *ustedes*, for both formal and informal address. Unlike the regional varieties of the Canary Islands, in Latin America, the verbal ending used with *ustedes* is not formed from *vosotros*. In other words, forms such as that shown in (103) are used, but not (104).

Another difference between Latin American and Spanish usage of subject pronouns is that in the former, asymmetric relationships are more predominant and social distances are still very noticeable (cf. Brown & Gilman, 1960). Schwenter (1993: 73) provides the following example, a dialogue that contrasts with that in (100):

(105)   Dependienta: *Buenas tardes* 'Good afternoon.'
        Clienta: *Buenas tardes* 'Good afternoon.'
        Dependienta: *¿En qué puedo servirle?* 'How can I help you-sg-f?'

The clerk in this exchange refers to the customer as *usted*, as seen by her use of the pronoun *le* (*servirle*), instead of the familiar *servirte*.

3.8.3.2 Voseo

From a sociolinguistic point of view, the situation regarding the use of *vos* varies greatly, because dialects differ widely in their acceptance of this verb form in standard speech. For many speakers, *voseo* forms part of their most informal register and is used as a form of address for very close friends and family members only. *Tuteo* is found in all other cases for the informal pronoun. This is because in most dialects speakers employ *vos* in addition to *tuteo*, so that it does not supplant it.

In Argentina, Uruguay and Costa Rica, *voseo* is used by all social classes. According to Alonso (1948), cited in Cotton and Sharp (1988), popular (linguistic) wisdom has it that in Buenos Aires, for example, where the use of *vos* is quite widespread, children are taught to spell *vos* with the letters *t* and *ú*.[93] In some other Latin American countries, such as Chile, however, *voseo* is not identified with educated speech, as it is far more common in an informal register and is avoided in formal speech. However, this Chilean *voseo* (which combines the informal pronoun *tú* with the *vos* verbal forms) is sometimes labeled *voseo culto* 'cultivated voseo' (which seems to be a contradiction), because it characterizes the speech of young, educated, urban, middle-class speakers (cf. Torrejón, 1986, 1991, discussed in detail in Lipski (1994: 202) for further details).

In the rest of Latin America, whereas *voseo* is the predominant system, the meaning of *tú*/*vos*/*usted* varies from one geographical region to the next. For example, Lipski (1994: 259) notes that in El Salvador, where *voseo* is in competition with *tuteo*, a new system seems to be appearing in which the scale of familiarity has *vos* on one end (the most familiar) and *usted* on the other (the most formal), with *tú* representing an intermediate degree.

In other countries, where *tú* and *vos* coexist, the meaning of *usted* is quite different from that found in other dialects of Spanish. For example, in the areas of Ecuador and Colombia, *voseo* and *tuteo* are still very much in competition. Yet in these same areas, *usted* is used in contexts that would require the use of *vos*/*tú* in most other dialects, because they convey the idea of closeness (for example, exchanges between spouses, exchanges from parents to children, etc.). Similarly, in Eastern and Central Colombia and rural Panama, *usted*, rather than *vos*/*tú*, seems to cover both formal and informal use. As a final example, consider the situation in Costa Rica, described by Penny (2000: 153), who notes that in this country *vos* is not the most familiar form. In Costa Rica, *usted* conveys a greater degree of closeness, and is used among family members, including exchanges from parents to children.

Due to the variety of verbal paradigms used with *vos*, as discussed above, and the extense territories where *voseo* is present, there is a great deal of what can be termed linguistic insecurity as to this phenomenon, making it difficult to pinpoint all the sociolinguistic and pragmatic details pertaining to its use. As Stewart (1999: 123) summarizes, 'the degree to which the use of *vos* is stigmatized or is accepted as the regional standard is in constant flux as societies evolve.' Paradigms vary from country to country, and even within the same country, and the values attached to the use of one conjugation or another also vary. This is not unexpected, given that language is a living thing, and is always undergoing change. We next consider the sociolinguistic aspects of possessive adjectives.

3.8.4 Sociolinguistic aspects of possessives

In Section 3.3 above, we discussed dialectal variation regarding the use of possessives. We noted that possessives are generally used across dialect areas much less than in English. In this section, we take into account sociolinguistic aspects of possessive use. For example, in familiar speech, especially when addressing children, possessive adjectives are frequently used in place of the article, in order to add an affective nuance. That is, to a child, instead of saying (106) or (108), in which the definite article would be the norm, we might well say (107) or (109), in which the possessive adjective is used:

(106)   *Dame la manita.* 'Give me your (literally, 'the') hand,' meaning 'Hold my hand.'
(107)   *Dame tu manita.* 'Give me your hand.'
(108)   *Termínate el desayuno.* 'Finish your (literally, 'the') breakfast.'
(109)   *Termínate tu desayuno.* 'Finish your breakfast.'

According to Cotton and Sharp (1988: 159), some linguists interpret this use of the possessive adjective in such constructions, at least in Mexico, as an influence of Náhuatl, a language where possessives are more common than Spanish. There is, however, no consensus among scholars in this regard, particularly as it is also found in Peninsular Spanish. We next turn to the use of diminutives in society.

3.8.5 Sociolinguistic aspects of diminutives

As discussed in detail in Section 3.4 above, affection and small size are the two main values that are associated with diminutive infixes. The use of diminutive forms, however, may also convey other notions, such as courtesy, or even irony, as in (110) and (111) below:

(110)   *¿Te apetece una copita?* Do you feel like a drink? May I offer you something to drink?
(111)   *Pues sí que es un problemita . . .* 'Well, that is quite a problem.'

In terms of regional use, we stated previously that diminutives are used more frequently in some areas of the Spanish-speaking world than in others (i.e., more in Mexico, Central and South America than in Spain).

However, we must emphasize that it is not just a question of regional variation. From the sociolinguistic point of view, it is interesting to note that in Spanish, for the most part, women tend to use diminutive forms more than men. Moreover, as is the case with possessive adjectives, diminutive forms are more commonly used to address children. We next turn to another aspect of morphosyntactic variation, namely the position of pronouns, or clitic climbing.

3.8.6 Clitic climbing

As a final example of morphosyntactic register variation, we will consider clitic climbing the fronting of pronouns as in *voy a hacerlo* 'I'm going to do it'→*lo voy a hacer* 'I'm going to do it' (literally, 'it I'm going to do'). Torres Cacoullos (1999) shows that clitic climbing is far less common in a formal register in auxiliary + gerund sequences in Spanish, particularly with auxiliaries other than *estar*. In her corpus, clitic climbing with the auxiliary + gerund sequence is found in 89% of the cases of spoken Spanish in Mexico City, as opposed to only 68% of possible cases in a series of written essays. This number diverges more dramatically for the auxiliary *seguir*: in 80% of cases of spoken Spanish in Mexico City, clitic climbing was found, compared to only 40% of instances in a series of written essays. Consider (112) and (113) below:

(112) (a) *Estoy leyéndolo* (formal register) 'I am reading it.'
       (b) *Lo estoy leyendo* (informal register) 'I am reading it.'
(113) (a) *Sigue diciéndolo* (formal register) '(S)he keeps saying it.'
       (b) *Lo sigue diciendo* (informal register) '(S)he keeps saying it.'

In examples like (112a) and (113a), according to Torres Cacoullos, the lack of clitic climbing is equated with a formal register. We next discuss L2 acquisition of morphology.

3.9 L2 Acquisition of Morphology

There are two main schools of thought regarding L2 acquisition of phonology. Broadly speaking, some scholars believe that L2 acquisition of morphosyntactic features such as word order, gender, number and aspect will be imperfect, regardless of the learner's proficiency level. For example, the Failed Features Hypothesis (FFH) of Hawkins & Chan (1997), Hawkins & Liszka (2003), Hawkins and Franceschina (2004), Franceschina (2001) and Tsimpli and Dimitrakopoulou (2007) suggests that after the Critical Period, acquisition of morphosyntactic features is lexically based, unlike the case of native speakers.[94] In other words, gender , for example, is learned noun by noun. Other schools of thought, such as proponents of Full Transfer Full Access (FTFA) including Flynn (1986), Lardiere (2000) and Prévost and White (2000), claim that L2 learners can acquire these types of features different from their L1 after the Critical Period.

Arteaga and Herschensohn (1995, 2006, 2007) take a middle-of-the road view, as their study of Advanced French L2 showed clearly that the learners (one with age of acquisition of 48) had mastered gender, agreement and number, although they did not perform according to native speaker standards. They argue that processing constraints and feature reassembly (Lardiere, 2000) explain this discrepancy. In other words, L2 speakers do not always match the correct ending to the surface form. This means that their competence (underlying knowledge of the linguistic system) is superior to their performance (actual production).

Given the controversy surrounding L2 morphological acquisition, let us review the facts. L2 morphological acquisition is less clearly defined than L1 morphological acquisition, which occurs in stages.[95] According to the seminal research completed on three English-speaking children, Adam, Eve and Sarah, in the early 1970s by Brown (1973), L1 English-speaking children learn morphology according to the following pattern:

(114)   Adam, Eve, Sarah
         – -ing *me going*
         – in/on *in the car*
         – plural *two doggies*
         – irregular past forms *Baby went*
         – possessive marker *Daddy's hat*
         – copula *Annie is happy*
         – articles *the bus*
         – regular past -ed *She walked*
         – third person singular marker *Johnny comes*
         – auxiliary be *He is coming*

As pointed out by Fromkin *et al.* (2007), among others, the fact that children first acquire the plural (e.g. *two doggies*) and then only later acquire the third person singular marker means that it is not a question of phonology (i.e., [z]), but of morphology. Children also master derivational morphology quite early and create utterances like the following:

(115)   *I have to pledge* (i.e. dust) *with the Pledge.*

L1 acquisition of morphology is generally complete by age 3.

With respect to syntax, L1 English-speaking children, as all children, begin with a holophrastic stage, or one-word utterances:

(116) *Wow-wow!* (= Dog)
(117) *Done!*

By the age of 2, children progress to the two-word stage, as in the following:

(118) *Hi, Rachel.*
(119) *Mommy home.*

Later, by the age of 3, children begin to form complete sentences, although they lack function words. This is referred to as Telegraphic speech by most researchers:

(120) *Put key in door.*

What happens in languages like Spanish, with rich morphology? The studies show conflicting results. According to recent research (see Hernández Pina, 1994; López-Ornat, 1997; Montrul, 2004; Smith *et al.*, 2003), children acquire agreement morphology between articles and nouns very early, even at 1.5 years of age, as in (102a).[96]

(121) (a) *el libro* 'the book'
       (b) *la niña bonita* 'the pretty girl,' literally 'the girl pretty.'

According to Hernández-Pina's (1985) study, however, agreement morphology between nouns and adjectives lagged a bit, and errors were evident in his data until the age of at least 2.8 years, with complete mastery by age 4 (121b).

With respect to L1 acquisition of Spanish verbal morphology and tense, again, there are opposing views. Some studies argue that it is mastered quite early, even by 2 years of age. Many studies, including those by Hernández-Pina (1994), Jacobsen (1986), Cortés (1989) and Eisenberg (1985), found that very young children produced many instances of infinitives, imperatives, past and present participles, and present tense forms, and some use of preterit and present perfect forms.[97] Other studies, including those by Fernández Martínez (1994) and Ezeizabarrena (1997), argue that person/number agreement does not develop by the age of 2, as had been previously argued for Italian by Hyams (1992), except for perhaps the first person. Differences in verbal aspect and tense, according to these studies, also occur after the age of 2. Finally, Gathercole *et al.* (1999) argue that children do not show stages with respect to verbs, but rather learn person, tense and aspect in a random order. Despite the conflicting viewpoints regarding Spanish L1 morphological acquisition, for the purposes of our discussion, we will adopt the order of acquisition followed by Kvaal *et al.* (1988), given below in (122):

(122)   demonstratives *este libro* 'this book'
         articles (including agreement) *la casa* 'the house'
         copulas *Está triste* 's/he is sad'
         regular present indicative *hablo* 'I speak'
         irregular present indicative *hago* 'I do'
         plurals *los chicos* 'the boys'
         possessive de *La bicicleta de Juan* 'Juan's bicycle' (literally, 'the bicy-
         cle of Juan')
         preposition en *Estamos en la escuela* 'we is at school'
         irregular preterit indicative *Fui* 'I went'

What is the relevance of L1 acquisition of morphosyntax for L2 acquisition? It has been argued that L2 learners also pass through stages of morphological and syntactic acquisition. For example, Lightbown and Spada (2006), following Krashen (1977), give the following order of acquisition by English L2 speakers:

(123)   ing (progressive) *She singing*
         plural *bushes*
         copula *She is here*
         auxiliary progressive *She is singing*
         irregular past *They took*
         regular past *We watched*
         third singular *She thinks*
         possessive singular *Ben's book*

By comparing (122) to (123) above, we can see the similarity in how L1 and L2 English speakers acquire morphosyntax. With respect to Spanish, Boyd (1975), in a study of L1 English children (L2 Spanish), found the following developmental order:

(124)   plural inflection of nouns *perros* 'dogs'
         progressive forms *cantando* 'singing'
         possessive *de la niña* 'of the girl' (= the girl's)
         present tense form *corre* 'he/she/you runs'
         past forms *hablaste* 'you spoke'
         subject–verb agreement (*ellos*) *hacen* 'they make'

Several recent studies have been conducted on verbal agreement/tense/aspect in adult Spanish L2. Regarding aspect, some influential studies are those of Andersen (1986, 1991) and Andersen and Shirai (1994), whose Lexical Aspect Hypothesis claims that Vendler's (1967) classification of verbs plays a role in L2 acquisition. According to Vendler (1967), the following are the classes of verbs:

(125)   stative verbs that describe existence or a state, such as *tener* 'to have'

activity verbs that describe an action that progresses through time, such as *cocinar* 'to cook'

accomplishment verbs that describe a completed action, indicating a process, as in *pintar un cuadro* 'paint a picture'

achievement verbs whose action is true for a given point in time, such as *Acabó la tarea* 'he finished his homework.'

One difference between states and activities *vis-à-vis* the other classes of verbs is that the former, given their lack of telicity, can be accompanied by a phrase like the *por una hora* 'for one hour,' as illustrated in (105). Achievements and accomplishments, on the other hand, cannot, due to the fact that their meaning encodes telicity.[98] See (126) below:

(126)   (a) *Corrió por una hora.* 'He ran for an hour.'
  (b) *Está (siempre) triste por una hora todas las noches.* 'He is sad for one hour at night.'
  (c) **Cambió el aceite del carro por tres horas.* 'S/he/you changed the oil in the car for three hours.'
  (d) **Ganó la carrera por tres horas.* 'He won the race for three hours.'

On the other hand, as noted by Vendler (1967), accomplishment verbs and achievement verbs, but not stative or activity verbs, can use '*in* phrases' (*en* in Spanish), as illustrated by (127):

(127)   (a) accomplishment: *Escribió un libro en un mes.* 'He wrote a book in one month.'
  (b) achievement: *Notó a la muchacha en dos minutos.* 'He noticed the girl in two minutes.'
  (c) activity: **Bailamos en un mes.* 'We danced in one month.'
  (d) stative: *Estaba/estuvo triste en un mes.

Finally, one difference between achievement and accomplishment verbs is that if an *en* 'in' phrase is used with these verbs, their meaning is very different. So if we say (127a), this means that he was writing the book in question for the entire month. However, if we say (127b), noticing the girl did not take two minutes, but rather occurred at one single point in time.[99]

With regard to L2 learning, Andersen's Lexical Aspect Hypothesis (1986, 1991) claims that there are eight stages through which learners pass, including the following: present, preterit (first with achievements and accomplishments, followed by activities and stative) and imperfect (first with statives, then activities, followed by achievements and accomplishments).[100] Anderson (1981) argues that L2 learners of Spanish will use the imperfect with stative verbs, only mastering the preterit with such verbs much later. They will first use use the preterit with verbs in the achievement class, later mastering the imperfect with such verbs.

In other words, L2 Spanish learners will say at first *estaba* 'I was,' but not *estuve* 'I was,' and *bailé* 'I danced,' but not *bailaba* 'I used to dance.' Regarding the validity of the Lexical Aspect Hypothesis, there is a mixed consensus. Some studies, such as those of Comajoan (2006), Collins (2002) and Ayoun and Salaberry (2005), argue that it can largely account for L2 acquisition of aspect.[101] Others, however, including Labeau (2005), Salaberry (2002) and Dietrich *et al.* (1995), claim that the model cannot explain several kinds of learner errors with respect to aspect.

A variety of studies have been conducted recently regarding adult L2 Spanish nominal agreement (number, gender) with articles and adjectives. One such study, by White *et al.* (2004), shows that beginning L2 Spanish learners make gender and number agreement at a much lower accuracy level than L1 speakers of Spanish (i.e. they produce errors like **la casas rojo* 'the red house' instead of the target *las casas rojas*). They found that students' accuracy improves greatly as their proficiency develops.

Sagarra and Herschensohn (2008) conducted a study in which students completed, at their own pace, a so-called 'moving window task.' Students were directed to read a computer screen that displayed sentences one word at a time. Each subsequent word was then shown on the computer screen as the learners, at their own pace, pressed a computer key. Sagarra and Herschensohn conclude that beginning students do not notice gender, whereas intermediate and advanced students pattern similarly to native speakers in this regard. Similarly, Keating (2006) argues that it is possible for L1 speakers of L2 Spanish to acquire gender. In his view, differences between L2 speech and the L1 target are due to a problem in performance rather than competence. All of these studies support the FTFA model discussed above.

Other researchers argue that Spanish gender/number agreement is never fully acquired by English L1 speakers, confirming the FFH (see above). Although she does not directly discuss the FTFA or FFH model,

Kurinski's (2007) results nonetheless show that speakers' production of accurate gender did not improve much as they became more proficient. Franceschina (2003) argues that only learners whose L1 has a grammatical category can acquire it in their L2. This, in turn, means that L1 speakers of English cannot acquire Spanish gender, which is borne out by the results of her study of adult L2 learners of Spanish from various linguistic backgrounds.

Similarly, Hawkins and Franceschina (2004), in a study of English and Italian L1 speakers learning Spanish and Spanish L1 speakers learning French, claim that according to the results of their study, speakers whose L1 had the category of gender (e.g. Spanish speakers learning French) were able to successfully acquire gender in an L2 that also possessed that category. On the other hand, they argue that L1 speakers of English, a language that lacks grammatical gender, were unable to acquire this grammatical feature. According to these scholars, their results support the FFH model discussed above.

Another characteristic of L2 acquisition of morphology, according to Van Patten's Input Processing Theory, is that L2 learners attend to semantic information before morphological information. In other words, in a sentence like the following, they will fail to process the past tense ending of the verb in (128a):

(128)   (a) *Hablaste inglés **ayer**.* 'You sp**oke** English **yesterday**.'
        (b) *Hablaste inglés.* 'You sp**oke** English.'

For Van Patten, for students to focus on the verbal ending *aste* they must not be given any other clues like *ayer*. Therefore he would recommend that instructors instead use a sentence like (128b). He also argues, in accordance with his First Noun Hypothesis, that L2 learners process the first noun in a string as the agent, as in the following:

(129)   ***Juan** me habló por teléfono.* 'Juan telephoned me.'

In (128) above, due to the First Noun Hypothesis, *Juan* is interpreted by L2 learners as the agent. Because of this tendency, Van Patten argues that students must be exposed to utterances that do not follow this pattern, as in the following:

(130)   *A Pedro ama **María**.* 'It is Pedro whom María loves.'

Finally, Van Patten argues that students tend to pay more attention to the beginnings and endings of words, which can be exploited in morphological acquisition, as most derivational and all inflectional morphemes in Spanish are either prefixes or suffixes.

Other scholars, noting that students do not seem to progress in their L2 without a focus on form, argue for the necessity of input flooding, which entails the use of several targeted forms in context (e.g. Trahey & White, 1993). In the L2, unlike the L1, according to this view, students seem to need negative evidence, in other words, explicit correction, although it is effective only 10% of the time (Oliver, 1995). The form that this correction should take is not clear; some studies, such as by Harley (1998), argue for the ineffectuality of metalinguistic explanations, which are based on traditional grammar. For example, consider the following:

(131)   *Fui a la tienda cuando era niño.* 'I went to the store when I was a child.'

In a metalinguistic correction, the instructor would give an explanation of the uses of the imperfect tense (*iba* 'I used to go') vs. the preterit (*fui* 'I went'). In other words, the discussion would be centered on the imperfect as a verb tense for habitual or ongoing actions, and on the preterit as the correct tense for completed actions.

Another form of correction is that of recasts. In such a method, the instructor produces the correct form of an incorrect student utterance, without making any comment. In other words, if a student says *la casa bonito* 'the pretty house', the instructor repeats *la casa bonita*, with no further commentary. Lyster and Ranta (1997) point to the low level of uptake (i.e. noticing a correction and incorporating it into one's speech) that recasts reap.

In other words, an interaction in which the instructor gives the correct form directly following the student's ungrammatical utterance such as saying *tú estás* 'you are' when the student produces *Tú estoy* 'you am.' They argue that negotiation, whereby the speaker and listener arrive at the correct form together, is the most effective form of correction (see also Pica *et al.*, 1987, among others). An example of negotiation would be the following exchange:

(132)   Student: *Tú estoy* 'you am'
        Instructor: *Tú es* – 'you are'
        L2 learner: *Tú estoy* '*you am'
        Instructor: *Tú hablas, tú cocinas, tú es* – 'You speak, you cook, you are'
        L2 learner: *Tú estás* 'you are'

In (132) above, the student produces an incorrect verb form for the verb *estar* 'to be' and the subject *tú* 'you.' The instructor does not produce the correct form, *tú estás* 'you are,' but rather leads the student to utter the grammatical form based on analogical forms such as *tú hablas* 'you speak.'

3.10 Conclusion

Morphosyntactic regional and social variation is less common than lexical variation, as discussed in detail in Chapter 4, but still exists across the Spanish-speaking world. In the preceding sections, we have presented some areas of variation among the different Spanish dialects, from noun morphology (including diminutive formation) to verb forms and usage (e.g. *está rompido* vs. *está roto*), to the pronominal system (including terms of address), and extending to some phenomena belonging to the clause level (such as *dequeísmo* and word order). We next presented sociolinguistic aspects of Spanish morphosyntax. We concluded our discussion with the topic of L2 morphological acquisition. In the next chapter, we address regional and sociolinguistic variation in the words of Spanish, or its lexicon.

Chapter 4

¿Frijol o habichuela?
Spanish Lexical Variety:
Potential and Pitfalls

4.1 Introduction to the Lexicon

Is *smarf* a word in English? If you are a native speaker, you probably took only seconds to decide that *smarf*, in fact, is not a word in English, although it is a possible word. By possible word, we mean a word that obeys all phonotactic constraints of English. In other words, the sounds used in the word exist in English, and the phoneme order, similarly, reflects English rules. If the word were *msarf*, we would know that not only is it not a word in English, it is not even a possible word. How can we as native speakers possibly decide in mere seconds if a word exists in our language, at least in our experience? We check the word against our entire mental dictionary, known as the lexicon. Word retrieval is extremely quick in our L1, which explains the rapidity of our answer.

How about the word *unropar* in Spanish? If we are L2 learners of Spanish, we may take considerably longer to answer that question. Further, we may be left with a great deal of doubt, because our lexicon in our L2 is quite a bit smaller than that of our L1. Finally, we may or may not be able to recognize whether or not the word is a possible word in Spanish, although our general proficiency may play a role here.

What information regarding word entries is contained in the lexicon?[102] First, if we know a word, we know how to pronounce it. Second, if we know a word, we know its meaning. We know that in the case of homonyms (or *homophones*), two words that sound the same, such as *cross* (either a symbol of Jesus or a person who is in a bad mood), have different meanings. On the other hand, we know that synonyms, such as *late* and *tardy*, which do not have the same form, have the same meaning.

We also know about gradable pairs, also known as scalar antonyms, such as *small* and *large*, which show a continuum of meaning. Some

94

antonyms are absolute, such as *living* and *dead*. In our L1, we further know the range of meanings of a word, as argued by Teichroew (1982), among others. For example, consider the word *break*. We know that it means to literally destroy something, and also that the voice of a boy has become that of a man, in other words, has permanently lowered in pitch. One way that we as native speakers relate one word to another is by means of semantic features. For example, the words *woman* and *girl* share the features *+human, +female*, but they differ in the features *±mature, ±young*.

Part of our knowledge of words means that we know that the meaning of idiomatic expressions or idioms (a combination of words whose meaning makes them a unity) cannot be derived from the combination of the words themselves included in the expression. For example, if we say to another person, *Go break a leg!*, we mean *Good luck!*, and not that we want the addressee to actually break his or her leg. For this reason, we must store idiomatic expressions as entries separate from the individual words contained therein in our lexicon. In other words, we store them as a chunk, meaning that we know the meaning of the entire expression.

Third, if we know a word, we know its grammatical category, even though we may not have the metalinguistic knowledge necessary to label this category. For example, we know intuitively that *race* can be a noun or a verb, because we can utter the phrases, *I raced my friend, I like to run races*. In the first use of *race*, we put the verb in the past tense, showing that part of our native speaker knowledge is that it is a verb and, as such, can take verbal endings. In the second example, we add the plural morpheme *-s* to the noun. Our lexical entry also contains the spelling of the word, if we are literate speakers. If not, this information will not be stored in the lexicon.

But our lexical information goes beyond pronunciation and grammar; it also contains information regarding pragmatics. In other words, we know that a word may be taboo, such as *bitch*, or used only in very informal speech (e.g. *Dude*). Further, we may have dialectal knowledge of a word, such as *poke* for *sack*, knowing that it is not used in our dialect, although it is a word in English. Unlike a dictionary, however, we most likely do not know the *etymology* (i.e. the historical source) of a word. In the next section, we turn to a discussion of the Spanish lexicon.

4.2 Introduction to the Spanish Lexicon

The total number of lexical items of the Spanish language (impossible to count, as is the case in any other language) would include, as Moreno de Alba (1992: 47) states, 'los vocablos propios de la lengua hablada y escrita, de todas las épocas, de todos los lugares, de todos los niveles socioculturales de los hablantes, de todas las especialidades, ocupaciones, profesiones, etc.'[103] As we have mentioned in Chapter 3, nowhere in the Spanish language is variation more noticeable than in the lexicon. Moreno de Alba devotes a whole chapter of his work to the 'Unidad y variedad léxica de la lengua española.'[104] In his discussion of this topic, he agrees with a number of well-known Hispanists (such as Menéndez Pidal or Lapesa) who highlight the essential unity of the Spanish language in its morphosyntax (where variation is proportionately more limited, as we have seen in Chapter 3), while pointing out the variation that is so dominant in the lexicon.

This heterogeneity in the lexicon of Spanish is not a surprising fact when one considers the number of speakers, the extension of the areas where the language is spoken, and the different indigenous languages spoken at the time of the Spanish conquest. We have presented in Chapter 1 the notions of descriptive and prescriptive approaches to language. We start this chapter by emphasizing that no one lexical variant is, per se, better or more correct than the other. Moreover, although there is variation in the lexicon, there is also an important core of lexical items common to all Spanish speakers, as discussed in detail in Chapter 6.

4.3   Introduction to Regional Lexical Variation in Spanish

As we have noted in Chapter 1, there are more than 330 million speakers of Spanish, inhabitants of more than 20 countries, where Spanish may be the only official language, or may share that status with other languages. It is not surprising, then, that the lexicon is one of the areas where variation is greatest. Indeed, it is not uncommon for an identical object to be designated differently in different areas of the Spanish language world. As an example, consider Table 4.1. It presents the most common terms used for the very same objects in five countries, four of them from Latin America.

Table 4.1 illustrates the fact that there are lexical items that are commonly used in one dialect, but totally unknown in another. Indeed, neither a Mexican nor a Spaniard would ever be able to recognize Argentinean *zoquetes* 'socks' for *calcetines*, or Salvadoran *chumpa* 'jacket' for *cazadora*. Moreover, the same word may mean different things in different areas. Once more, Argentinian *piloto* and Puerto Rican *medias* have different referents in Spain, where *piloto* is the person in charge of a plane, 'pilot', and *medias* is an exclusively feminine clothing item, 'pantyhose.'

4.3.1   Latin American Spanish vs. Peninsular Spanish

Traditionally, a lexical dichotomy was established between the Spanish from Spain and the Spanish of the Americas (a supposedly homogeneous

Table 4.1   Lexical variation: most common terms in five countries[105]

España	Argentina	Puerto Rico	México	El Salvador
acera	vereda	acera	banqueta	acera
autocar	colectivo	guagua	camión	camioneta
americana	saco	gabán	saco	saco
bañador	malla	traje de baño	traje de baño	calzoneta
cajón	cajón	gaveta	cajón	cajón
calcetines	zoquetes	medias	calcetines	calcetines
cazadora	campera	jacket	chamarra	chumpa
gabardina	piloto	capa	impermeable	capa
gafas	lentes, anteojos	espejuelos	lentes, anteojos	anteojos
manzana	cuadra	manzana	cuadra	manzana
piscina	pileta	piscina	alberca	piscina
piso	departamento	apartamento	departamento	apartamento

variant). This view has been challenged, however, by many dialectologists, such us Fontanella de Weinberg (1976) or Zamora and Guitart (1982). These scholars view the idea that Spain and Spanish America represent two dialect areas as simplistic, since both continents are characterized by a variety of geographical and linguistic considerations. Azevedo (1992: 346), in turn, notes that this traditional division has been replaced by a more dynamic notion, that of a common linguistic system that allows for a variety of speech utterances. This idea is also highlighted by Moreno de Alba (1992: 48), who states that we cannot speak of American Spanish as a whole, as a linguistic block that can be opposed to European Spanish, which is similarly not monolithic.

Indeed, vocabulary of the speakers of any region will always include some words peculiar to that particular place, together with a large number of lexical items that are shared by all the speakers of that language, regardless of their origins. Here we will concentrate on those lexical items that are characteristically Latin American, that is, common in one or more Latin American countries, but not in Spain (either because they are not known in this regional variety or because their use is different). Sometimes, these words are referred to as 'Americanisms,' although many have been incorporated into the lexicon of all Spanish-speaking areas. This is the case of some indigenisms or words whose origin can be found in the indigenous languages of Latin America. For example, *chocolate* 'chocolate' or *tomate*, lexical items borrowed originally from Náhuatl), which would not be exclusive of Latin America. In other words, they would be considered 'Americanisms' from a historical point of view, but not in present-day usage.[106]

Table 4.2 offers some examples of lexical items that are characteristic in Latin American use, broadly speaking, but not in Spain (the Peninsular counterpart is also given).[107]

Table 4.2   Latin American vs. Peninsular Spanish

Latin American Spanish	*Peninsular Spanish*	*English translation*
apartamento	piso	*apartment*
apurarse	apresurarse	*hurry up*
bomba (de gasolina)	surtidor	*gas pump*
camarones	gambas	*shrimp*
carpeta/alfombrado	moqueta	*carpet*
carro	coche	*car*
chequera	talonario de cheques	*check book*
demorarse	tardar	*take time, be late*
elevador	ascensor	*elevator*
enojado	enfadado	*angry*
extrañar	echar de menos	*miss*
fósforo	cerilla	*match*
jalar	tirar	*pull*
lindo	guapo	*pretty*
llamada de larga distancia	conferencia	*long distance call*
manejar	conducir	*drive*
pararse	levantarse	*stand up*
pelear	reñir	*have an argument*
pena (dar pena)	vergüenza	*be embarrassed*
timón	volante	*driving wheel*

The examples in Table 4.2 are instances of the situation mentioned above: the Latin American terms either are not used at all in Spain (e.g. *jalar* 'to pull') or are used with a different meaning (e.g. *pararse* is used in Spain with the idea of 'to stop', *pena* has the sense of 'pity', a *carro* is a 'cart').

Although we have spoken of the Latin American variety as if it were unified, for the purposes of contrasting it with the Peninsular one, this does not give an accurate picture. We must highlight the existence of important internal contrasts. This is illustrated in Table 4.1, which presents the most common terms used for the very same objects in five countries, four of them from Latin America. But in addition to having one referent and many lexical variants to denominate it, we may find among the dialects of Latin America the opposite situation. We may have the same lexical item but very distinct referents in different dialects.

Two clear examples are the words *guagua* and *gringo*. *Guagua* is used as an equivalent for 'bus' in Caribbean Spanish (as well as in the Canary Islands). However, in most of the Andean region (i.e. Ecuador, Peru, Bolivia, and Chile) it refers to a 'baby'. *Gringo*, in turn, is used to refer to people from the United States in most of Latin America. Yet in Argentina, its meaning is rather 'European' or 'of fair skin color'.

The reader should note that this type of presentation is necessarily simplistic, in that regional variation exists even from one community to the other within the same country in the Spanish-speaking world. Even a simple word can illustrate the extent of lexical variation within Spanish. For example, Lope Blanch (1988: 148) reports in the *Atlas Lingüístico de México* that there are approximately 50 lexical variants for *luciérnaga* 'glow worm.' Beyond this difference in terms, the Spanish of the Americas has two lexical features that are clearly distinctive and that are not part of the Peninsular variety. One is the presence of indigenisms and the other is the use of the so-called archaisms (words from earlier centuries in Spanish no longer used in Spain).[108]

4.3.2 Indigenisms

Another source of variation present in the Spanish of the Americas has to do with the contact of Spanish with other languages, due to the specific circumstances of certain geographical areas or countries.[109] This can take the form of a substratum, which is a language spoken by native peoples of a region that is replaced by another language (in this case, Spanish). Such indigenous languages, while lost, do influence, to a greater or lesser extent, the exported language.

The frequency of indigenisms can be explained by the fact that upon their arrival to the Americas, Spaniards found a variety of objects (plants, animals, etc.) that were unknown to them. They therefore borrowed from the natives both the objects and their name. As we have pointed out above, some of these words have been incorporated into the common language (e.g. words such as *chocolate, tomate* from Náhuatl, spoken at the time of the Conquest in central Mexico, *llama, alpaca* from Quechua, spoken in the Andes, *canoa, hamaca* from Taino, spoken in the Caribbean, or *jaguar, tapioca* from Guarani, spoken in Paraguay).[110] Some indigenisms, however, are used only in the region of the original language, as noted by Rosenblat (1958: 12). For example, in the Antilles and in the Northern coast of Venezuela and Colombia, there are many words whose origin can be traced to the Arahuaq and Caribe languages (e.g. *guano, manigua* or *mangle*[111]).

In Mexico and Guatemala, in turn, Náhuatl and the Mayan languages are the source of words such as *elote, guajolote* or *mole*, which are not common in other areas.[112] As to the Andean region, we find words stemming from Quechua and Aymara (for instance, *chacra, choclo* or *carisina*).[113] These are not the only languages whose influence on Spanish is relevant at the local levels. The Chibcha languages, Mapuche and Guaraní are also very important in their respective areas. In bilingual regions, certainly, the number of indigenisms is higher. That is, for example, the case of Southern Mexico and Guatemala (Maya influence), the mountainous Andean region, where Spanish is in contact with Quechua and Aymara, and Paraguay, where Spanish and Guaraní are both official languages.[114]

4.3.3 Archaisms

The use of archaisms, or words that have ceased to be used in some dialects, is another defining feature of the Spanish from the Americas.[115] Teschner *et al.* (1975), for example, make reference to the lexical items represented in Table 4.3 below:

Table 4.3 Archaisms in the Americas: 1

	LA Spanish	*Peninsular Spanish*
(i)	lindo	bonito
(ii)	masas	pasteles
(iii)	pararse	ponerse de pie
(iv)	prieto	negro
(v)	prometer	asegurar

Azevedo (1992), in turn, offers examples of lexical items that have acquired a different meaning in Latin American Spanish, and therefore contrast with the original meaning preserved in Peninsular Spanish. Table 4.4 shows what these words mean on both sides of the Atlantic:

Table 4.4   Archaisms in the Americas: 2[117]

	Latin American use	*Peninsular use*
carro	automóvil	vehículo grande, de dos ruedas, para transportar cargas
zócalo	plaza mayor	base o cuerpo inferior de un edificio
jirón	calle (Peru)	desgarrón

In other words, in Table 4.4., we see words such as *carro*, which continue to be used in both Latin American and Peninsular Spanish, albeit with different meanings (e.g. 'auto' vs. 'large vehicle').

Moreover, there are instances of the opposite situation, that is, cases in which the lexical item has evolved in Peninsular Spanish. Examples can be seen in Table 4.5:

Table 4.5   Archaisms in the Americas: 3[118]

	Latin American use	*Peninsular use*
bravo	enfadado	valiente
provocar	apetecer	incitar
dilatar	tardar	aumentar el volumen de un cuerpo

As Table 4.5 shows, the words *bravo*, *provocar*, and *dilatar* still have their original meaning in Peninsular Spanish (i.e. 'brave,' 'to provoke,' and 'to expand,' whereas in the Spanish of Latin America, they have become different lexical referents (i.e. 'angry,' 'tempt,' and 'take (time)'). We next turn to vocabulary that has entered the Spanish language from other languages.

4.3.4   Lexical items borrowed from foreign languages

Many foreign languages have contributed words to the Spanish language in general, and to Latin American Spanish in particular. Some of these languages are considered to form part of the superstratum, or a language superimposed on another. For political or cultural reasons, it does not supplant the original language (e.g. Arabic). Others constitute the adstratum, or a language that coexists with another. The most important of these languages at present are the African languages, Arabic, French, Basque, Portuguese, Italian and English.

At the time of the Conquest of America, black slaves were taken to all parts of the continent. Nowadays, the black population in Latin America is limited mostly to the Antilles, the Caribbean, Panama, and the coastal areas of Colombia and Ecuador. Some lexical items from the languages spoken by these slaves have been introduced in the Spanish language of those areas. As was the case with the indigenisms, some *afronegrismos* (as Zamora Munné & Guitart (1982: 155) call them) have spread all over the Spanish-speaking world. That is the case of some musical terms, given the popularity of Afrohispanic music. Some examples would be the musical instruments *conga, bongo* and *marimba*. But many other lexical items of this type are exclusive of the areas mentioned above, where words such as *bembé* 'party,' *cumbancha* 'fun,' *guineo* 'banana' or *guarapo* 'sugar cane juice' are frequently used.

In general terms, the influence of African languages in the Latin American Spanish lexicon is not as important as that of the indigenous languages, but it is still considerable. We have mentioned music as a semantic field where terms of this origin are relevant. In addition, we should also bear in mind religion, for in some of the areas mentioned above, the African religions are still preserved, together with their ritual language. The latter contains many such as *babalao* 'wise man,' 'priest'.[119]

During their occupation lasting more than seven centuries, the Arabs gave many words to Spanish. Indeed, scholars estimate that more than 4000 Spanish words are of Arabic origin, such as *alcalde* 'mayor.' Other words whose source is Arabic include *álgebra* 'algebra,' *almohada* 'pillow,' and *alberca* 'swimming pool' or 'water reservoir.' One way to recognize Arabic words in Spanish is that most words beginning with *al-* stem from that language, as it is the definite article in Arabic. However, there are also words like *azafata* 'stewardess' (originally 'the lady in attendance') whose source is Arabic, although they do not begin with *al-*.

Until recently, French was considered the predominant language of culture, and up to the 19th century this language was the main source of foreign terms in Peninsular Spanish. There are some Gallicisms, however, that are more common in Latin American Spanish than in Peninsular Spanish. Some examples, provided by Zamora Munné and Guitart (1982: 157), are the use of *adición* for *cuenta* 'check' in the River Plate area, the use of *bayú* for *prostíbulo* 'brothel' in Cuba, *chofer* rather than *chófer* 'driver,' *fuete* for *látigo* 'whip,' *musiú* for *extranjero* 'foreigner' in Venezuela, and *petipuá* for *guisante* or *arveja* 'pea' in the Antilles.

Basque became a co-official language in the Spanish Basque Country in 1978. There has been an increase regarding the contact between Spanish and Basque due to the increasing number of bilingual individuals. Indeed, there are many Basque words that have been incorporated into the Spanish spoken in this area of Spain; they are related to all aspects of daily life (Llorente, 2005). Some examples are *ikastola* for 'Basque school,' *bidegorri*, a term that refers to 'the lane specifically devoted to bicycle users,' or *bertsolari* for 'oral poet'. These borrowings are particularly abundant in the area of politics, since both nationalistic and non-nationalistic mass media (written or spoken) make use of Spanish in their portrayal of political life. Some lexical items related to this field are the adjective *abertzale* 'nationalistic' (literally, it means 'lover of the homeland'), *kale borroka* 'street violence,' *euskaldún* 'Basque,' and *lehendakari* 'president.'

Many of these terms have been adopted in their original orthographic form, but others have been adapted to Spanish patterns. In some occasions, they are also integrated morphologically in the Spanish language. Thus, some adjectives receive inflection for gender and number, for example, or become nouns by means of the addition of a Spanish suffix: *batasuno(a)/s* 'radical nationalist,' *abertzalismo* 'nationalism.' With regard to Basque loans, we must remember that this language also contributed many terms to the core lexicon of Spanish. Therefore, some Basque words like *izquierda* 'left,' *guijarro* 'stone,' *Javier* 'Xavier' (either a person or place name), whose origin is Basque, are now present in all varieties of the Spanish language.

Some examples of Portuguese terms borrowed by Latin American Spanish are *cachaza* 'sugar cane spirit,' *conchabarse* 'offer oneself as a hired hand,' *facón* 'big knife,' *buraco* 'hole' and *mucama* 'servant.' In the border areas between Brazil, Uruguay and Paraguay, the influence of Portuguese is greater, as should be expected, and a mixed system between the two languages has been created. This system, called *fronterizo* or *fronteiriço* by the linguists who study it, is a mixture between Uruguayan Spanish and the Portuguese variety of the area of Rio Grande do Sul. In many cases, monolingual native speakers of either Spanish or Portuguese are unable to comprehend this mixed system.[120]

Italian immigrants arrived in thousands at the end of the 19th century to some Latin American areas, particularly the Argentinean coasts, and the southern part of Uruguay. Thus, for a few decades, many Argentineans were almost bilingual. Fontanella de Weinberg (1995: 172) points out that according to the 1897 Census of the city of Buenos Aires, 32% of the population was actually Italian, a number that includes only those born in Italy. If we were to add their children, born already in the new continent, that percentage would increase to almost 40%.

For the most part, these borrowed terms belonged to semantic areas related to daily life, such as food items and the family. Some examples are *chao* for 'goodbye,' *manyar* for 'eat,' *capuchino* for 'coffee with milk in a small cup,' *pibe* for 'child,' *nono(a)* for 'grandfather'/'grandmother' and *laburo* for 'work.' A mixed Spanish and Italian language, *cocoliche*, also appeared. *Cocoliche* is similar to *fronterizo*, the Spanish and Portuguese mixture. It is considered to be a transition language, without much currency at present.

The language that has provided Spanish with the most borrowed terms is, no doubt, English. On one hand, English, due to US advances in technology and other areas, is considered prestigious. For this reason, it has greatly influenced both Peninsular Spanish and the different Latin American varieties. On the other hand, the situation of bilingual areas, such as Puerto Rico or the Southwest of the United States, must be taken into account. As to the first case, there are some Anglicisms that are common in Peninsular Spanish (such as *camping* 'camp' or *parking* 'parking lot') but are not used in Latin America. Conversely, some words borrowed from English that Peninsular Spanish does not have (e.g. *chance* 'opportunity' or *closet* 'wardrobe') exist in the Latin American dialects. But there are many terms borrowed from English that are common to both sides of the Atlantic: *week-end*, *self-service*, *best-seller*, *hit-parade*, *training* and *márketing* are some instances.

English has had an even greater influence in the bilingual regions of the United States, as is to be expected. English terms are thus common, either with or without phonetic/orthographic adaptation. Examples include *bil* 'bill,' *ganga* 'gang,' *troca* 'truck,' *friser* 'freezer,' *guachar* 'watch,' *jit* 'hit' and *jonrón* 'home run.' In the Spanish of the Southwest, specifically, there has been an extensive exchange of words between Spanish and English as this region of the United States was originally colonized by Spaniards.

According to scholars, the variety of Spanish spoken in this area is both innovative and conservative. Speakers from this region typically use many Anglicisms, as discussed above, as well as archaic forms (such as *truje* for *traje* 'I brought' or *haiga* for *haya* 'subjunctive of *there is/are*') and false cognates (such as *letra* for *carta* 'letter' or *parientes* for *padres* 'parents'). Sometimes the use of such lexical items is labeled 'Spanglish,' a term that generally reflects a negative view of the mixture of English and Spanish.[121] It goes without saying that such an opinion has no linguistic basis, particularly given the other languages that have influenced Spanish. We next turn to regional register variation and the Spanish lexicon.

4.4 Register Variation in the Spanish Lexicon

The degree of formality in our speech has lexical consequences. Our language varies according to where we are using it (our house, our workplace, at a party) and to whom we are addressing. We do not talk the same way to our family and to our instructors, or to our friends. When learning our native language, we learn that we cannot talk equally to all listeners. Given the permeation of Spanish throughout the United States, but particularly in the Southwest, Spanish instructors face unique challenges. Our students are far more likely than those of other languages to be exposed to a variety of Spanish registers, both informally and through work-related contexts.

As we have discussed in Chapter 1, lexical variation is one way in which Spanish speakers of Spanish clearly distinguish among registers. Consider, for example, (7) and (8):

(7)   (a) *Deja ver tu **patita***[122] (informal register)
      (b) *Deja ver tu **pie*** (formal register)
(8)   (a) *Está más loco que una cabra, el **crío ése***[123] (informal register)
      (b) *Ese **niño** está muy loco* (formal register)

Lexical choices may vary at the word level, as in (7) (e.g. the use of *patita* for *pie*) or in (8) (e.g., the use of *crío* for *niño*). There are scores of such words in Spanish. Moreover, we find dialectal differences here, too. For example, informal words for formal *dinero* 'money' include *lana* (most common in Andean and Mexican Spanish) *pasta* (in Spain), and *guita* (in Argentina). As another example, consider *problema* 'problem,' belonging to the formal register, which is *marrón* in Spain and *quilombo* in Argentina in informal speech. A final example is *chamba* 'job' (verb: *chambear* 'to work'), used familiarly in many regions of Latin America for *trabajo* and *trabajar*. In Spain the word for the same referent is *curro* (verb: *currar*) when speaking informally.

Another option used in Spanish to indicate a register difference is the increased use of idioms (expressions whose meaning cannot be understood by the individual words it contains) for the informal register, as in (9) and (10):[124]

(9)   (a) *Me vale un cacahuate* (informal register)
      (b) *Me importa muy poco* (formal register)
(10) (a) *No tienen (en) donde caerse muertos* (informal register)
      (b) *Son muy pobres* (formal register)

Idioms serve another function in language besides marking an informal register. For L2 speakers, the use of idiomatic expressions can make their speech sound more native-like. In Chapter 6, we discuss specifically how to teach idioms, basing our discussion on dictionary use. In the next section, we turn to euphemisms, or words used in place of taboo words.

4.4.1 Euphemisms

Spanish, as many other languages, has topics or terms of discussion that are prohibited or made taboo for some sociocultural reason. In most cultures, these areas include religion, body excretions and sexual acts, among others. In order to avoid the terms that are considered harsh, offensive, and socially unacceptable, euphemisms are used. The use of euphemisms is directly linked to the topic of register variation as well, as they are typically not used in informal speech. For example, if we want to express the idea that somebody has died, we may do so informally by the use of an idiom, such as *estirar la pata* 'to croak' (literally, 'to stretch one's leg'). In a formal register, however, we will not use an idiom to express the idea of dying. Similarly, we will avoid the register neutral word *morir* 'to die'. In its place, we may use other verbs, such as *fallecer* 'perish,' *dejar de existir* 'stop being' or *pasar a mejor vida* 'to go to a better place'.

The same would apply, for example, to express the idea of having sex, which, in a formal register, would be conveyed by expressions such as *hacer el amor* 'make love' or *tener relaciones íntimas* 'have intimate relations'. In informal speech, on the other hand, we may very well substitute the taboo expressions *follar* or *echar un polvo* in Spain, and by *chingar* in Mexico. All of the latter could be translated as 'to fornicate, to perform the sexual act.' The words used in the formal register, in both examples, are obviously euphemisms. The ones used informally may have a jocular nuance to them.

As the above example illustrates, regional variation exists in this regard as well, although most euphemisms are shared by all varieties of the Spanish language, as Zamora and Guitart (1982: 162) state. The expressions that are considered taboo may vary from variety to variety in the Spanish-speaking world, and might be a source of embarrassment, or at least confusion or misunderstanding, on many occasions. A word such as *coger* lacks any sexual innuendo in Spain, where it expresses the idea of 'grab, catch.' The term *coger*, however, is used to indicate 'perform the sexual act' in Mexico (as a synonym for the even more informal *chingar*, as discussed above). Since *coger* is a taboo word in Mexico, *agarrar* ('to grab') replaces it in the other context. In other words, where a Spaniard would say *coger el autobús* 'take the bus,' a Mexican would say *agarrar el autobús*. We next turn our attention to the lexicon of heritage speakers.

4.5   Heritage Speakers and the Lexicon

How do we organize our lexicon if we are truly bilingual? Early research (e.g. Potter *et al.*, 1984) indicated that bilinguals have separate lexical stores from a very young age, maybe even from the beginning of their language acquisition. These researchers argued for a mixed lexicon among young bilingual children, because they may lack a term for one concept or another in one of their languages. For example, they may have in their lexicon the word *leche* but not the word *milk*. Assuming that the mature bilingual lexicon contains a form level (the words themselves) and a content level (the meanings of the words), as argued by Potter *et al.* (1984), each word is believed to be segregated (i.e. different) at the form level but joined at the concept level.

Kroll *et al.* (2005) express a different viewpoint, noting that bilinguals proficient in their L1 and L2 only speak words in the wrong language on rare occasions. This does not mean, however, that information about both languages is inactive in tasks such as reading and speaking, as shown by the studies in Brysbaert *et al.* (1999), Colomé (2001), Hermans *et al.* (1998) and Van Heuvent *et al.* (1998). This is perhaps surprising, given that bilinguals possess no mechanism to switch off one of their two languages. In other words, words in both languages are activated in a parallel manner.

In Dijkstra (1998), Dutch-English bilinguals were asked if words were real. When they had to perform the task in their second language, English, seemingly little evidence of activation of the alternative meaning of homographs (words spelled identically) but significant facilitation for cognates relative to controls were found. So-called Stroop tasks (first used in Stroop, 1935) involve the task of naming a picture in one language; a distracting word is presented at some point before, during or after the picture is presented.

Several studies (e.g. Costa & Caramazza, 2000; Hermans *et al.*, 1998) argue that if distractors are semantically related, they interfere in picture naming; yet if they are phonologically related, they actually facilitate the process. In other words, suppose that the desired word is *casa* 'house'. In such a case, if the word *domicilio* 'domicile' is given as a distractor, it could adversely affect the naming task, whereas if the word *taza* 'cup' were presented, it would facilitate the naming task. Miller and Kroll (2002) found that similar results were found even when the distractor words were in the L2 (e.g. *domicile*).

Scholars have interpreted these results in conflicting manners. For example, Hermans *et al.* (1998) argue that such results argue for a language non-selective model of production, whereas Costa *et al.* (1999)

claim that only a language selective model can account for the data, although non-target alternatives that do not lead to selection are activated. Schwartz *et al.* (2007) note that the distracter required in Stroop data causes bottom-up processing, or processes from the words and morphemes to the sentence itself, which is problematic. Kroll *et al.* argue that the Stroop results in fact provide evidence for the Bilingual Interactive Activation Model (BIA; Dijkstra & Van Heuven, 1998). In such a model, the word *bike* first activates the language nodes so as to identify the target language.

According to Schwartz *et al.* (2007), the same language nodes then collect evidence about whether or not the word in question exists in each language. A further function of these language nodes is inhibiting the other language. These nodes, in their view, are sensitive to top-down influences so that information is made available to the bilingual regarding the context in which the word in question appears. The latter, however, is necessarily dependent upon which, if any, of the languages are dominant. Indeed, researchers such as Kroll (1993) and Kroll *et al.* (2005) argue that much depends on the bilingual's level of competence. Kroll claims that if we are dominant in one language, our L1 knowledge is inextricably linked to our second language. In other words, in his view, we always first access, in one way or another, our L1 lexicon before coming up with a word in our L2. This is known as a Word Association Model. In this model only the L1 is linked directly to the conceptual level. Moreover, the L2 word is assigned the L1 meaning.

In a Concept Mediation Model (Potter *et al.*, 1984), on the other hand, the L1 and L2 words are not directly linked, either at the form level or at the concept level. Instead, both are connected directly to the meaning level. In the Asymmetrical Model (Kroll, 1993), it is argued that the organization of our lexicon depends on our competence in the L2. At early stages, our L1 lexicon feeds directly into our L2 lexicon, but this can change as our knowledge of the L2 deepens. The model is asymmetrical in that L1 to L2 translations were quicker than L2 to L1 translations. Finally, De Groot and Barry (1992) argue for a Distributional Model, in which L1 words and L2 words can be assigned to different concepts, assuming that the competence of the L2 learner allows this. In other words, entries that do not entirely share meanings, such as *cita* (both 'date' and 'appointment' in Spanish) and *date*, will be therefore linked to different concepts.

As is often the case, studies supporting one model over another have yielded conflicting results. For example, it has been claimed that translation priming (i.e. prior repetition of a word pair, such as *orange/naranja*) has a positive effect on the speed of processing. The studies in Gerard and Scarborough (1989) and Kirsner *et al.* (1980) show the opposite results, in other words, that translation priming has no effect on processing speed. Given our experience as both L1 and L2 learners and teachers of various languages, we agree with Kroll (1993) in believing that at early levels of competence, an Asymmetrical Model makes the most sense. As a learner's L2 competence develops, a Concept-Mediation or Distribution level best reflects the organization of our L2 lexicon, in our view. We next turn to L2 lexical acquisition.

4.6 L2 Lexical Acquisition

The importance of L2 lexical acquisition cannot be over-emphasized. After all, as pointed out by Gass (1988) and Gass and Selinker (2001), among others, miscommunication arises more often from lexical errors than from morphosyntactic errors. Consider the following utterances produced by non-native speakers of English (Spanish L1):

(11) *Can you tell me where is the train station?* (Gass & Selinker, 2001: 372)
(12) *I feel sorry for people who live in the suburbs.* (Gairns & Redman, 1986: 3)

In (11) above, although there is a syntax error, the question is perfectly understandable to L1 speakers of English. However, such is not the case for (12). The speaker in (12) does not mean to express pity for people who live in the suburbs, but rather for those who live in the *suburbio*, or slum area. The lexical error in (12), unlike the syntactic error in (11), seriously impedes communication.

In terms of quantity, according to Gass and Selinker (2001: 372), these types of lexical errors are not only the most common ones when learning an L2, but also the ones that native speakers and learners alike view as the most disruptive when trying to communicate. In addition to being crucial for communication, lexical skills are also pivotal for comprehension or production of input, either written or oral (cf. Lafford & Salaberry, 2003, and references therein). In other words, the more lexical items that an L2 speaker knows, the better his or her comprehension of the L2 will be.

With regard to L2 acquisition, some scholars make a distinction between an active vs. passive command of L2 vocabulary. For Teichroew (1982), there is not so much a dichotomy between these concepts as a continuum. In the initial stage, the L2 learner recognizes the lexical item, but it is only in the final stage that he or she is capable of producing it independently. By production, Teichroew also means the capacity to produce the range of associated meanings of a word.[125] For example, consider (13), which is adapted from Kellerman (1979):

(13)   (a) *He broke his leg.*
       (b) *She broke his heart.*
       (c) *His voice broke.*

These are but three examples of the range of meanings associated with the English verb *to break*. In order for an L2 learner to be at the final stage of lexical acquisition, in Teichroew's view, he or she would need to master all of these meanings. At the initial stage, on the other hand, the L2 learner may only know the meaning in (13a).

For Laufer and Paribakht (1998), there are three types of vocabulary knowledge: passive, controlled active and free active. If an L2 learner has passive knowledge, he or she understands the most common meaning of a word, whereas with controlled active, the L2 learner can produce the word, but only on 'cued recall.' For example, the L2 learner may be able to complete the sentence (cf. Laufer & Paribakt, 1998) in (14):

(14)   (a) *On my food, I like salt and pe_____.*
       (b) *En mi comida, me gusta poner sal y pim_____* (=14a)

In (14a) the initial letters rule out other possibilities, so that the L2 learner will use the word **bacon**. Similarly, in (14b), the only vocabulary item that could complete the utterance is *pimienta*. The most sophisticated L2 lexical knowledge is exemplified by free active mastery in this view, which means that the L2 learner has complete access to the word and can produce it at will. In Laufer and Paribakht's study, L2 learners most quickly developed passive knowledge. However, active and free active knowledge developed at a much slower rate. Immersion settings (e.g. study or extended travel abroad) positively contributed to the development of these kinds of lexical acquisition.

Bahrik (1984) argues that learning vocabulary is a function of how deeply the learner processes it. Low-level processing, or simply repeating words, is ineffective in this view. For Bahrick, learners process vocabulary better if they have to place words in a grammatical structure, by actually using words in sentences. The best, deepest, processing, however, comes from matching the meaning of words with the meaning of the entire sentence. Bahrick also found that recycling is essential to the vocabulary learning process. In particular, frequency of use is less important than reviewing vocabulary every 30 days. Cook (2001) proposes that students be taught the complexity of word meanings, where possible (cf. Teichroew).

Another aspect to take into account is prototype theory (Rosch, 1983), according to which vocabulary is divided into basic level terms vs. class level terms. An example of the difference would be basic level *cubiertos* 'cutlery' vs. class level (or superordinate level) *tenedor* 'fork.' Another example would be basic level *rosa* 'rose' vs. class level *flores* 'flowers.' It is widely accepted that children learn basic-level terms before class-level terms (Rosch, 1983). Given their concreteness, this would seem to be applicable to the L2 learning process as well, as it is well known that L2 learners learn concrete terms before abstract ones (see De Groot & Keijzer, 2000, among others).

Word associations are another way in which L1 vs. L2 responses are different. In our L1, we have the following word associations: *secret* > *agent*, a syntagmatic response that completes a syntactic structure, a paradigmatic response that shows organization of the lexicon according to paradigms or sets of words, such as *hot* > *cold*, and finally, a klang response in which the associated word rhymes with the other word, such as book and hook (Cook, 2001: 52). In our L1, we develop the ability to use paradigmatic responses, first beginning with the syntagmatic ones, a pattern of development that seems to be similar in our L2 (Cook, 2001: 53).

4.7 Conclusion

The focus of this chapter has been the Spanish lexicon. We began our discussion with a general linguistic presentation of the lexicon itself, including what knowledge is contained. We next considered the great variation found in the Spanish lexicon, beginning with regional variation. We showed that lexical differences are extensive among dialects. One dichotomy is the lexicon found in Peninsular *vis à vis* Latin America, due, in part, to the use of archaisms in the latter dialect. However, to view Latin America as one monolithic dialect group with respect to lexical variation is an oversimplification that cannot be maintained. Indeed, dialects of Latin America also evince considerable regional variation in their respective lexicons. This difference among dialects can be attributed in part to indigenisms used in Latin America and language contact, which varies depending on the country in question.

We then discussed sociolinguistic aspects of the Spanish lexicon, including the use of euphemisms and the fact that taboo words, although they exist, are generally avoided in all but the most informal speech. We also addressed idiomatic expressions, which belong to an informal register. Our next topic was the bilingual lexicon, specifically the different models of organization of the lexicon in heritage speakers. We concluded our discussion with L2 acquisition of vocabulary, noting that the knowledge of words is crucial to comprehension and production of speech. In the next chapter, we turn to the role that earlier forms of a language should play in language instruction.

Chapter 5

They Said haiga *in* El Mío Cid? *The History of Spanish as a Window to Variation*

5.1 Introduction

This chapter has a slightly different focus from preceding chapters. We consider the question of whether courses dealing with the history of the Spanish language are an artifact in the curriculum which should be discontinued, or whether they should instead figure in the curriculum of the modern Spanish department (Arteaga & Llorente, 2004, 2005). We begin our discussion with a historical overview of the role of diachronic linguistics in the foreign language curriculum over the past century. We then turn our attention to the current curricular situation in Spanish departments across the country with respect to courses on the history of the Spanish language. We present several arguments in favor of the inclusion of diachronic information in the Spanish language classroom. We end our chapter with a fairly radical proposal, namely that courses focusing on the evolution of the Spanish language should be taught at both the graduate and the undergraduate levels. Our reasons for this are twofold. First, historical information about Spanish can clarify many of its current linguistic features. Second, the increased metalinguistic awareness gained from exposure to the history of Spanish will help students appreciate the synchronic variation found in Spanish as well as its continuing evolution.

5.2 Historical Overview

The curriculum in foreign languages has, to a certain extent, been subject to the vagaries of teaching methodology. At the beginning of the 20th century, the dominant teaching methodology was the Grammar-Translation method, which placed a primacy on the academic knowledge of a language. A great deal of importance was accorded to reading and translation. Since academic knowledge regarding a language was the purpose of language classes, considered more important than the ability to speak or understand language, the preparation of teachers of foreign languages was far different from what it is today.[126]

This method emphasized almost exclusively the academic knowledge of the foreign language in question (i.e. formal grammar and reading), as opposed to oral production and comprehension of the spoken word.[127] For example, students trained under this method were able to recite the myriad uses of the subjunctive mood, although they may not have been able to spontaneously utter, or understand, a phrase containing the subjunctive.[128] The Grammar-Translation method favored field-independent thinkers, who excel at abstract concepts, as opposed to field-dependent speakers, who require a context for learning (Cook, 2001: 137–140). Courses in the Grammar-Translation method were taught in English, in a manner much like Latin is today. Despite the fact that this method is rarely used today, it has left its imprint on many of the grammar sections in current textbooks, which are quite prescriptive in their presentation of grammar and lexical items.

One hundred years ago, conversational proficiency was not a priority in teacher training; knowledge of grammar, however, was considered essential, as was knowledge of the history of language. Indeed, a review of relevant articles from the period in the *Modern Language Journal* indicates that historical linguistic knowledge was taken for granted for foreign language majors, at both the graduate and undergraduate levels. For example, Keniston (1922: 1), outlining the necessary background that modern language teachers should acquire in graduate school, tops the list with what he refers to as 'linguistic background,' by which he means diachronic linguistics:

> First of all, there is the linguistic background. If we would really illumine, if we hope even to understand our texts, we must know the ancestry of words. And so the student of the Germanic tongues must know Gothic and Old High German, and, to feel their affinity to our own speech, must study Anglo-Saxon; the student of the Romance languages must know Vulgar Latin, Old French, Old Spanish, and Old Italian. With the phonological and morphological study will go the study of historical grammar, for the phrase, like the word, is only a stage in an eternal process....

Aron (1922: 79) echoes this view, underscoring the importance of historical linguistics for the (high school) language teacher:

> What teacher has not been asked the reason for the grammatical gender of German, French, and Spanish? A brief exposition of Brugmann's

well-known theory of the rise of grammatical gender invariably satis-
fies the question....

This same view held for undergraduate study. Bronk (1921: 184) considers
knowledge of the history of a language to be among the 'attainable goals'
in college foreign language instruction, and one that affords certain advan-
tages for less orally proficient students:

> Another attainable college aim in teaching a modern language is to
> make students intelligent regarding its origin. This involves recourse to
> history, anthropology, and phonetic science, as well as to other lan-
> guages, thereby conducing to general intelligence and culture. This kind
> of work gives students seemingly without oral gifts a chance to shine.

Here Bronk espouses a common theme of the period, namely the belief that
exposure to historical linguistics has positive cognitive effects generally.

This widespread view of the importance of historical linguistics is
echoed by Crawford (1925: 188). Reporting on foreign language study, he
includes as an ultimate objective for undergraduate language study, 'a
clearer understanding of the history and nature of language.' It seems that
in no era has our profession truly been satisfied with training of foreign
language teachers. The early part of the last century was no different. For
example, Purin (1928) details the status at that time of a report regarding
preparation and training of (high school) foreign language teachers, which
was undertaken by the American and Canadian Committees of the
Modern Foreign Language Study. The results of the study deemed current
teacher training at the time to be unsatisfactory. Knowledge of historical
linguistics figures among the recommendations set forward by the com-
mittee (Purin, 1928: 16):

> The aims of these courses [i.e. to train foreign language teachers]
> should be to give the prospective teachers adequate training in lan-
> guage (including oral command), in literature, in the history of the
> foreign civilization, in history of language....

Hagboldt (1928: 194) agrees, emphasizing that a 'master teacher' of foreign
languages:

> ... is a trained philologist and knows the foreign language according
> to the history of its sounds, forms, dialects, and in its relations to other
> languages in the same group, especially to English. This training
> enables him to answer satisfactorily any intelligent question asked by
> his students about grammar and syntax and it allows him to make
> extremely valuable comparisons between the forms and constructions

of English and the corresponding forms of the foreign language or other modern languages.

This view was even held at the period for high-school *students* of foreign languages. For example, Crawford (1925: 173) insists that Spanish high-school students be exposed to philology; in his words:

> They should be made to realize in the early stages of their study that Spanish is not only the sole medium of communication between persons in a very considerable portion of the world, but that the language itself is the product of many centuries of growth and change. The position of Spanish as a daughter of Latin should be made clear from the outset....

Introducing students to diachronic phonological rules (such as initial /f/ in Latin/English becoming /h/ and then mute (i.e. non-pronounced) in Spanish), Crawford argues, will foster their vocabulary acquisition (e.g. *fabulare/hablar* 'to speak'). Some ten years later, in the 1930s, historical linguistics continued to be viewed as essential to the foreign language curriculum. Aspinwall (1937: 560) mentions the necessity of future language teachers (in this case, of French), mastering 'Phonetics, grammar, and the development of the French language.'

Michie (1938) goes so far as to recommend a program of study of philology that she had developed for an eighth-grade English course, which began with a four-week introduction into the Indo-European language family, followed by seven-week courses on the Romance languages and the Celtic languages and a nine-week study of the Germanic languages, including English. She claims that in addition to improving students' oral and written expression, there was another benefit to the emphasis on philology (Michie, 1938: 346):

> The mental health of several pupils was noticeably improved by the gradual dissolving of linguistic difficulties (semantic blockages), through increasing familiarity with and understanding of the actual function of language.

The unintentional humor of Michie's quote notwithstanding, her point is that historical linguistics improves students' metalinguistic knowledge *about* language.

Greiner (1938: 209) aptly sums up the view of many scholars of the era regarding the goals of the Grammar-Translation method, with its academic, abstract focus:

> The main objective in modern foreign language study today should be to become intelligent *about* language. What was once the by-product

should become the main object of pursuit. While the student is becoming intelligent about language, he can be learning some German,
French, or Spanish, and other things.

Like many scholars of his era, Greiner emphasizes the link between historical knowledge of a language and greater metalinguistic understanding that languages evolve through time (Greiner, 1938: 209):

> I know men who have been out of school for twenty-five years and
> who still know that *columba* is Latin for dove and *casa* is Spanish for
> house. Yet they cannot understand that likely *feel badly* will in the near
> future be correct, simply because it is becoming usage in good
> society ... they had not become intelligent about language ....

Schutz (1939: 498), reporting on the foreign language curriculum at the
Ohio state universities, indicates that historical linguistics, or 'emphasis
on historical aids to grammar,' is regularly incorporated into grammar
study in the 5th quarter undergraduate sequence of classes; he advocates
diachronic information as 'an aid to simplicity.' McCuaig (1940: 111)
argues that etymology 'will naturally follow in any Spanish course.'
Indeed, this was the prevailing attitude until the war. Freeman (1941:
301) states that 'the Romance language teacher who has not had a good
course in Romance philology should lose no time attacking the subject
by himself.'

The situation of language teaching changed radically after the beginning of WWII. Kurz (1943: 463) strongly criticizes the Grammar-Translation
approach, noting that it does little to improve fluency or comprehension
(Kurz, 1943: 209):

> The program of present course must be changed from the emphasis
> on grammar, reducing the number of hours devoted to acquiring the
> rules, and incorporating more the cultural background or milieu in
> which the language is spoken ... Reading knowledge is public enemy
> number one.

The emphasis during the war was on the ability to *use* language, to speak
and understand. Intensive courses were developed. In the case of Spanish,
two developments were seen (U.S. Office of Education, 1943: 431):

> There is every likelihood, however, that two tendencies brought into
> prominence by the war and current problems will have a lasting effect
> upon the teaching of Spanish. The first of these is emphasis upon an
> oral, conversational approach ... The second is greater emphasis upon
> the Spanish-speaking countries of the New World ....

In the curriculum proposed by the above report from 1943, the history of the Spanish language is not mentioned. Similarly, Mapes (1943: 538) argues that in times of war, oral/aural skills must be emphasized, as well as a 'specialized military vocabulary.' Jordan (1944: 342), addressing curricular needs in postwar America, echoes this sentiment (cf. Duggan, 1944; Morgan, 1944):

> The practical viewpoint advocates rightly that foreign languages be taught 'for use' … The majority of all college students taking foreign language courses should aim at a speaking knowledge ….

Indeed, (the largely academic style of) foreign language teaching found itself on the defensive during WWII, because of its inability to produce students who could speak and understand a language. To be sure, many scholars, such as Pargment (1945), were highly critical of the purported success of the 'intensive' method employed by the armed forces. As he noted, the groups of soldiers to whom "intensive language training" was given shared many characteristics which students of language programs oftentimes lacked (Pargment, 1945: 201):

- A very high percentage of 'army beginners' had had previous language training ….
- The amount of time given to the A.S.T.P. [Army's Specialized Training Program] men – from 15 to 17 h a week – is from three to four times that given the regular classes in normal time ….
- The size of the A.S.T.P classes was from three to four times smaller than that of our ordinary classes ….
- In the army program, reading and writing were not objectives ….
- The students had been selected with great care both for general intelligence and for linguistic background or aptitude ….
- All students had the same objective, and gave their full cooperation.

Huebner (1945) agreed, noting that the 'unselected student-body' who takes a foreign language makes it impossible for the schools to adopt a 'conversational aim.' Yet the experience of the war did have a profound effect on language teaching, in part because foreign languages were suddenly seen as *relevant*. As noted by Simpson (1945: 382–383):

> Whether our aloofness be best described as consecration to the contemplative life, or sulking in our tents, we have been violently recalled to use and duty by – *mirabile dictum* – the armed forces …. There are indications that … we are groping nostalgically for our comfortable seclusion.

With this sudden relevance came accountability, despite the lack of parallels between the army's specialized units and the typical university setting, as noted by Simpson (1945: 383):

> We cannot compete with the army specialized units, but we can do better at what we do....

Again, the call here is for a shift of focus to the oral/aural aspects of language acquisition. Singer (1946: 338) is equally critical of the results of the Grammar-Translation method:

> Any teacher, surely, would be proud to develop students who could speak with reasonable fluency and correctness of intonation and pronunciation; write a respectable page of prose; read without the necessity of translating every word into English, mentally if not orally, and finally, have a sympathetic understanding of the culture and viewpoint of the Spanish-speaking world. Such students are rarely produced in our classes today.

Given the sudden primacy of the oral/aural, scholars began to disregard any role for historical linguistics in the curriculum. Knowledge of culture and geography was considered to be essential, as was understanding of basic phonetics. With respect to teacher training, many scholars bemoaned the lack of fluency of the instructors themselves, who were a product, in their view, of the failed Grammar-Translation method (Tharp, 1949: 419–420):

> The current vogue of emphasis on the oral approach requires a teacher competent in the oral skills... Such a teacher should know the techniques of developing good pronunciation and of promoting oral expression. These are the hardest of all objectives and should not be attempted by ill-trained teachers.

This view continued to be held well after the war. Freeman (1949: 263) decries the lack of 'proper training' for foreign language teaching. In his view, the most important aspects for the curriculum for prospective foreign language teaching were the following: pronunciation, oral fluency, basic grammatical competence, knowledge of the culture and civilization, an understanding of the contribution to intellectual ideas of the literature of the country and, finally, foreign language teaching methodology. No mention is made of familiarity with historical linguistics.

Interestingly, in the decade of the 1950s, there was some renewed interest in the role of the history of the language for the language teacher, perhaps due to the rise of linguistics as a separate field of study. Giduz

(1952: 66) mentions 'etymology' as one of several 'other abilities that will be of great value' to the foreign language teacher. Nabholz (1953: 350) discusses the explanatory value of knowledge such as Grimm's law in the case of German:

> In conclusion, let it be stated that references to the interrelationship of the languages and to the laws governing these relationships as well as to the history of words tend to make the language instruction more fruitful and interesting for the student and instructor alike.

Prince (1954) echoes this view, stressing the importance of a 'linguistic approach,' including a diachronic perspective on the origin and inter-relatedness of words, to language even in the elementary language classroom. He argues that language departments should include historical linguistics in their curricula, particularly at the graduate level, so that teachers will be prepared to provide meaningful explanations to students. For example, instructors will be able to point out the fact that the endings of the synthetic future tense in French are based on the verb *avoir* 'to have' or that *aujourd'hui* 'today' is a reinforced form. London *et al.* (1955: 136), in a discussion of what courses the Spanish major should take, also points to the importance of historical facts about Spanish. They argue that a "considerable knowledge" of such aspects of language is essential. They go so far as to recommend that Spanish majors peruse such journals as *Romance Philology* during their course of study!

Indeed, in the *Modern Language Journal*'s report on the Qualifications for Secondary School Teachers of Modern Foreign Language (MLJ, 1955), 'language analysis' is listed as an essential criterion. The report recommends a grading scale of sorts for prospective teachers (minimal, good, superior), in which levels beyond 'minimal' require competence in both historical and synchronic linguistics (MLJ, 1955: 291):

> *Good*: A basic knowledge of the historical development and present characteristics of the language, and an awareness of the difference between the language as spoken and as written.
> *Superior*: Ability to apply knowledge of descriptive, comparative and historical linguistics to the language-teaching situation.

In the post-Sputnik decade of the 1960s, there was a renewed interest in foreign languages in general. With the advent of the new technology resulting in language laboratories, the Audio-lingual approach became dominant. In many ways, this approach was diametrically opposed to the Grammar-Translation method, in that understanding was viewed as a requisite for speaking, only after which reading and writing could presumably follow.[129] Within such a pedagogical framework, the role of historical linguistics was necessarily diminished, although some scholars, such as Bieler (1964: 134), continued to argue for its relevance:

> The trend seems to point toward a more and more extensive use of pattern drills, based purely on stimulus response…The most effective and direct methods should be adopted… But after a mainly synchronic approach, diachronic interpretation should be in order. After the student has acquired the skills and after he has learned how the language is used, it would be logical to offer him an explanation why it is used in this particular way… A course in the history of the French language offering this explanation seems essential for students preparing to teach the language, and highly desirable for all who wish to render their previous study meaningful.

Interestingly, Bieler makes a distinction between a course in the history of French and a course on Old French, recommending the former over the latter. Yet he was fully aware of the fact that his recommendations ran contrary to the pedagogical practice of the era. As he notes, only 12 out of 218 universities offered such a course at the undergraduate level, 9 at the graduate level and 3 at both levels.

MacAllister (1964), addressing the preparation of college professors, does not discuss familiarity with the history of the language of study. He considers only a backround in synchronic linguistics to be essential. Similarly, the *Modern Language Journal*'s (1966) report on teacher education fails to mention historical knowledge of the language, as do Banathy (1968) and Pillet (1970). Brooks (1966), discussing the training of foreign language teachers in general, does mention philology. However, he deems it to be of equal importance to psychology and cultural anthropology.

In the decade of the 1970s, many scholars began to call for a course on general linguistics, including historical linguistics in the foreign language curriculum, to raise what Cook (2001) terms 'language awareness,' or raising awareness of language itself. For example, Haile (1970) reports on a course he created for college freshmen at the University of Illinois, called 'Introduction to the Study of German.' Philology, by which he means the 'historical study of language and literature,' is one of four major content areas of the course, along with Linguistics, Literary Criticism and the History of Language Teaching (Haile, 1970: 120).

By the decade of the 1980s, the Communicative Approach had largely supplanted the Audio-lingual method. It had become generally accepted that language was not a skill that could be 'drilled' into students, in recognition of the fact that the Audio-lingual method did not generally result in communicative competence. This was the decade in which the ACTFL (American Council on the Teaching of Foreign Languages) Proficiency Guidelines were first developed; the initial guidelines, from 1983 and revised in 1985, make no mention of knowledge of the history of a language, although linguistics is mentioned in the distinguished level of Reading (ACTFL, 1983):

> **Reading.** *Distinguished level.* Able to read fluently and accurately most styles and forms of the language pertinent to academic and professional needs. Able to relate inferences in the text to real-world knowledge and understand almost all sociolinguistic and cultural references by processing language from within the cultural framework. Able to understand a writer's use of nuance and subtlety. Can readily follow unpredictable turns of thought and author intent in such materials as sophisticated editorials, specialized journal articles, and literary texts such as novels, plays, poems, as well as in any subject matter area directed to the general reader.

Perhaps in part due to the great influence that ACTFL has enjoyed in the field of foreign language instruction, Di Pietro *et al.* (1983), reviewing graduate foreign language curriculum in the United States, consider the courses offered in philology (8% of total courses) to be artifacts, arguing instead for the development of courses in applied linguistics.

Indeed, the Communicative Approach of the 1980s, unlike the audiovisual approach, emphasized *production* (e.g. conversation, communication) in the classroom. Grammar was relegated to footnotes or units separate from the main chapters, and typically assigned as homework, not discussed in class. Yet the emphasis on communication seemed to sacrifice grammatical accuracy. In response to this, in the decade of the 1990s, the focus was on global proficiency. Many scholars argued for a renewed *focus on form*, and for the importance of integrating grammatical explanations into a communicative framework (e.g. Doughty & Williams, 1998; Ellis, 1993; Herron & Tomasello, 1992).

In the 1990s, culture (especially through the study of literature) was also accorded major importance in the curriculum (see Omaggio Hadley, 1993; Swaffar *et al.*, 1991; Shanahan, 1997, among others). Although synchronic linguistics was accepted as part of the curriculum during this period, most scholars did not consider courses on the history of the language to be relevant (two exceptions are Rini, 1990, and Arteaga & Herschensohn, 1995). In fact, it was argued during this period that university Latin should be taught as a living language, as was the case in the New York school district (see Abbott & Davis, 1996; see Ball & Ellsworth, 1996, for an opposing view).

Schulz (2000), in a thorough review of articles on foreign language teacher training in the *Modern Language Journal* from 1916 to 1999, does not mention knowledge of history of the language in her list of priorities for teacher development in the future.

In this section, we have seen how specialists in the field viewed historical linguistics in the foreign language classroom over the last century. There was felt to be a direct link between philology and the Grammar-Translation method of prewar America. For students to be well-versed in abstract information *about* the language was considered of paramount importance. This view changed radically, however, with the advent of WWII, where the focus was on *using* language skills. Diachronic linguistics was viewed as emblematic of the failed language instruction of the previous decades. This view remains largely unchanged today, although for a brief period in the 1950s, with the rise of theoretical linguistics, scholars once again promoted historical linguistics for foreign language students. This view was supplanted, in the 1960s, by the Audio-lingual method and its focus on oral/aural skills.

In the Communicative Approach, which dominated our field in the 1980s, the emphasis on conversational competence was incompatible with both grammatical instruction and historical linguistics. Even in the past two decades, however, with its emphasis on marrying a *focus on form* with communicative competence, few scholars have argued for the importance of diachronic linguistics. In the next section, we consider curricular offerings across the nation in modern language departments to gauge the extent to which courses in the history of language continue to be offered.

5.3   Current Curricular Trends

In our review of the curricular offerings in Spanish departments across the United States, we found that many Spanish departments currently offer courses entitled 'History of the Spanish language.' The description of such a course varies in length, from a detailed account of its content (1) to a brief statement (2) and (3):

(1)   Introduction to the origin and evolution of the Spanish language. Focus on phonological, morphological and syntactic changes that Latin underwent, which gradually gave way to modern Spanish, and on the historical circumstances for the birth and spread of the Spanish language around the world (Northern Illinois University).

(2)   Historical development of the Spanish language from its origins to the present in Spain and Latin America (Marquette University).

(3)   The phonological, morphological, syntactic and semantic evolution of the Spanish language from Latin (University of Florida).

Whatever the institution, from the description of the above courses, we can infer that the approach to its content is rather traditional (e.g. theoretical and philological in nature). Common textbooks used in these courses are those by Resnick (1981) and Lathrop (1980). Reading lists include chapters from Menéndez Pidal (1940), Lapesa (1980) and Lloyd (1987). At some institutions, the title of the course clearly points toward a traditional approach. For example, the corresponding course at Brown University is entitled 'Spanish Philology,' whereas other institutions, such as the University of Tennessee, offer 'Old Spanish.'

For the most part, History of the Spanish Language courses are offered at universities with graduate programs. In some institutions (e.g. the University of Illinois at Urbana), the course is taught with a shared code, for both undergraduate and graduate students. Rarely do we find a four-year Spanish program where such courses are taught, although Illinois Wesleyan University, in Bloomington, is an exception, offering a course entitled 'History of the Spanish Language' for undergraduate students. Study abroad programs in different Spanish universities frequently include courses on the history of the Spanish language among their offerings, perhaps because this subject is compulsory in Spain to complete the degree in Hispanic Philology. That is the case, for example, of the program used by the University of Virginia, at the University of Sevilla.

Generally speaking, where the course is offered at the graduate level, it is not a requirement, but is rather an optional course that can fulfill a requirement related to Linguistics. For example, at Brown University, 'Spanish Philology' (Spanish 201), considered a graduate course, appears as an alternative to fulfill one required area (seven courses are listed in their catalogue as options, and three should be selected). This only applies to the Hispanic Studies Concentration in Language and Linguistics (one of three possibilities at this university). At Tulane University, one of the few universities to offer a course on the history of Spanish at the undergraduate level, the course is optional for undergraduate students as well. In order to major in Spanish, students need to select at least three credits in several areas; one of those areas is labeled 'Language, Linguistics and Literary Theory.' 'History of the Spanish Language' (Spanish 561) is one of *twelve* possible courses.

In this section, we have seen that in the United States, courses on the history of the Spanish language are offered generally at the graduate level, with few exceptions. From the course description and textbooks used in the classes, we can assume that most of these courses are traditional philology courses. But even at the graduate level, there is a tendency across the country to make courses on the historical development of Spanish optional rather than required. In the next section, we argue against this trend, suggesting that a course on the history of Spanish should be required, at both the graduate and undergraduate levels.

5.4 The Relevance of Diachronic Linguistics

We believe that the knowledge of the history of Spanish is essential for students at both the undergraduate and graduate levels. In beginning classes, this may take the form of simple diachronic explanations regarding features of Spanish (see below). But at upper-division levels, we argue that if linguistics is to be taught at the undergraduate level in Spanish, it should take the form of a history of Spanish course, for many reasons. First, according to the current ACFTL Proficiency guidelines, knowledge of *culture* is deemed to be essential in all but the lowest proficiency level in Reading and Speaking. Of the range of possible linguistics courses, the one with the most direct link to culture is the history of Spanish, as argued by Arteaga and Herschensohn (1995: 212) for French. These scholars make the point that the current emphasis on *culture* makes historical linguistics *more*, not *less*, relevant:

> ... there is an inextricable link between historical information and culture ... In a proficiency based classroom, the cultural context of a language is of paramount importance and is intertwined with the history of the people ....

As a concrete example, the role of the *Real Academia de la Lengua* and its grammar, prescriptive in nature, figures as an interesting linguistic and historical topic to be discussed. In our view, the conservative nature of the *Real Academia* can be understood as an attempt to maintain the link between the diachronic and synchronic forms of the Spanish language, so that the connection among Spanish-speaking areas is not lost. This tension is clearly illustrated by the preface to the Statutes:[130]

> La institución ha ido adaptando sus funciones a los tiempos que le ha tocado vivir. Actualmente, y según lo establecido por el artículo primero de sus Estatutos, la Academia 'tiene como misión principal velar porque los cambios que experimente la Lengua Española en su constante adaptación a las necesidades de sus hablantes no quiebren la esencial unidad que mantiene en todo el ámbito hispánico'.

Moreover, diachronic linguistics is a window to synchronic variation, which has been argued to be essential for the Spanish language curriculum (Arteaga & Llorente, 2003), given the pluricentric nature of Spanish that we have emphasized in this book. Indeed, a course in the history of Spanish can give students a greater understanding of language variability in several ways. First, many dialectal differences can be traced to their historical roots.

As Arteaga and Herschensohn (1995: 219) argue, a course in the history of a language also serves to illustrate to students that language is 'organic and constantly evolving.' Indeed, these scholars echo Michie (1938) in their belief that historical explanations serve a purpose beyond accounting for linguistic facts, namely increasing students' metalinguistic awareness (Arteaga & Herschensohn, 1995: 219):

> In our view such [i.e. historical] explanations serve a greater purpose than merely imparting interesting facts about language; they also provide students with a firsthand understanding that languages are organic and are constantly evolving. A perhaps unexpected benefit from this approach is that students become able to accept the variability found in Modern French, such as the notion that certain structures (negation, for example) seem to be undergoing change at the present time.

Finally, the explanatory value of historical facts cannot be understated, as noted by several scholars, including Rini (1990) and Arteaga and Herschensohn (1995). As summed up by Rini (1990: 843), who argues for relevant diachronic explanations in the Spanish language classroom:

> I maintain that the application of such historical linguistic information will replace the typical inaccurate, uninteresting, and unhelpful responses like those mentioned at the beginning of this article [e.g. That's just the way it is, learn it! It's just irregular!] with enlightening, helpful, ones, which will enrich the study of the target language for the teacher and students alike.
>
> Indeed, there are a series of linguistic facts which cannot be adequately explained to students without recourse to diachronic facts about Spanish (see Rini for a discussion of some of these facts). We turn to these next.

5.4.1 Spanish phonology from a diachronic perspective

The commonalities between the phonology of the dialects of the so-called *tierras bajas* in Latin America or coastal dialects and that of Andalusia (e.g. aspiration of syllable-final /s/, lambdacism, velarization of syllable-final nasals, and deletion of intervocalic /ð/) can naturally be explored in a course focusing on the history of the language.[131] The reasons for these shared characteristics are still somewhat controversial, but all make reference to historical facts. For example, one theory points out that immigration patterns from Spain to Latin America meant that 40–67% of immigrants to the new world were from Andalucía (Cotton & Sharp, 1988). Another view (Alonso, 1982) notes the great similarities between the Spanish spoken in

Mexico City and Lima and that of Castile (e.g. retention of syllable-final *s*, general consonantism). He argues that these features cannot be explained without recourse to the fact that these Latin American cities were the seats of the *virreinatos* 'viceroyalties' during the colonization period, and therefore had much contact with Castile.

Consider once more phonological characteristics such as the *distinción* of Castile, the *seseo* of Latin America and the *ceceo* of Andalusia (Alonso, 1967: 122), as in (4):

(4)   *distinción* [ká sa] *casa* 'he marries' [ká θa] *caza* 'he hunts'
       seseo [ká sa] *casa* 'he marries' [ká sa] *caza* 'he hunts'
       ceceo [ká θa] *casa* 'he marries' [ká θa] *caza* 'he hunts'

The above variants cannot be adequately explained, at least at the graduate level, without reference to the 16th century *reajuste de sibilantes* 'realignment of the sibilants' of Alonso (1947).

Before the 16th century, the grapheme *z* represented the affricates [ts] and [dz], depending on their phonemic environment. When these affricates were simplified in the 16th century, the dialect of Andalusia replaced them with a voiceless dental [ŝ], whereas the dialect of Castile replaced them with the interdental [θ]. From a historical point of view, both developments are natural, for two reasons. First, the initial consonant in the affricate was dental, and second, the simplification of an affricate (stop + fricative) is common diachronically among languages.[132]

Indeed, students with an appreciation of the evolution of a language can better understand the more recent development of dialectal characteristics, such as the *žeísmo* of the *Río de la Plata* region in Latin America (roughly, Uruguay, Paraguay and Argentina).[133] *Žeísmo*, or the spirantization, or the evolution to a fricative (and sometimes devoicing) of the palatal glide /j/ is a fairly recent development in the Spanish language (Lloyd, 1987: 346). The developmental link between *lleísmo* (which contrasts the palatal lateral /ʎ/ with the palatal glide /j/) and *yeísmo* (which has no palatal lateral) is a clear one, historically speaking, and has been evidenced in other languages (e.g. French). But as we saw in Chapter 2, the development of žeísmo is unique to Latin American Spanish (5):

(5)   *žeísmo* [ká ʒe] *calle* 'street'
       lleísmo [ká ʎe] *calle* 'street'
       yeísmo [ká je] *calle* 'street'

From an evolutionary standpoint, the development of [j] to [j] to [ʒ] is again expected. The point of articulation of both sounds is palatal, so that the change is a minor one. One reason why a glide may evolve into a fricative is due to the phonological process of reinforcement, or making a consonant more resistant to change. Devoicing the segment to [ʃ] further strengthens the consonant from a diachronic point of view.

Historical explanations can also explain writing conventions in Modern Spanish, making orthography more transparent. For example, although Spanish orthography is generally phonemic, students are often puzzled by the dual value of 'x,' which corresponds to either [x] or [ks] (6):

(6) *México* [méx iko] 'Mexico'
     Xavier [xaβ jér] 'Xavier'
     taxi [ták si] 'taxi'
     exigente [ek si xén te] 'demanding'

The reason for this bifurcation is purely historical. In Old Spanish, the spelling *x* corresponded to the phoneme [š], as in the modern English word *sherry* from Xeréz [šeréts]. During the 16th century, the series of changes affecting affricates resulted in the velarization of [š] to [x]. On the other hand, the group [ks] is directly inherited from (Vulgar) Latin, as in *excelencia* 'excellence' [ek θe lén θja]

In some cases, phonological change has led to morphological variation. In morphology, there are several facts that have historical explanations. For example, students are often puzzled as to why the indirect object *le* 'to him, to her' becomes *se* 'oneself' when it precedes the direct object *lo(s)* 'him/them' or *la(s)* 'her/them,' as in (7) (cf. Rini, 1990):

(7) (a) *Le di el libro.* 'I gave him the book.'
     (b) *Se lo di.* 'I gave it to him.'
     (c) *Les regalé el libro.* 'I gave them the book.'
     (d) *Se lo regalé.* 'I gave it to them.'

Students often confuse this *se* with the reflexive, although its origin, in fact, is quite different, as summarized by Resnick (1981: 88):

(8) illī-illum> [iḷe iḷo]> [ḷe ḷo]> [želo] > [sélo] > [se lo]

In (8), the palatalization of the group [le] resulting in [zˇ] undergoes devoicing and then depalatalization, arguably by analogy with the pronoun *se*. The fact that these phonological changes were regular in the history of Spanish might very well serve as solace to the beleaguered Spanish student!

Phonology has played a role in another morphological development in Spanish, namely in so-called stem-changing verbs. Such verbs, which are quite frequent, show an alternation in the stem vowel between the first and second person plural, on the one hand, and the remaining forms (9):

(9)   (a) *poder* 'to sleep'
           singular   plural
           puedo 'I can'   *podemos* 'we can'
           puedes 'you can'   *podéis* 'you all can'
           puede 's/he/you can'   *pueden* 'they/you can'
      (b) *empezar* 'to begin'
           singular   plural
           empiezo 'I begin'   *empezamos* 'we begin'
           empiezas 'you begin'   *empezáis* 'you all begin'
           empieza 's/he/you begin' *empiezan* 'they/you begin'

The above examples illustrate two very common alternations in Spanish, *o/ue* and *e/ie*. These alternations developed historically as a regular phonological change, in which short lax vowels in Latin underwent diphthongization in Spanish when stressed (cf. Rini, 1990). A diachronic explanation not only serves to dispel notions that Spanish verbs are chaotically irregular, but also underlines the synchronic fact, which is that only forms in which the stem vowel is stressed show the alternation. Forms in which the stem vowel is unstressed pattern like the infinitive.

In other verb forms, although the development of alternation is more opaque (i.e. because it is due to palatalization or metaphony, the raising of a vowel, such as e to i), as in the example in (10):

(10) *pedir* 'to ask for'
      singular   plural
      pido 'I ask for'   *pedimos* 'we ask for'
      pides 'you ask for'   *pedís* 'you all ask for'
      pide 's/he/you ask for'   *piden* 'they ask for'

In the example in (10), students can readily recognize that the alternation of vowels (*i/e*) can be seen where they are stressed (e.g. *pido*) and where they are not (e.g. *pedimos*). It is important to note that despite the explanation of the diachronic rule, students will nonetheless need to memorize which verbs evince this alternation (e.g. *morir* 'to die') and which do not (e.g. *morar* 'to inhabit'). We next turn to historical accounts of morphological variation found today in Spanish.

5.4.2 Diachrony and Spanish morphology

As discussed in detail in Chapter 3, Spanish dialects evince a great deal of morphological variation. Students will come to appreciate such variation, without passing judgment, if they are led to view such forms as a natural part of the evolutionary process. For example, in the dialect of Spanish spoken in the Southwest United States, several archaic verb forms are found, such as *haiga* 'there is/there are (subj),' *dijistes* 'you (inf.) said' and *creiba* 'he believed' (11):[135]

(11)   Archaic verb forms in the Spanish of the Southwest United States
       (a) *haiga* 'there is/there are, subj.'
       (b) *dijistes* 'you (inf.) said'
       (c) *creiba* 'he believed'
           (cf. Penny, 2000: 220).

In our view, if students and instructors understand the historical sources of these verb forms commonly used in the Southwest, they will be more apt to view the dialect favorably.

Another instance of dialectal differences in morphology, as discussed in Chapters 1 and 3, can be found in forms of address. To recap our discussion from those chapters, we note that the use of the pronoun *vosotros* 'you all,' the second person plural informal pronoun, is a characteristic of the dialects of Spain (12):

(12)   Spain: *vosotros habláis* 'you (pl., informal) speak'
       LA: *ustedes hablan* 'you (pl., informal/formal) speak'

While *vosotros* does not exist in Latin America, *vos* exists for the majority of speakers of Latin American Spanish (with the exception of México), and is used as the second person singular (informal) form (13). In Spain, as well as in Mexico, the form used is *tú*.

(13)   *vos hablas (habláis, hablás)* 'you speak' (Latin America)
       = *tú hablas* (Spain, most of México)

Again, the explanation for the linguistic variation is historical.[136] Latin had two ways of addressing a second person: tu│ , to talk to a single person, and vo│ s, to address more than one, regardless of the formality of the speech. During the evolution of the Latin language, however, the pronoun *vos* acquired an additional value, that of deference or formality. In formal speech, vo│ s came to be used to address just one person. This evolution is indicated by (14):

(14)   (a) Classical Latin forms of address
           tu│ singular, formal/informal vo│ s plural, formal/informal
       (b) Late Latin forms of address
           tu│ singular, informal vo│ s plural, formal/informal
           vo│ s singular, formal

The situation in (14b) is that found in Old Spanish (before the 15th century) as well. At that time, *tú* was the second person singular non-deferential pronoun, with *vos* as its plural counterpart. For deferential exchanges, *vos* was the appropriate pronoun, both to address just one individual and to address more than one person.

As the language evolved, however, the use of *vos* spread to informal contexts as well, giving rise to the system in (15):

(15)   Old Spanish forms of address (15th century and later)
       tú singular, informal   *vos* plural, formal/informal
       vos singular, formal/informal

By the 15th century, *vos* had lost much of its deferential value, and was almost equivalent to *tú*. Given the emergence of social classes in Spain, there was a need, then, to create new alternatives to express the idea of formality. Several nouns were used for that purpose, among them *señoría* 'lordship,' *merced* 'grace' and *excelencia* 'excellence.' These were combined with the feminine form of the possessive adjective corresponding to the second person plural, *vuestra*, for both *señoría* and *merced* are feminine nouns. *Vuestra merced* ('your grace') was the form that finally became predominant, with a new plural counterpart *vuestras mercedes* ('your graces'). These combinations are the sources of present-day *usted* and *ustedes*. Finally, the pronoun *vos* was reinforced with *otros* (from Latin *alteros*) in the plural, to distinguish it from the singular *vos*. This evolution is summarized in (16) below:

(16)   Sixteenth century forms of address in Old Spanish
       tú singular, informal *vosotros* plural, informal
       vos singular, informal
       vuestra merced/vuestra señoría/excelencia singular, formal
       vuestras mercedes/vuestras señorías/excelencías plural, formal

Thus, at the beginning of the Golden Age, the time when the Spaniards arrived in the New World, the terms of address commonly used for the second person singular non-deferential singular were *tú* or *vos*. The corresponding plural counterpart was *vosotros* (a pronoun that had previously had a purely contrastive value) and *vuestra merced/vuestras mercedes* as deferential terms of address.

However, at this point it time, a distinction developed between the forms *vos* and *tú* in Spain only. *Vos* came to be used for persons who were considered to be socially inferior, whereas *tú* was the preferred informal form for those of equal social status. In fact, in 1579 a nobleman who referred to another with *vos* was subsequently challenged to a duel!

(Cotton & Sharp, 1988: 148). According to Correas (1626) in his *Arte grande de la lengua castellana* (cited in Cotton & Sharp, 1988; Pountain, 2001):[137] 'De vos, tratamos a los criados, y a los labradores y personas semejantes y entre amigos a donde no hay gravedad ni cumplimiento si se trata de VOS.' How did *vos* become so widespread in Latin America? According to historical linguists, *vos* was the most common form of address used when speaking to the indigenous peoples of Latin America, whom the Spanish enslaved (Walsh, 1985).

Another area of morphological variation among Spanish dialects concerns the third person accusative and dative forms, as discussed in detail in Chapter 3. Students of the language are frequently confused with their use (particularly when the third person is concerned), but so are native speakers! In the Old Spanish system, also called the etymological usage, there was a clear delineation of cases (see (74) in Chapter 3 for a summary). For the accusative (direct object), only *lo(s)* and *la(s)* as masculine or feminine accusative forms were used. For the dative (indirect object), *le(s)* was found. From a diachronic perspective, taking as a basis the forms given above, the logical possibilities are either a system that overgeneralizes case (e.g. *leísmo*) or a system that overgeneralizes gender (e.g. *laísmo/loísmo*). In the evolution of the Spanish language, both variants emerged.

La *Real Academia* accepts both the *uso etimológico* and *leísmo* as standard, provided the pronoun *le(s)* is replacing a person. However, the scholarly organization considers *leísmo* to be a grammatical mistake when the pronoun substitutes an inanimate object (17) and (18):

(17) *Leísmo*, considered standard usage as per the *Real Academia*
*Ayer, vimos **a Juan**. **Le** vimos en el parque.* 'Yesterday we saw Juan. We saw him in the park.'

(18) *Leísmo*, considered substandard usage, as per the *Real Academia*
Vi **un vestido muy bonito y **le** compré.* 'I saw a very pretty dress and I bought it.'

This pronouncement is somewhat arbitrary, given the logic of *leísmo*. Similarly, from a historical standpoint, *laísmo* and *loísmo* are natural developments, although again la *Real Academia* does not accept them, as in (19) and (20):

(19) *Loísmo*, considered substandard by la *Real Academia*
****Lo** di el dinero (**a Pedro**).* 'I gave him (Pedro) the money.'

(20) *Laísmo*, considered substandard by la *Real Academia*
****La** envié la carta (**a Elena**) por correo.*
'I sent Elena the letter by mail.'

Indeed, la *Real Academia* considers this substitution of the accusative for the dative to be a serious grammar mistake, despite the fact that it is not only quite frequent in some Spanish dialects (mostly in Spain), but also a natural bifurcation from *el uso etimológico*.

It is clear from the above discussion that a thorough discussion of the third person direct and indirect object pronouns must include both synchronic and diachronic data. The question of which variants to teach in the Spanish language classroom is discussed below in Chapter 6. However, approaching this topic from a historical perspective can illustrate both the somewhat unfounded prescriptivism of la *Real Academia* and the fact that grammars of dialects have typically undergone changes that are to be expected.

Another morphological fact that often puzzles students is why some feminine singular words, such as *agua* 'water', seemingly take a masculine definite article: *el agua* 'the water' (cf. Rini, 1990). Synchronically this can be explained by the fact that the words in question begin with a stressed /a/, as discussed in detail in Chapter 3. From a diachronic perspective, however, the article used with such nouns is actually a result of one of two regular developments of the Latin feminine singular demonstrative *illa* 'that' (21):

(21) ĭlla [é:lla] → *el* 'the' (by apocope 'loss of final syllable')
       ĭlla [é:lla] → *la* 'the' (by aphaeresis 'loss of first syllable')

Therefore, although *el* is synchronically masculine, diachronically it was also feminine. Another morphological fact about Spanish that has historical roots is the formation of adverbs in *mente*. Students are told that the feminine form of the adjective combines with *mente* to form the adverb (e.g., *rápidamente* 'quickly' from *rápido* 'quick') and are generally given no explanation (22):

(22) *rápido* 'quick' → *rápidamente* 'quickly'
       lento 'slow' → *lentamente* 'slowly'

From a diachronic perspective, however, the reason for this is clear: *mente*, the basis for the adverbial ending, was a feminine noun in Latin.

The gender of nouns in Spanish is often puzzling for beginning students. They often want to know *why* a noun is either feminine or masculine, particularly since English nouns lack grammatical gender. Recourse to diachronic information can illustrate for the student that gender is inherited directly from Latin and shared by other Romance languages and not some bizarre feature designed to thwart their language-learning attempts! This is particularly helpful in cases such as *el día* 'the day' or *la mano* 'the hand' where there is a clash between the grammatical form and the gender, because unlike regular *puerta* 'door' or *libro* 'book,' these nouns did not belong to the first or second declension in Latin.

Moreover, students often ask why trees are masculine while their corresponding fruit is feminine, such as *cerezo* 'cherry tree' and *cereza* 'cherry.' The answer once again lies in the history of the language. Nouns such as *cerasius* 'cherry tree' were feminine, but formed part of the fourth declension. They became regularized to second declension masculine nouns because of their ending in *us* (*o* in Vulgar Latin.)

In our view, it is also highly useful for students to understand the concept of a neuter grammatical gender and to differentiate it from the masculine, for example, in (23):

(23) (a) *Lo/la creo.* 'I believe him/her.'
      (b) *Lo creo.* 'I believe it.'
      (c) *Lo que quiere es mudarse.* 'What he wants is to move.'
      (d) *No te puedo hablar de aquello.* 'I can't tell you about that (issue).'
      (e) *No te puedo hablar de aquél/aquélla.* 'I can't tell you about that one (m. or f.).'

The neuter pronoun in (23a–e) above contrasts with the masculine or feminine pronouns, which refer to antecedents in the discourse. In our view, the nominalizing characteristic of the neuter in Spanish cannot be adequately explained without recourse to diachronic facts. Other remnants of the neuter gender include expressions such as *tomarse algo a pechos* 'to take something to heart' or *en tiempos de* 'in times of'. We next turn to the historical roots of the Spanish lexicon.

5.4.3 The Spanish lexicon through history

With respect to semantics, through a presentation of historical linguistic facts, Spanish students can gain an appreciation for the varied sources of the lexicon of Spanish. For example, as discussed in Chapter 4, the present-day lexicon in Spanish is a result of the admixture of various languages. Due to the Moorish occupation of the Iberian Peninsula, Spanish has over 4000 words of Arabic origin, such as *álgebra* 'algebra' or *almacenaje* 'storage.' During the time of colonization of the Americas, Spanish was in contact with various African languages, which have contributed words such as *conga* 'a type of drum.'

During the same period, the indigenous languages of Latin America contributed scores of words to Spanish (see Chapter 4 and Cotton & Sharp, 1988, for a discussion). For example, *aguacate* 'avocado' and *elote* 'corn' hail from Náhuatl, spoken in Central Mexico. From Quechua, an indigenous language in the Andean region, Spanish has such words as *chompipe* 'turkey' and *carisina* 'inefficient or masculine woman.'[138] Taino, from the Caribbean area, has contributed several commonly used words to Spanish, for example, *jaiba* 'crab' and *huracán* 'hurricane'. Guaraní, the substratum language from Paraguay, has given Spanish such terms as *jacaranda* 'rosewood tree' and *piraña* 'piranha'.[139] A diachronic view equates this lexical variation with the cultural richness of the native languages spoken during the colonization of the Americas.

Finally, as we touched upon in Chapter 4, other languages, such as English, French and Italian, have contributed a great many lexical items to the Spanish language over the past centuries. Words such as *cheque* 'check,' *bombón* 'candy' and *mafia* 'mafia' are found both in Peninsular Spanish and in many dialects of Latin American Spanish. Sometimes the borrowings are a characteristic of a given dialect, and not Spanish as a whole. Where these languages are in close contact with Spanish, such as in the Southwest of the United States, vocabulary items often reflect this merger. For example, such words as *baquennpaura* for 'baking powder' or *mopear* 'to mop' are in common use in this geographical area.

Archaims, by their very definition, hearken back to earlier forms of a language. Spanish, particularly the varieties spoken in Latin America, has a vocabulary that in many cases differs little from that used in Spain centuries ago. Such vocabulary items include *¿Mande?* 'what did you say' and *balde* 'bucket,' words that no longer have currency in Spain (see Chapter 4 for discussion).

5.5 The Role of Diachronic Linguistics in Today's Spanish Curriculum

In the preceding sections, we have presented several arguments for the relevance of the history of the Spanish language in the undergraduate curriculum. We again emphasize that for beginning students, many of these explanations may not be necessary. Indeed, they may be confusing. But for third- and fourth-year Spanish majors, as well as for graduate students, a course in the History of Spanish should be required. However, we are not advocating a return to the types of courses taught under the rubric of the term *philology* in the past century. Such courses were often highly theoretical and abstract, and used textbooks such as those by Penny (1991), Lathrop (1980) or Lapesa (1980). They continue to be appropriate for graduate programs in Hispanic Linguistics, in our view, but should not be offered for non-specialists. At the graduate level, we advocate a more theoretical approach after the initial introduction. For example, graduate students should be exposed to current research in diachronic linguistics in Spanish.

Rather, at the undergraduate level, we advocate a course that briefly introduces the subfields of phonology, morphology, semantics and syntax for the first several weeks of class, before focusing on the history of the Spanish language from an evolutionary standpoint. The kind of course we envision could use Hualde *et al.*'s (2001) for the first weeks, followed by excerpts from Resnick (1981). This, in turn, would be supplemented by texts from the various periods of the Spanish language (cf. Pountain, 2001) up to the present cyberspeak.

By proposing these kinds of courses, we echo Rini (1990), who states that while it is clear that the facts discussed in this section can be *delineated* without reference to historical information, it is equally clear that they cannot be *explained*, in any real sense, with only a synchronic reference. Students who are not given historical information see *voseo* or *yeísmo* as seemingly arbitrary, isolated characteristics of the language.

5.6 Conclusion

In this chapter, we have considered the role of diachronic linguistics in the curriculum of foreign language programs. We have noted that at the turn of the last century, with the dominance of the Grammar-Translation method, knowledge of historical linguistics was deemed to be essential, but as an abstract, purely academic exercise. WWII, while focusing attention on the importance of foreign languages, shifted the pedagogical focus from knowledge *about* language to the ability to *use* the language in a practical sense. The armed forces implemented intensive language training programs that focused on the development of the oral/aural skills.

In the decade following WWII, scholars once again stressed the importance of the inclusion of historical linguistics in the foreign language curriculum, perhaps due to the growing prominence of linguistics as a field of study. However, the shift toward the Audio-lingual methods of the 1960s meant that language was viewed as a skill to be mastered through drill and repetition; there was no role for historical linguistics to play in the curriculum. With the Communicative Approaches developed as a result of the proficiency-oriented curricula of the 1980s and 1990s, the focus shifted to communicative and cultural competence.

In this chapter, we have claimed that a cultural approach, far from ostracizing historical linguistics, in fact necessitates its inclusion in the curriculum, because of the link between culture and history (cf. Arteaga & Herschensohn, 1995). We have further argued, following Rini (1990), that certain linguistic facts about Spanish can only be addressed by recourse to historical information. Finally, in our view, the metalinguistic awareness that undergraduate students will obtain by exposure to the history of the language will help them appreciate the variation that exists in the Spanish language today, as without insight into the evolution of Spanish, students will be unable to embed synchronic variation into a historical context. In the next chapter, we turn to concrete tips for integrating variation in the Spanish language classroom. We also provide an evaluation of three popular first-year texts, *Impresiones*, *Plazas* and *Puntos de partida*, with respect to their presentation of regional and sociolinguistic variety in Spanish.

Chapter 6

Textbooks and Tips: How to Use and Enhance Available Resources in the University-level Class

6.1 Introduction

In this chapter, we move from theory to practice. Specifically, we discuss how the notion of variation, which we have argued is so crucial to Spanish in today's world, can best be incorporated into the Spanish language classroom. This chapter is therefore particularly relevant to current and future Spanish language teachers. In our discussion, we draw from both classroom research presented in prior chapters and our extensive experience as university-level Spanish language instructors and coordinators of Spanish language programs. Our goal is to leave the reader with enough specific tips that he or she can successfully address variation in the Spanish language classroom at all levels. In so doing, we revisit the topics presented in earlier chapters from a pedagogical perspective. We present concrete suggestions for integrating variation into the Spanish language classroom from the beginning levels.

We end this chapter by a review of variation in three of the university Spanish language textbooks that address the issue of variation, *Impresiones*, *Plazas* and *Puntos de partida*. We begin by considering their presentation of dialectal differences. We then evaluate their discussion of sociolinguistic variation. Thirdly, we consider whether or not the special needs of heritage speakers are addressed. Finally, we give an evaluation of the diachronic information, if any, given to instructors and students. We give concrete suggestions for using the variation presented in these texts and for supplementing the information. We next turn to a discussion of how to address dialects in the Spanish language classroom.

6.2 Dialectal Variation in the Spanish Language Classroom

While we believe in integrating information about dialects into the Spanish language classroom, we must emphasize that a Spanish language class is not a course in dialectology.[140] Whatever information is presented regarding dialectal variation must not be overwhelming, but rather must be manageable and helpful to the student. In our view, any presentation should be both accurate and simple, and should be recycled (i.e. given regular practice after the first time) often throughout the text (see Cook, 2001). It is essential that presentations are linguistically sound. Students who continue their Spanish studies will then find that they already have a basis for regional (and social) variation in speech, topics that often come up in more detail in upper-division literature and linguistics classes. Moreover, as we have argued throughout this text, an understanding of Spanish dialects is crucial to speakers' communicative competence.

Many studies have addressed the question of regional variability within Spanish language instruction. For example, D'Ambrosio (2004) argues that dialectal variation can help students understand the current use of the second person pronouns used widely in Spain and Latin America (i.e. *usted, ustedes, tú* and *vos, vosotros*). Arteaga (2000) has stressed the importance of regional variation in pronunciation training in Spanish language classrooms in the United States. Arteaga and Llorente (2004) have similarly emphasized the importance of incorporating dialectal variation into the Spanish language classroom, both for English L1 speakers and for heritage speakers.

Although there are hundreds (if not thousands) of dialects in Spanish, for pedagogical purposes it is neither necessary nor desirable to provide information regarding every instance of regional variation in Spanish in the beginning language classroom. What we advocate in this chapter is a broad, macrodialectal approach, in which only salient dialectal features are stressed. Such an approach would focus first and foremost on the notion of dialectal variation itself, particularly in first-semester language classes. The immediate goal is to raise the level of students' metalinguistic awareness regarding dialectal variation per se (what Cook, 2001, calls 'language awareness'). Given our general pedagogical approach, which presupposes moving from the known to the unknown, we advocate first presenting students with the notion of regional variation in English.

Beginning linguistic texts, such as *Language Files* (Bergmann *et al.*, 2007), have exercises that can be easily used in the Spanish language classroom.

Alternatively, instructors may put together simple exercises like the following (1):

(1) Dialects (regional varieties) of language vary in systematic ways. Try to identify the following dialects:
(a) *I'm a' fixin' to go soon.* [am ə fík sin tə gə́ʊ sún]
(b) *Have you parked the car?* [hǽv ju pákt ðə ká]
(c) *It's about time.* [ɪts ə bóʊt tájm]
(d) I am a student of linguistics. [aj ǽm ə stu dənt əv lɪŋ gwíst ɪks]

The example in (1a) represents the dialect spoken in the Southern United States. Both phonological (pronunciation) and morphosyntactic (word forms and word order) clues are characteristic of this dialect. Can you find them? The example in (1b), conversely, represents the dialect spoken in the Boston area. Example (1c) represents the dialect spoken in the north central United States (e.g., Minnesota). Finally, the example in (2d) represents the dialect spoken in the western United States. What dialectal characteristics can you identify in these examples?

Which dialect do you speak? Do you have a negative opinion of any of the other dialects in (1)? Why do you think that may be so? Can you identify the rules illustrated by (1a)–(1d) above? For example, in the dialect of the Southern United States, the diphthong [aj] is systematically (i.e., every instance) replaced by [a]. By viewing dialects as differing from each other in this way, we can come to appreciate the variety of language without judging one variety as superior to others.

The instructor will need to pronounce the transcriptions given in (1), as we cannot expect beginning language students to have mastery of the IPA. Invariably, such an exercise taps into knowledge that students already possess regarding regional variation of speech. It has the added benefit of framing such knowledge in a linguistic context that accepts dialectal variation as fact, making no value judgments. Using such an exercise as a springboard, instructors can easily begin to introduce students to dialectal variation in Spanish. One effective way of doing this is to play tapes of strikingly different dialects. Even beginning students can readily perceive that the dialects 'sound' different. One good collection of dialect recordings, which is also available on CD, is that found in Teschner (2000).

Ideally, after this kind of general introduction to the notion of regional variation (covered in more depth in second-year and advanced courses), students and instructors should be able to rely on textbooks for information regarding dialectal features. A general presentation of this topic follows from the cultural focus of given chapters. We address this aspect in Section 6.16, where we present a review of three first-year Spanish textbooks that are a resource for students and instructors with regard to dialectology.

One point of caution is in order. It is well known that within a given dialect, certain features are marked, as pointed out by Hildalgo (1990), Guitart (1981, 1983) and Terrell (1982). So, as Lipski (1997) notes, while an educated Mexican might consider the pronunciation of [θ] in *zapato* by a *madrileño* to be a quaint dialectal variation, his or her reaction to *polecía* 'policeman' for *policía* or *probe* 'poor' for *pobre* is likely to be negative.

How should such marked dialectal features be presented in a Spanish language classroom? After all, the goal is to teach the prestige variety, expanding the students' (both L1 and L2) range, without portraying negatively the dialectal features that may characterize the individual student's idiolect. In our view, the answer to this question lies in the presentation of the notion of a variable rule, as discussed in detail in Chapter 2, in which the intersection of dialectology and register may be seen. In other words, students should be led to equate the alternative forms with familiar speech. The goal is for students to understand, but not necessarily produce, these variants. We next discuss sociolinguistic variation and Spanish language courses.

6.3   Register Variation and the Spanish Language Classroom

In Spanish, register variation is sharply defined. Given the variety of registers with which one may come into contact, the issue of which register to teach is not an easy one to resolve. In our view, students must be able to recognize and to manipulate a variety of registers. Because of the permeation of Spanish throughout the United States, both Spanish instructors and students face unique challenges. We believe that students of Spanish are far likelier than those of other languages to be exposed to a variety of registers, as their interactions with native speakers may well occur in a wide range of social contexts, such as at school, at work, while traveling or at informal gatherings.

In language classrooms, however, instructors typically adopt a prescriptive approach of language at the expense of a descriptive one. Therefore, natural speech is not only not allowed, it may well be considered to be a mistake, regardless of the register being used. For example, consider (2a) and (2b) below (cf. Chapter 1):[141]

(2)   (a) *¿Qué hubo?* 'What's up?' [kjú βo]
      (b) *¿Cómo va todo?'* (= 2a)

In the first example, we see the informal greeting often used between friends or young people in Mexico. In (2b), we see a more formal equivalent. In the communicative-oriented classroom dominant today, students are typically presented with informal conversational activities, although the textbooks themselves generally present only formal structures. D'Ambrosio (2004) and Arteaga (2005) argue that textbooks fail to present a good overview of register difference.

It is important to emphasize that register variation is slightly more complex than dialectal variation because of the existence of marked register differences. In other words, differences in register are not always neutrally received by the listener, as argued by Holman (1996). However, the solution cannot be to fail to present this kind of variation, because, as we have argued in previous chapters, students are more likely to come into contact with a variety of registers in Spanish than in other languages. So how are we, as instructors, to proceed?

In our opinion, it is first necessary to raise students' language awareness, in the sense of Cook (2001). This can be done with respect to register variation by providing exercises such as those found in many beginning linguistic textbooks. Consider (3):

(3)   Below are sentences that might be spoken between two male friends chatting informally:
Yo, dude. Sup?
Not much, dude. Just chillin'
Wanna hang with us?
Sure, man. Whatcha doin'?
Gonna go to the beach.
Cool, catcha in 10.

On the other hand, the same conversation can have a strikingly different tone:

Hello, Dr Martínez. What are you doing?
Nothing important. How about you?
Would you like to go to the beach with us?
That would be very nice, thank you. I'll meet you in 10 minutes.
Great!

The instructor can ask students to give more examples of informal vs. formal conversations in English. Once students understand the notion of register variation, they can be provided with examples in Spanish. The goal at the lower level classes should be to understand, but not necessarily use, informal registers of Spanish. In other words, passive recognition of register difference is generally a viable alternative, particularly for beginning levels, but it must include the ability to recognize differences in register. At more advanced levels, however, the goal should be true communicative competence, meaning that students should be able to engage in style shifting. We next turn to the subfields of language, discussing how variation, both dialectal and sociolinguistic, should be incorporated into the Spanish language classroom.

6.4　Phonology in the Spanish L2 Classroom

In the first part of the last century before WWII, the teaching methodology regularly employed in L2 classrooms was the Grammar-Translation method. As we have discussed in Chapter 5, this method emphasized metalinguistic (i.e., information about language) over communicative competence. Briefly put, all languages were taught like Latin is today. The target L2 was not spoken in the classroom. The Grammar-Translation method met its goals. Given the emphasis on reading and writing, speaking was not stressed, meaning that pronunciation was not typically taught. Interestingly, however, most texts from this period do include basic phonetic information, either at the beginning of the text or at the end, and left to the discretion of the instructor.

The focus (and goals) of L2 teaching, however, changed when the Audio-lingual method was introduced in the 1960s. Indeed, in this method, pronunciation was deemed to be essential to L2 acquisition. As an example, note that in the Modern Language Association's Spanish textbook, *Modern Spanish*, Unit 1 explains in detail Spanish pronunciation, using technical terminology (such as 'voiceless stops' and 'voiced fricatives') regarding the Spanish sound system and phonology. Unit 1 presents not only the concepts of phoneme and allophone but also suprasegmentals (e.g., rhythm, stress, and intonation) in English and Spanish.

One interesting feature is the recycling of pronunciation within this text. Indeed, after Unit 1, every chapter recycles pronunciation until Unit 11 (of 27 units). At times, by today's standards the discussion may appear to be over-done in a beginning language class. For example, in Unit 3, we find a ten-page discussion on intonation. Nonetheless, pronunciation is actively presented and recycled, which matches the stated goals of speaking and listening in this method.

The Audio-lingual approach gave way to the Communicative Approach in the 1980s. Oddly enough, no importance was accorded to pronunciation in this method, despite its stated goals of communicative competence. This seeming disconnect has been pointed out by several scholars, including Terrell (1989), Arteaga (2000), Dansereau (1995) and Krashen (1980).

Since the 1990s, the ACTFL has greatly influenced the teaching of all foreign languages, including Spanish. Unfortunately, from our viewpoint, books organized around proficiency guidelines barely allude to pronunciation, despite their focus on intelligibility, which students are not expected to master at the Novice or Intermediate levels (ACTFL Proficiency Guidelines; Rivers *et al.* 1989: 351–372).

Indeed, ACTFL only expects the L2 speaker to be intelligible at the Advanced level, and does not expect that pronunciation may be native-like even at the Superior level, which is contrary to the findings of Bongaerts (1999). Fluency, however, is mentioned (as being lacking) in the description at the Intermediate Mid level ('Speech is often characterized by long pauses,' p. 355); ACFTL does expect students to be fluent at the Advanced Plus level, in which the speaker 'Often shows remarkable fluency and ease of speech' (p. 357). So how do we teach pronunciation in today's classroom, which emphasizes both a focus on form (i.e., grammar) and communicative competence? It is clear that suprasegmentals must be taught early in the course, as they affect intelligibility. How, specifically, can suprasegmentals be taught from the beginning levels?

It has long been accepted that perception (i.e. the ability to *hear* the difference between two sounds) must precede production for L1 phonological acquisition (see Bever, 1981; Churchland, 1986; Edelmann, 1989; Kuijpers, 1996). Recent research affirms this notion for L2 acquisition as well (see Estarellas, 1972; Oyama, 1982a, 1982b, among others). Flege (1995) argues that for L2 learners to create new phonetic categories for L2 sounds (cf. Rochet, 1995), they must first perceive the cross-linguistic difference.

A recent study of the pronunciation of English vowels by adult L2 learners by Flege *et al.* (1997) confirmed the link between perception and accuracy in speech production. The results from this study show that only speakers who were able to accurately perceive the varied spectral quality of English vowels were also able to accurately produce them. However, unlike the case in L1 acquisition, an L2 learner's accurate perception of sounds does not always lead to accurate production of sounds, as Flege (1995) notes.

Arteaga (2000), following Bergen (1974), provides a sweeping proposal for Spanish language classrooms, arguing that in beginning Spanish classes, a simplified phonetics program (i.e. a 'learner's dialect') should be presented. She recommends including the following topics, which are discussed in detail in Chapter 2 above:

(6) (a) suprasegmentals
    (b) tap [r] and trilled [r̄].

(c) alveolar [l].
(d) vowel tension and absence of vowel reduction
(e) spirantization of stops
(f) nasal assimilation

To present this learner's dialect, Arteaga argues that explicit phonetics instruction of the process in question should be presented in non-technical (but accurate) language. Consider as an example the phonological process of spirantization of stops discussed in Chapter 2 (e.g. the alternation of b/β, *d*/ð/ and g/ɣ). According to Arteaga, the phonetics instruction in this case should take the form of a simple, non-technical explanation of a stop vs. a fricative. Students could be taught to equate the category *stop* with closure of two articulatory organs, using [b] and [β] as a starting point. The discussion should include an overview of the distribution of stops and fricatives in Spanish (see Chapter 2 for a discussion), a concept that should be revisited several times during the course of the year. Recall that we have argued that production must follow perception, a point of view that is confirmed by several recent studies.

This means that the first step toward having students correctly articulate sounds is to ensure their ability to perceive them. Crucial to our approach are listening comprehension exercises, which contrast the sounds in question. For individual segments, exercises like the following, modeled after those presented in Dalbor (1996), uses simple words known to the student.

(7)

To be read by instructor (without translation)	To be completed by student [b]	[β]
1. *beso* 'kiss'	x	
2. *vago* 'lazy'	x	
3. *boca* 'mouth'	x	
4. *hablar* 'to speak'		x
5. *billete* 'ticket'	x	
6. *hubo* 'there was/were'		x
7. *cabello* 'hair'		x
8. *abrir* 'to open'		x
9. *bonito* 'pretty'	x	
10. *haba* 'bean'		x

The exercise in (7) should be given orally to students. They should be directed to number 1-10 on a piece of scrap paper and to indicate [b] and [β] as column headings.

Take, as another example again, an exercise modeled from Dalbor (1996), which contrasts English and Spanish vowels (8):

(8)

To be read by instructor without translation.	To be completed by student	
	English [ej]	Spanish [e]
1. *de* 'of'		x
2. *ray*	x	
3. *p* 'Spanish letter 'p'	x	
4. *pay*		x
5. *se* 'himself/herself/yourself'		x
6. *que* 'that'		x
7. *lay*	x	
8. *say*	x	
9. *le* 'him/her/you formal'		x
10. *day*	x	

In (8) above, the contrasting sounds are the Spanish monophthong [e] and the corresponding English vowel [ej], which is a diphthong.

As noted by Arteaga, Spanish textbooks are not consistent in the presentation of such exercises. Indeed in many cases, they are totally missing. Examples may be found, however, in phonetics texts, so that instructors should have no difficulty creating similar practice activities. Once perception has been established, students are ready to proceed with accurate production of speech sounds. It is essential that any production exercises include only words that the students have actively learned. In this way, pronunciation exercises will be meaningful to the student (cf. Terrell, 1989). For more advanced students, tongue twisters or even proverbs can be used (cf. Teschner, 2000).

With respect to suprasegmentals, exercises such as (9) can be presented, in which a question and a declarative sentence are only distinguished by intonation:

(9)   (a) *¿Hablas español?* 'Do you speak Spanish?'
     (b) *Hablas español.* 'You speak Spanish.'

At more advanced levels, the concepts of synalephy (vowel linking across word boundaries) and syneresis (vowel linking within a word) should be addressed (e.g. *me imagino* 'I imagine' [mej ma xí no]) as discussed in some detail in Chapter 2. At this level, students must know of the preferred open-syllable structure of Spanish and the fact that it applies across word boundaries as in *los hombres hablan* [lo sóm bre sá βlan] 'the men talk,' and that elision is found in sequences like *la Havana* [la βá na].[142]

More advanced language students can be presented with utterances whose pronunciation is identical, notwithstanding the fact that the word boundaries vary:[143]

(10) (a) *loco loco* 'crazy crazy'
      (b) *lo coloco* 'I put it in'

Suprasegmentals are clearly important, and therefore must be one of several aspects of Spanish that is addressed.

In order to introduce more complex phonological processes in Spanish, it will be necessary to use larger utterances, although simple phrases will suffice for processes such as nasal assimilation (e.g. *un vestido* 'a dress' [um bes tí ðo] see Chapter 2). As recommended by Barrutia and Schwegler (1994), free conversation exercises that direct the student to concentrate on a particular sound or process should also be used as their linguistic competence increases. In addition, they allow for additional recycling. Recycling is essential for both grammar and vocabulary (Van Patten, 2004a, 2004b; Bahrick, 1984). It is no less important for pronunciation (Arteaga, 2000).

It is unreasonable to assume that students will master sounds on the first pass. Therefore, phonetics should be addressed in every chapter, with many topics revisited several times as necessary. After all, most students will fail if they are expected to master /r̄/ after a single lesson. However, as discussed by Arteaga, instructors may have to supplement those exercises given in textbooks or create exercises on their own. Incorporating phonetics instruction into the Spanish language classroom from the beginning levels may seem like a daunting task in Spanish language classrooms, where typically instructors feel pressed to cover the grammar points on the syllabus.

However, it is Arteaga's viewpoint, which we share, that phonetics instruction is so important to both the L2 process and the L2 learner (Oyama, 1982a, 1982b) that we must find 10 minutes two or three times a week to address it, and not only in the first semester. Finally, by using vocabulary that the students know, phonetics instruction will facilitate the recycling of vocabulary, which Bahrick (1984) argues is essential to the learning process. We next discuss the issue of phonological processes and heritage speakers.

6.5   Heritage Speakers and Phonology in the Spanish L2 Classroom

For heritage speakers, phonetics instruction is no less important than for L2 learners. This may come as a surprise to instructors, given that many of these students show no trace of English pronunciation in Spanish. One reason why overt instruction in phonetics is beneficial even for those students with native-like pronunciation is that it will improve their skills in reading aloud (Nash, 1973; Hudelson, 1981). This, in turn, will facilitate another goal of SNS classrooms presented in Valdés (1997), namely the transfer of literacy skills.

For Nash (1973: 134), phonology should be used to counteract orthographic interference in bilinguals. She recommends that when teaching orthography

> We need to design better materials for teaching pronunciation that deal with problems of spelling contrasts as well as problems of sound contrasts. A complete description of phonological performance recognizes the equal partnership of phonology and orthography in the representation of language.

Similarly, according to Azurdia (1998), phonetics helps bilingual students learn the necessary orthographic–phonemic correspondences to learn to read in Spanish. She argues that this is the case, regardless of the particular method used to teach reading (phonics vs. structural), because it is through phonetics that bilingual students come to best identify letters, syllables and words.

To reach that goal, she claims that students must come to be able to master the following skills to read in Spanish (Azurdia, 1998: 90–91): (i) distinguish between a high and a mid vowel, as in *por aquí paso un coquí* 'a type of frog indigtenous to Puerto Rico passed by here'; (ii) understand that each spelling or digraph represents a single sound *sale humo de la chimenea* 'smoke comes out of the chimney'; and (iii) know the sounds of the Spanish alphabet.

Further, in Azurdia's view, bilingual students must also be able to do the following: (iv) identify consonants and vowels, and their allophones; (v) understand the effect that a preceding or following letter may have on a sound, as in *gente* 'people' vs. *gata* 'cat'; (vi) properly identify syllables; (vii) understand the phonemic role of suprasegmentals, such as stress, as in *público* 'public' vs. *publico* 'I publish'; (viii) identify diphthongs, triphthongs and consonantal groups; (ix) recognize which consonant clusters can be syllable initial or syllable final; (x) recognize which phonemes can be represented by different graphs; (xi) identify the phonemes /r̄/ and /r/ based on their distribution; and (xii) distinguish between similar spellings such as *que, gue, güe* on the one hand and *qui, gui, güi* on the other, as in *guerra* 'war' vs. *vergüenza* 'shame'.

Finally, Azurdia (1998: 97) views the use of phonetics as one of many tools for teaching reading to bilinguals. She argues that 'la fonética como estrategia al nivel de lectura sirve para desarrollar la comprensión en forma auténtica.'[145] In keeping with what we have argued above, she points not only to the necessity of thorough phonetics training for SNS teachers, but also to the necessity of a background in dialectology, and an understanding of registers. The goal, in her view (Azurdia, 1998: 98), is to teach the student 'la variación normal para que logre precisar el idioma a modo de comunicarse con otros de habla española sin tacharle al estudiante el habla que ya trae.'[146]

We next turn to the issue of dialectal phonological variation in the Spanish language classroom.[147]

6.6 Teaching Phonological Dialectal Variation as an Aid to Comprehension

As we have argued throughout this book, dialectal variation is particularly relevant in the Spanish classroom because of the pluricentricity of Spanish. We know that Spanish students are very likely to be exposed to Spanish from vastly different dialect areas either within the classroom setting from one semester to the next or in a natural setting outside the classroom. At first glance, it may seem that dialects in Spanish exhibit an astonishing amount of phonological variation, even within a single country. Who has not been struck by the phonological differences of Northern Mexico vs. the Coastal areas of Mexico, not to mention the Yucatán Peninsula? A *madrileño* speaks in marked contrast to an *andaluz*, and the phonology of a speaker from Buenos Aires differs clearly from that of a speaker from Lima.

For this reason, popular third-year Spanish phonetics texts (Barrutia & Schwegler, 1994; Dalbor, 1996; Teschner, 2000) have chosen to present a model pronunciation loosely based on that of the so-called *tierras altas* (highlands), while providing an overview of the salient phonological features of Spanish dialects. But even first-year Spanish students, in order to comprehend native speakers who hail from various regions, should be exposed to Spanish dialectal variation, while being encouraged to maintain consistency in their own pronunciation. In order to avoid the mixing of dialectal features that never co-occur in a single Spanish dialect (e.g. the *distinción* from North Central Spain and the *žeísmo* of the River Plate countries), it is imperative that instructors explain to students which features characterize regional speech.

As discussed in detail in Chapter 2, Spanish dialects, like all dialects, are characterized by a variety of phonological processes. In order to improve communication with speakers from different dialect areas, students should ideally be taught to recognize native speech reflecting the following three phonological processes, discussed in detail in Chapter 2:[148]

(11) (a) Aspiration/deletion of syllable-final consonants.
    (b) *Distinción/seseo.*
    (c) *Yeísmo/žeísmo/lleísmo.*

Other dialectal processes can be addressed either when encountered in the Spanish language classroom or when students inquire about them. Sometimes, the instructor will recognize that the features of his or her dialect are not of the *tierras altas*, and will wish to explain. Again, the focus should be on student consistency of pronunciation and comprehension of other dialects, not on the production of all possible variants.

6.7 Phonological Register Variation in the Spanish L2 Classroom

Phonological register variation in Spanish, as discussed in detail in Chapter 2, is well defined. However, that does not mean that this variation is neutrally received by listeners. Assuming that we are giving students the tools to engage in style shifting, at whatever basic level, we need to actively teach phonological register variation, at least passively, for comprehension. A presentation can be given, and recycled during the years of basic Spanish instruction, of the typical forms that phonological register variation can take. The instructor must clearly make a difference, however, between phonological processes (i.e. elision) found in rapid speech and those found in informal speech, as these are not identical (see Chapter 2 for discussion). With respect to true register variation in phonology, we have to consider the consequences of our instruction. Are we truly to teach students for active production forms like *tiatro* 'theater' for *teatro* or *grodo* 'fat' for *gordo*, which may be stigmatized?

In such a case, we advise against presenting such variants unless students, including heritage students, specifically ask about them or show evidence of them in their speech. Here we differ from Hidalgo (1990), who claims that phonological variation should not be a focus of SNS classrooms. Again, our point that such variants are not neutrally received is highly important. Heritage speakers need to understand that their speech may be overly familiar. The way to teach this is to stress the acquisition of the academic register, without being judgmental regarding the familiar register that the student may speak. Non-native speakers may adopt informal speech patterns as well, and they will have to be instructed to exercise caution when using them, particularly since they will also, most likely, have accented speech.

For these reasons, we do not present specific tips for teaching phonological register variation in the Spanish language classroom, other than to identify and actively model the processes that are present in rapid speech. It does a disservice to students, in our opinion, for the instructor to model only slow, artificial speech, as students will not be able to understand speech spoken at a normal rate of speed. Again, while dialects may vary with respect to the rapidity of speech, no dialect exhibits the kind of artificial speech often found in Spanish language classrooms, particularly at the beginning levels. We next consider the teaching of Spanish morphosyntax.

6.8 On Teaching Morphosyntax in the Spanish L2 Classroom

The L2 acquisition of morphosyntax is addressed in detail in Chapter 3. Here we focus on what we are to do concretely in our classes in order to foster morphological acquisition. We know that input flooding is needed (Trahey & White, 1993). With respect to classroom instruction, many teachers find the theories of Van Patten (2004a, 2004b) useful. As we discussed in Chapter 3, the central claim of Van Patten is that students attend to semantic details before morphological or syntactic ones. What this means in the classroom is that we must remove semantic clues from utterances if we want the students to notice and then acquire the form.

In other words, if we are teaching the subjunctive vs. the indicative, we will not use examples like (12), but will instead use examples like (13a) – (13b):

(12) *Quiero que vengas a la fiesta.* 'I want you to come to the party.'
(13) (a) *No creo que vengas a la fiesta.* 'I don't think you will come to the party.'
      (b) *No creo que vienes a la fiesta.* 'I don't think you will come to the party.'

For Van Patten, the examples in (13) would be preferable because both the subjunctive and indicative are possible after *no creo* 'I don't believe.' As discussed in Chapter 3, according to this framework, students must not use semantic cues to decide which form is needed. As for corrections, recasts, in which the instructor merely repeats the utterance, but in its correct form, are ineffective (Pica *et al.*, 1987; Lyster & Ranta, 1997; see Chapter 3 for a complete discussion). Students need to negotiate the correct form in order for there to be uptake.

If we follow Krashen (1982), who proposes that the input given students should be slightly above their current level (comprehensible input, or $i + 1$), we have a frame of reference from which to proceed. In other words, until students are ready to master a structure, it should not be presented.[149] We must keep in mind at all times, however, the likelihood that our students will never completely master the morphosyntax of the L2. They are not making mistakes due to their carelessness. They may have instead fossilized (e.g. integrated into their grammar a non-native form) incorrect forms and are therefore incapable of correcting them. We next address morphosyntactic dialectal variation in the Spanish language classroom.

6.9 Morphosyntactic Dialectal Variation in the Spanish L2 Classroom

As we have seen in Chapter 3, there is a great deal of regional variation in Spanish. We must emphasize, as stated in Section 6.2, that a Spanish language class is not a course in dialectology. On the other hand, students will undoubtedly come into contact with speakers of other dialects of Spanish, whose speech may evince regional morphosyntactic varieties. How are we to proceed? We recommend actively presenting the morphosyntactic features of the most dominant dialect in the area where the Spanish language is taught.

For example, in Spain, *vosotros* should be actively taught. In the United States, it should be presented for passive knowledge only, as *vosotros* and its related forms are not used in Latin America. Students who do not travel to Europe or will not otherwise come into contact with Spaniards will not hear these forms. The decision of whether or not to teach *vosotros* and its related forms cannot be made lightly, as dialects either use *vosotros* or do not. For those that do, its use is obligatory when referring to the second person plural informal (see Chapters 3 and 5 above).

Other dialectal variation, such as diminutives, e.g. *ito* vs. *illo*, discussed in detail in Chapter 3 as well, will undoubtedly arise in readings at the second- and third-year levels and should be presented at that time. Again, the goal is not for students to actively *produce* all regional morphosyntactic variation, but rather to *understand* alternative forms. More challenging, perhaps, is how to address morphosyntactic register variation in the classroom; we turn to this in the next section.

6.10 Addressing Morphological Register Variation in the Spanish L2 Classroom

The question of morphological variation necessarily raises the question of standard, academic language. What are we to teach our students? In our opinion, it does not serve students' interest to teach them variants like *ponido* 'put' for *puesto* or *freído* 'fried' for *frito*. The problem with these forms is that they are associated with a low level of education. The goal in our Spanish language classrooms is to develop both communicative competence and academic competence. In other words, we want our students to become literate in Spanish, while developing the ability to converse naturally with native speakers.

However, all morphosyntactic register variation is not created equal. Consider *voseo*, regularly used by over two-thirds of Latin America. *Voseo* is at once a dialectal issue and a register issue, particularly for countries where its usage is sociolinguistically marked (i.e. most countries other than Argentina). On the other hand, many of our students are young and will often engage in informal speech or have informal speech directed at them. They must, therefore, be able to associate *vos* with *tú*. The solution, again, is to create exercises for our students, if they do not already exist in textbooks. For example, the following is a sample exercise that instructors could use regarding *voseo:*

(14)   For many Spanish speakers, *vos* is used in place of *tú* for informal speech; this pronoun refers to the second person singular. It may have a variety of verb endings, such as present tense *áis*, *ás*, *as*, for *ar* verbs, *éis*, *és*, *es*, for *ir/er* verbs depending on the country. For purposes of this class, you should be able to relate *tú* to *vos*, but you should not actively use *vos* unless instructed to do so. The following questions test your understanding of Spanish forms of address.

     (1) María, ¿*vos estáis* lista?

     The equivalent pronoun in Standard (academic) Spanish is the following:

       (a) *vosotros estáis* b. *tú estás* c. *Usted está* d. *Ustedes están*
          The plural of the italicized form vos estáis is the following:

       (a) *vosotros estáis* b. *tú estás* c. *Ustedes están* d. a or c depending on speakers' dialect
          The formal of the italicized form *vos estáis* is the following:

       (a) *ustedes están* b. *usted está* c. *tú estás* d *vosotros estáis*.

Other topics of morphosyntactic variation should be considered on a case-by-case basis. For example, the issue of which third person object pronouns to use is slightly more complex than forms of address. We have presented the variants (e.g. *el uso etimológico, el leísmo, el laísmo, el loísmo*) above in Chapter 3 and discussed their historical evolution in Chapter 5. However, all variants do not have equal currency in the Spanish-speaking world. With respect to the direct object pronouns, academic Spanish accepts only *lo/las/los/las* or *le* and *les*. In other words, *loísmo* and *laísmo*, in which the direct object pronouns *lo* and *la* are used as indirect objects (e.g. *La dije, Lo hablé*), are not found outside Spain, even in highly informal speech.

Leísmo, on the other hand, in which the indirect objects *le* and *les* are used to refer to direct object pronouns referring to persons (i.e. *le vi, les quiero*), are widely accepted, even in academic speech, in both Spain and Latin America. In our view, while the *uso etimológico* (e.g. *le dije, lo vi*) should be actively taught, *leísmo* can be presented for passive recognition. Indeed, it simplifies the object pronoun system, and therefore may be a viable alternative for students. For heritage speakers, who use *leísmo* as a matter of course, instructors may choose to present the *uso etimológico* in parentheses when correcting student papers. Yet they should not, in our view, take points off for direct and indirect object variation other than *laísmo* or *loísmo*, which, as we have argued above, are marked morphological features.

Other exercises dealing with Spanish morphosyntactic register variation, like the following, can also be incorporated into the classroom:

(15) For some native speakers of Spanish, alternative verb forms may be used, which differ from the academic forms. Many times these forms are analogical formations (i.e., irregular verb forms made regular), such as *breaked* for *broke*. In the following exercise, the verb in parentheses is not the academic form, and would therefore be unacceptable in formal writing, although it may be heard in informal conversation. In each case, choose the academic alternative:

(1) He *freído* el pescado.[150]
　　a. *frito* b. *cocido* c. *escogido* d. *comprado*
(2) ¿Has *ponido la* mesa?
　　a. *comprado* b. *roto* c. *puesto* d. *pintado*
(3) ¿*Dijistes* la verdad?
　　a. *Dijeron* b. *Dijisteis* c. *Dijo* d. *Dijiste*
(4) El banco no estaba *abrido*
　　a. *cerrado* b. *abrida* c. *abierto* d. *abrito*

Such an exercise is in keeping with our perspective on the importance of variation in Spanish. Throughout this book, we have used the term 'academic' to refer to what is often known as 'standard' Spanish. We believe that it provides a way to teach morphosyntactic variation without expressing a negative judgment regarding the variety spoken by our students, particularly our native speakers. Exercises like those given above in Section 6.5 should be used as a springboard, because they raise linguistic awareness in our students regarding register differences. Oftentimes, professors complain that students' English is too familiar. However, students generally know how to engage in style shifting, at least to a limited extent, in English. Moreover, it may be the case that students only come to appreciate register differences in English through a presentation of register differences in Spanish. We next turn to the issue of lexical dialectal variation in the L2 classroom.

6.11 Dialectal Variation and the Lexicon in the Spanish L2 Classroom

The lexical variety of Spanish, while providing richness for the Spanish language, also poses challenges for the university-level classroom. For example, given the lexical variation in Spanish today, in the first semester of our university-level Spanish language classes, when we present food vocabulary, which word for *bean* are we to teach: *frijol*, *haba*, *poroto*, *alubia* or *habichuela*? In the unit on clothes, what word should we use for *jeans*: *pantalón de mezclilla*, *jeans*, *vaqueros*, *tejanos* or *bluyines*? When we introduce vocabulary regarding the household, how do we translate *bedroom*: *habitación*, *recámara*, *cuarto*, *dormitorio*, *pieza* or *alcoba*? When we discuss educational systems, how do we refer to *high school*: *colegio*, *secundario (mixto)*, *liceo*, *instituto* or *preparatoria*? Textbooks often present a dialectal hodgepodge of vocabulary, so that instructors cannot usually turn to them for guidance (see Arteaga & Llorente, 2003, for a discussion).

Given the extensive lexical variety among dialects in Spanish, it is unreasonable to expect instructors to be familiar with all the lexical alternatives for a certain item. Oftentimes, instructors, particularly native speakers, insist instead that students use the variants found in their dialect, which is clearly unreasonable, given the regional lexical variety of Spanish. Yet if we as instructors choose a lexicon from a particular region of Spanish, what are we to do when students use lexical items from a different dialect, either orally or in writing? Given the pluricentric nature of Spanish, our students may have learned some of these variants from their textbooks, from other instructors, from Spanish-speaking co-workers or at home from family members. The heritage students in our classroom who speak Spanish at home may use lexical variants that are not presented in textbooks. Some of these regional terms may not have great currency among dialects.

For the reasons outlined above in Chapter 1, variation in Spanish is a reality in the United States at present. This variation, which is based on geographical, linguistic and social variables, is often not acknowledged in the textbooks used to teach the language. Given the current focus on culture that dominates Spanish textbooks, it would seem natural for them to also include relevant information on dialectal variation itself, where it would be intertwined with the focus on given countries. However, the solution is not to use a 'cafeteria approach,' in which a hodgepodge of lexical items in different dialects is presented. We must similarly reject the alternative of capturing an idealized form of the language (favoring the written norm while doing so) that is not loyal to any one dialect in particular, but rather comprises features of the most prestigious norms (typically Peninsular Spanish). Our proposal for effective vocabularly teaching is presented next.

6.12 A Neutral Dialect

As we have seen, the greatest difference among dialects of Spanish is lexical. It is impossible to expect our beginning L2 Spanish students to acquire free active vocabulary knowledge of all Spanish dialects. In our view, development of such extensive lexical knowledge should focus instead on dialectally neutral terms (Arteaga-Capen & Llorente, 2007a).[151] One danger is that students may feel overwhelmed by the dialectal variation in the Spanish vocabulary. It is therefore important to explain to them that while lexical variation exists within Spanish, there are regionally unmarked terms that will help them communicate effectively across dialects.

We propose that Spanish textbooks should present students with a dialectally neutral lexicon, which they should actively master, in the sense of Laufer and Paribakht (1998), discussed in more detail in Chapter 4. We further advocate that common lexical items from regional varieties of Spanish should be presented for students' passive understanding and recognition. This, in turn, will result in basic understanding of dialectology in general, as well as familiarity with the regional varieties of Spanish frequently encountered in the United States.

The decision of which terms to consider as dialectally neutral will depend on the region in which Spanish is being taught as an L2.[152] For example, in the United States, we believe that common terms used throughout Latin America should form the basis of the vocabulary presented to students. For example, consider (16):

(16)   *Necesito rentar* **un apartamento**.
       'I need to rent an apartment.'
       Mexico: *departamento*
       Spain: *piso*

As the word *apartamento* is understood throughout Latin America, we believe that it should be presented as the equivalent of *apartment*.

Some students will already employ a dialectal variant of a vocabulary item that is presented in the text, because they have been exposed to another dialect of Spanish, at home, at work or abroad. For example, let's say that a student in our class has experience with the Peninsular Spanish variety, and uses the word *piscina* 'pool' instead of *alberca*.[153] In our view, Spanish L2 instructors must be sensitive to the pluricentric nature of Spanish as evidenced by its lexicon. Only instructors with an extensive background in dialectology will be able to recognize all the regional variants that they may come across. This means that others would need to investigate (e.g. by the use of a dictionary, see Section 6.13 below), if necessary, whether or not a vocabulary item used by the student is in fact indicative of a dialect other than the one that they speak.

Furthermore, we recommend that dialectal variants of vocabulary not be counted as mistakes and, as such, marked wrong (cf. Hidalgo, 1990). However, as Spanish instructors, we believe that it is our responsibility to make the student aware of dialectally neutral equivalents because such equivalents can facilitate communication among speakers of different dialects of Spanish. In other words, we can make the point to our students that while a lexical item may be perfectly valid for a given dialect of Spanish (cf. *piso*), there is a dialectally neutral term that native speakers in Latin America with whom they will come into contact will be more likely to understand (e.g. *apartamento*).

In summary, in this section, we have advocated a three-pronged approach to lexical variation in Spanish: first, provide students with a general understanding of dialectal variation; second, teach a dialectally neutral lexicon for active mastery; and third, teach common lexical variants for passive recognition only. In doing so, we agree with Salaberry and Lafford (2003: 15) that the students will not be confused, because the pedagogical goal is 'raising students' awareness of other dialects (as opposed to productive use of alternative dialects).' We next consider how dictionaries should be used in L2 classrooms.

6.13 Effective Dictionary Use and L2 Learners

The usefulness of dictionaries has been the subject of recent debate. Paribakht and Wesche (1999) argue that dictionary use does not facilitate lexical acquisition, while Gu and Johnson (1996) and Hulstijn and Greidanus (1996) take the opposing view. Underhill (1980), Herbst and Stein (1987), Moulin (1987), Hunt (1996) and Llorente and Parra (2006a) claim that effective dictionary use by the L2 learner is a component of overall language competence, but emphasize that explicit training is necessary. We share these scholars' point of view.

First of all, we agree with Herbst and Stein's (1987) argument in favor of having students actively use dictionaries in the classroom, not just to add an extra element to the foreign language syllabus, but as one more way of enabling students to master foreign language situations they might face. As they argue

> What is needed to improve the necessary competence of learners is not so much the development of special methods of teaching dictionary use, as the recognition that the foreign learners competence in dictionary use is part of their wider competence as speakers, readers or writers of the foreign language. (Herbst & Stein, 1987: 127)

It is our belief that students need to be taught to use their dictionaries effectively, because an inadequate use of them may lead to errors. For example, Hunt (1996: 20) observes that sometimes students trust their dictionaries too much, as they hold the erroneous view that every word in their language has an exact correspondence in their L2. Odlin (2001: 280), in turn, argues that dictionaries can help students to sort out problems related to other areas beyond the use of adequate lexical items. In his view, they are also useful in order to make proper decisions related to the morphological or syntactic characteristics of a text.

Instructing students in correct dictionary use may take the form of asking the students to examine the entries in a good bilingual dictionary. Let's say, for example, that students need to use the expression *pay attention* in one of their Spanish assignments. They could be directed to look up the word *pay*, included under (17) below, and to note the number and variety of entries. They would need to identify the abbreviations and select the entry that is most appropriate for the phrase they are trying to translate. According to the *Oxford Spanish Dictionary* (1388, 1389), this would be under (2) below (*prestar atención*):

(17) Entry for *pay*

pay¹ /peɪ/ *(past and past p* **paid**) *vt* **1 (a)** *(tax/rent)* pagar; *(amount/fees)* pagar, abonar (frml); *(bill)* pagar, saldar; *(debt)* pagar, saldar, cancelar;

I paid the amount in full pagué *or* aboné (frml) el importe en su totalidad; *this account ~ s 8% interest* esta cuenta da or produce un interés del 8%; *to ~ sth for sth/to plus INF; how much did you ~ for the painting?* ¿cuánto te costó el cuadro?, ¿cuánt pagaste por el cuadro?; *I paid a fortune to have it cleaned* me costó un dineral hacerlo limpiar, me cobraron un dineral por limpiarlo; *to ~ sth INTO sth: they ~ my salary into the bank* me depositan *or (esp Esp) me* ingresan el sueldo directamente en el banco; **paid** pagado **(b)** *(employee/creditor/tradesperson)* pagarle a; *they still haven't paid the builders* todavía no les han pagado a los albañiles; *you'll have to wait until I get paid* vas a tener que esperar hasta que cobre *or* me paguen; *we're paid by the hour* nos pagan por horas; *I wouldn't eat in that restaurant if they paid me* yo no comería en ese restaurante ni aunque me pagasen; *to ~ sb FOR sth pagarle algo a algn; when are you going to ~ me for the tickets?* ¿cuándo me vas a pagar las entradas?; *I paid him $20 for the table* le di 20 dólares por la mesa; *he was handsomely paid for his services* fue generosamente retribuido por sus servicios; *to ~ one's way: he paid his way through college* se pagó *or* se costeó él mismo los estudios; *I've never lived off him, I've always paid my own way* nunca he vivido a costa de él, siempre he pagado lo que me correspondía
2 *(respects)* presentar; *(attention)* prestar; *to ~ sbd a visit o call* hacerle una visita a algn; *I must ~ a visit o a call before we leave* (BrE colloq & euph) tengo que pasar al baño antes de irnos.

Correct dictionary use can also help students with idiomatic expressions. As discussed in Chapter 4, these combinations of two or more words, whose special meaning cannot generally be guessed from the isolated meanings of the individual words, are particularly challenging for students. They need training in how to deal with them as a whole, and practice in trying to find the key word in the idiomatic expression in question. Examples of these kinds of expression would be *you are pulling my leg* or *me estás tomando el pelo* ('you are kidding me' or, literally, 'you are taking my hair') where students would identify *pelo* and *leg* as key words. The dictionary entries from the *Oxford Spanish Dictionary* for these words appear under (18) and (19) (1280, 570):

(18)   Entry for *leg*

leg[1] /leg/ *n* **1** (Anat) (a person) *f:* (of animal, bird) pata, *f:* **break a ~** (set phrase: colloq & hum) ¡(buena suerte)!: *he; she can talk the hind ~ s of a donkey* (colloq) habla como una cotorra *or* (hasta) por los codos (fam); *not to have a ~ to stand on* (colloq) llevar todas las de perder; *shake a ~ !* (colloq) ¡muévete! (fam), apúrate (AmL); *show a ~ !* (BrE colloq) ¡a levantarse!, ¡vamos arriba! (fam); *to be on one's/it's last ~ s* (colloq) estar *en las últimas (fam); *to get a 0 one's ~ over* (BrE sl) echarse un polvo (arg); *to get on one's hind ~ s* (to stand up) (colloq) ponserse *de pie, pararse (AmL); (to go into a rage) (AmE) ponerse *bravo (fam); *to pull sb's ~* (colloq) tomarle el pelo a algn (fam); *to stretch one's ~ s* estirar las piernas; *to walk one's ~ s off* (colloq) matarse caminando *or* (esp Esp) andando (fam); *(before n) (muscle)* de la pierna; *(injury)* en la pierna; *~* **irons** grilletes *mpl*; (Med) aparato *m* ortopédico *(para la pierna)* **2 (a)** (Cullin) (of lamb, pork) pierna *f*. pernil *m* (Col); (of chicken) pata *f*, muslo *m* **(b)** (Clothing) pierna f; (measurement) entropierna *f* **(c)** (of chair, table) pata *f* **3** (stage-of competition, race) manga *f*, vuelta *f*; (-of journey) capa *f*; **I ran the second ~ of the relay** corrí el segundo relevo

(19) Entry for *pelo* 'hair'
m 1. *(de personas-filamento)* hair; *(-conjunto)* hair; *~ rizado/liso* or *lacio* curly/straight hair; *tengo que ir a cortarme el ~*; I have to go and have my hair cut; *tiene un ~ divino* she has lovely o beautiful hair; *tiene mucho ~* he really has thick hair; *siempre lleva el ~ suelto* she always wears her hair down o loose; *me encontré un ~ en la sopa* I found a hair in my soup; *al ~* (fam) great (colloq); *la falda le quedó al ~* the extra money is just what I need; *¿cómo se portó el coche? –* al *~* (Col) how did the car go? – just great *o* spot on (colloq) *andar o estar con los ~ de punta* (CS fam) to be in a real state (colloq); *caérsele el ~ a algn; se le está cayendo el ~* he's losing his hair; *como te descubran se te va a caer el ~* if you get found out, you'll be for it o you've had it (colloq); con estos ~ (fam) *¡llegan dentro de media hora, y yo con estos ~ !* they're arriving in half an hour and look at the state I'm in ! *con ~ y señales* (fam): *me contó su viaje con ~ y señales* she gave me a blow-by-blow account of her trip, she described her trip down to the last detail; *lo describió con pelos y señales*; she gave a very detailed description of him; *de medio ~* (fam) *(película/jugador)* second-rate; *le regaló un anillo de medio ~* he gave her a rather tacky ring; *echar el ~* (Chi fam) to live it up (colloq), to have a good time (colloq*); no tiene ~ en la lengua* (fam) he doesn't mince his words; *no tiene/tienes (ni) un ~ de tonto* (fam) you're he's no fool, there are no flies on you/him (colloq); *no verle el ~ a algn* (fam) not to see hide nor hair of sb (colloq*); hace mucho que no se le ve el ~* nobody's seen hide nor hair of him for ages; *ya*

no te vemos el ~ por aquí we never see you around her any more;
ponerle a algn los ~ de punta (fam) (*aterrorizar*) to make sb's hair
stand on end (colloq); (**poner neurótico**) (AmL) to drive sb crazy or
mad; *una película que te pone los ~ de punta* a spine-chilling movie;
por los ~ s (fam) only just; *se liberó por los ~ de que lo detuvieran* he
narrowly *o* only just escaped being arrested; *aprobó el examen por*
los pelos he just scraped through the exam (by the skin of his teeth);
por un ~ (AmL) just; *me salvé por un ~* I escaped by the skin of my
teeth (colloq); perdí el autobus por un ~ I just missed the bus, I
missed the bus by a few seconds; *por un ~ ne llego al banco* I only
just got to the bank in time; *se me /le erizaron los ~* (fam) it sent
shivers down my spine, it made my/his hair stand on end; *se me/le*
ponen los ~ de punta (fam) it sends shivers down my/his spine, it
makes my/his hair stand on end; *tirado de los ~* s (fam) farfetched;
tirarse de los ~ (fam); *estaba que se tiraba de los ~* he was at wit's
end, he was tearing his hair out in; *tirarse los ~ (de rabia)* (Chi fam)
to be furious; *tocarle* un ~ a algn to lay a finger on sb; **tomarle el ~ a**
alg (fam): *no va en serio, te están tomando el ~* they don't mean it,
they're only jokig *o* teasing *o* (colloq) pulling your leg: me están
tomando el ~, *ya me han caminado la fecha cuatro veces* the're
messing me about, this is the fourth time they've changed the date;
traído por o de los ~ s farfetched; *el argumento es de lo más traído*
de los ~ the plot is very farfetched **2** (fam) (*poco*): *se han pasado un*
~ they've gone a bit too far *o* (BrE colloq) a bit over the top; *no me*
fío (ni) un ~ de ese tipo I don't trust that guy an inch: *no quiso aflo-*
jar (ni) un ~ he refused to budge an inch: *te queda un pelito corta* it's
a tiny *o* a wee bit short for you **3.** (Zool) (*filamento*) hair: (pelaje—de
un perro, gato) hair, fur: (*-de un conejo, oso*) fur: *el gato va*
dejando ~ the cat leaves hairs all over the house; *la perra me dejó*
llena de ~ s I got covered with dog-hairs; *un perro pequeño de ~ largo*
a small, long-haired dog; *montar a o* (RPI) *en ~* to ride bareback;
ser ~ de la cola (Chi fam) to be nothing.

By analyzing these entries, students not only would get the proper translation for the idiom they are looking for, but they will also realize how much
dialectal information they contain, a point touched upon below.

Good use of the dictionary may also enable students to produce better
syntactic structures. A simple translation exercise could help them see this
point. For example, the sentences included under (20) contain expressions
that exist both in Spanish and in English, although in some of them the
order is curiously reversed (Mott, 1996: 177–178). This poses no problem

for heritage speakers, but L2 students of Spanish who are still working on their linguistic competence may very well translate word-for-word, producing a sentence whose unnatural word order sounds odd. If we were to ask students to do the translation exercise given in (20) below, we could underline or highlight key words that they should look up before they write the Spanish version of these sentences.

(20) Translation exercise[154]
Traduce las siguientes oraciones al español. ¡Ojo! Tienen expresiones idiomáticas. Antes de escribir tu traducción, consulta el diccionario.

(1) *My friend had an accident on the way home but he arrived safe and sound.*
(2) *My father works night and day.*
(3) *My grandparents still have a black and white television.*

The Spanish equivalents of these sentences, listed in (21), could be produced by students in an elementary Spanish class:

(21) (1) *Mi amigo tuvo un accidente cuando iba a casa, pero llegó sano y salvo.*
(2) *Mi padre trabaja noche y día.*
(3) *Mis abuelos todavía tienen una televisión en blanco y negro.*

With respect to idioms, a 'key word technique' can be used for helping even beginning students come up with the correct version of idiomatic expressions, including sayings and proverbs. By 'key word' we mean the word that forms the basis of the idiom in question. In the dictionary entry of such words, students can find expressions in which they appear. Students must learn, however, to identify the key word themselves. The *Oxford Spanish Dictionary* gives the first noun as the key word.

(22) (1) *It is raining **cats** and dogs.*
(2) *Kill two **birds** with the same stone.*

If there is no noun, the first verb, adjective, or adverb will determine where to find the expression:

(23) (1) ***Live** and learn.*
(2) *Better **safe** than sorry.*

Students should not have any problems finding the equivalent expressions in Spanish for (22) and (23), which are listed below, in (24) and (25):

(24) (1) *Está lloviendo **a cántaros** (or a mares).*
(2) ***Matar dos pájaros de un tiro.***

(25)   (1) *Todos los días se aprende **algo nuevo**.*
        (2) ***Más vale prevenir que curar.***

In dealing with idioms, students in an advanced class can employ the same 'key word technique' in exercises such as the one listed below, under (26):

(26)   Exercises on idioms

        Las expresiones idiomáticas

        Tanto el inglés como el español son muy ricos en expresiones idiomáticas. Estas expresiones son una combinación de dos o más palabras con un significado especial, que no se puede adivinar, por lo general, a partir del significado de las palabras individuales.

        En general, debemos aprender las expresiones idiomáticas como un todo; alterar el orden de las palabras, omitir o añadir alguna, puede hacer que la expresión sea incomprensible.

        El diccionario te puede ayudar mucho porque te proporciona el orden de las palabras de la expresión, su significado, y también ejemplos de su uso.

        ¿Cómo se buscan las expresiones idiomáticas?
        Primero debes decidir cuál es la palabra clave de la expresión. Si al buscarla, no encuentras la expresión que buscas, tal vez te has equivocado de palabra clave y debes intentarlo de nuevo.

        ¡Ojo! Recuerda que las expresiones idiomáticas aparecen *en letra cursiva*

        Ejercicio 1: Cómo buscar la palabra clave

    (1)   Estudia las expresiones idiomáticas que aparecen en las siguientes oraciones.
    (2)   Decide cuál es la palabra clave.
    (3)   Encuentra esa palabra en tu diccionario; mira la entrada por encima, centrándote exclusivamente en los grupos de palabras que están en negrita.
    (4)   Si la expresión idiomática no está en esa entrada, busca otra palabra clave.
    (5)   Cuando encuentres la palabra clave correcta, escríbela en la columna apropiada.
    (6)   ¿Cuál es la traducción más adecuada para las expresiones de este ejercicio?

Expresión	Palabra clave	Traducción
Ej. ¡Me estás *tomando el pelo*!	pelo	You are pulling my leg
1. No *se anduvo con rodeos*		
2. Soy *todo oídos*		
3. Le *dieron gato por liebre*		
4. Su madre *puso el grito en el cielo*		
5. Terminaron *en menos que canta un gallo*		
6. Te he pillado *con las manos en la masa*		

(7)　Ahora, haz lo mismo con las siguientes expresiones en inglés:

Expresión	Palabra clave	Traducción
Ej. She talks *non-stop*	talk	Habla por los codos
1. María worries about everything. She *makes a mountain out of a molehill.*		
2. My mother called me on an emergency, but it just was *a big fuss about nothing.*		
3. My boss always *makes a fool of me* on purpose		
4. His story was a little *far-fetched*		
5. I did not agree with her, but I *humored her* because I did not want to argue		
6. He wants to become a doctor, like his father. *Like father, like son.*		

Another possible exercise for advanced students would be that in (27)

(27)　Ejercicio 2: Expresiones idiomáticas (cont.)
　　　(1) Busca en tu diccionario las expresiones idiomáticas que aparecen en estas oraciones.
　　　(2) Estudia sus significados.
　　　(3) Explica su significado usando tus propias palabras.

Ejemplo:

No puedo tomar una decisión en este momento. Necesito *consultarlo con la almohada*.

Necesito más tiempo para pensar cuál es la decisión correcta

1. María siempre *se sale con la suya*.

· ·
· ·

2. José Luis es *un manitas*. Nunca necesita llamar al electricista.

· ·
· ·

3. Ayer fui al gimnasio y hoy *tengo los huesos molidos*.

· ·
· ·

4. El profesor *lo tiene entre ceja y ceja*, por eso nunca tiene buenas notas.

· ·
· ·

5. Sus hijos se quieren mucho pero *se llevan como el perro y el gato*.

· ·
· ·

Para recordar estas expresiones, escribe sus equivalentes en la siguiente tabla:

Consultar algo con la almohada
Salirse con la suya
Ser un manitas
Tener los huesos molidos
Tener entre ceja y ceja
Llevarse como el perro y el gato

Finally, we agree with Gu and Johnson (1996), Hulstijn *et al.* (1996) and Hunt (1996) (see Chapter 4 for further discussion), who take the view that dictionary use can facilitate lexical acquisition. We argue that dictionaries can be an important source of information regarding lexical varieties of Spanish, as well as differences in register if students are given proper training in their use.

Thus, going back to our original argument, what are students to do when they come into contact with the lexicon of a speaker or an instructor from a different dialect area? As instructors, where do we draw the line between acceptable alternates and regionalisms that should be avoided, either because they are known only in a geographically restricted area or because they are offensive to other dialects? Simply put, how do we help our students to communicate effectively while showing respect for other dialect areas?

In Section 6.2 above, we have argued that one of our goals as language teachers is raising our students' general language awareness, and in particular an understanding and appreciation of dialectal variation. We have advocated first raising their metalinguistic awareness by presenting this idea in a descriptive manner, without any judgment values, tapping into knowledge that native speakers possess regarding their own language. Examples similar to that given in (28), centered on the Spanish lexicon, could be used to raise this awareness; students would need to use their dictionaries:

(28)   Términos y países
       Usa tu diccionario y decide en qué países se utilizan los términos en cursiva
       Modelo: Put *peas* down on the shopping list.
       _____(1) Escribe *chícharos* en la lista de la compra.
       _____(2) Escribe *guisantes* en la lista de la compra.

   a. México b. España c. Bolivia
   (1) Don't forget *the shoe polish!*
   _____ (1) No te olvides de *la pasta de zapatos.*
   _____ (2) Y no te olvides de *la pomada.*
       a. Argentina b. Chile c. España
   (2) Estoy *enfadado* con mi novia. 'I am angry with my girlfriend.'
       a. México b. Ecuador c. España
   (3) ¿Viene tu amiga con nosotros? ¡*Chévere!*
       a. Colombia b. Panamá c. Argentina
   (4) I have just bought a new car
   _____ (1) Me acabo de comprar *un coche nuevo*
   _____ (2) Me acabo de comprar *un auto nuevo*
   _____ (3) Me acabo de comprar *un carro nuevo*
       a. México b. Argentina c. España
   (5) '*Los duraznos* que compraste no están maduros'
       a. España b. México c. Chile

By integrating exercises given in Section 6.11 above as well as exercises like (28), we can show students that while lexical variety is found among dialects of Spanish, there are many sources of information, including dictionaries, to help them cope.

As argued in Chapter 4, we believe that viewing passive and active vocabulary acquisition as a dichotomy (cf. Laufer & Paribakht) rather than as a continuum (Teichroew's view) is advantageous because of its important practical applications for the Spanish L2 classroom. Unity and diversity are important concepts in the lexicon of the Spanish-speaking world. We therefore advocate presenting L2 learners of Spanish with a neutral lexicon for active mastery, while systematically exposing them to regional variants as well for passive knowledge.

Indeed, in order to address the pluricentric nature of Spanish we must, in our view, make use of the notions of active and passive vocabulary. In other words, we advocate presenting common dialectal alternates to students, but for passive recognition only. This could be done as an enrichment exercise, through a linguistic note, either in the textbook or in the laboratory manual.[155] For example, consider (29):

(29)   Dialectal note:
       The vocabulary in this chapter will allow you to communicate with speakers of most dialects of Latin American Spanish. However, there are regional equivalents for many of the words you have learned in this chapter. From contextual clues, try to guess the dialectally neutral equivalent of the following words:
       (1) *Voy a rentar **un apartamento** (un departamento, un piso, una casa)*
       (2) *Le gusta comer **judías** (fruta, frijoles, habas)*
       (3) ***El fogón** no está caliente todavía (el horno, la estufa, el calentador de agua)*
       (4) *Queremos nadar en **la piscina** (la alberca, el río, el lago)*

We next consider how sociolinguistic aspects of vocabulary can be addressed in the L2 classroom.

6.14   Register Variation in the Lexicon in the Spanish L2 Classroom

With respect to the lexicon, as discussed in detail in Chapter 4, students are very likely to come into contact with the informal register. Students who express themselves in this register, including many heritage speakers, may not have other lexical choices at their disposal. Again, we emphasize the importance of presenting the most neutral variant for active acquisition and the familiar variants for passive recognition. For example, we discussed in Chapter 4 that the word *panza* may be used informally for *estómago*. Students should be taught to understand *panza*, particularly in more advanced language classrooms, but they should know to substitute *estómago*, particularly since they may otherwise overuse the informal term in formal settings (Holman, 1996). Heritage speakers will undoubtedly know both terms. However, some academic terms of a scientific nature may not be generally understood by L1 or L2 students. Exercises like the following may be given:

(30) In Spanish, as in English, informal lexical variants are used by native speakers, such as *Dude* for 'you.' Complete the exercise below, relating the academic word to the informal one; you are free to use dictionaries:

(1) Me duele *la panza*.
a. *la cabeza* b. *el estómago* c. *el pie* d. *la muela*
(2) Me vale un *cacahuate*.
a. *muy poco* b. *una manzana* c. *una pera* d. *un automóvil*
(3) *¿Qúe hubo?*
a. *¿Cómo estás?* b. *¿A dónde vas?* c. *¿Qué quieres?* d. *¿Cómo te llamas?*
(4) ¿Te duele *el coco*?
a. *la cabeza* b. *la espalda* c. *el brazo* d. *el dedo*
(5) Dame *la patita*.
a. *la muñeca* b. *el libro* c. *el pie* d. *la falda*

In the next section, we address the integration of diachronic information in the Spanish language classroom.

6.15 Diachronic Linguistics as a Snapshot of the Current Variation in Spanish

As discussed thoroughly in Chapter 5, Spanish instructors and advanced students of Spanish may be surprised to learn that most of the variation in Spanish today, both dialectal and sociolinguistic, can be traced directly back to earlier forms of the language. In fact, without recourse to historical information, many facts about Spanish cannot be adequately explained, as argued by Rini (1990). Indeed, information regarding the history of Spanish can give instructors and students a greater understanding of the roots of language variability and a greater appreciation for the organic, changing nature of language in general. As discussed in Chapter 5, any course, from beginning levels onward, that integrates culture into the classroom needs to touch upon historical explanations for certain phenomena.

However, it is also the case that explanations must be tailored to the students' general competence in Spanish. For beginning students, appropriate points of discussion are many of those that we gave in Chapter 5.[156] Among the topics that can be clarified to students through historical information include *lleísmo, voseo,* the various forms of address, variation of object pronouns, the article *el* used with feminine nouns and stem-changing verbs. It is neither necessary nor desirable for instructors to give highly complex explanations, including the entire process of evolution of *se* (Chapter 5, example (8)). Yet we nonetheless believe that instructors of Spanish should be aware of some basic diachronic information, particularly as it can broaden their perspective on language variation and change. When and where relevant, bits of historical information can be presented to students, which should help increase their acceptance of the variation that is found in Spanish today. In the next section, we present a detailed review of three popular first-year textbooks used in the United States, which, in our view, incorporate well the notion of variation.

6.16 Textbook Review

6.16.1 Introduction

For the purposes of our study, we have focused our attention on three first-year Spanish textbooks: *Impresiones* (Salaberry *et al.*, 2004), *Plazas* (Hershberger *et al.*, 2008) and *Puntos de partida* (Knorre *et al.*, 2008). All of these texts are published in the United States. They are addressed to a very specific audience: beginning Spanish language students at the university level who are L1 speakers of English. As we have seen in preceding chapters, our classrooms are becoming more diverse, and also include many heritage speakers of Spanish.

The reason that we have concentrated on these three textbooks is that they address variation in Spanish. Our evaluation of their presentation was in accordance with the parameters presented in previous chapters. Specifically, we sought to answer the following questions through our review (31):

(31)

(1) Is dialectal variation adequately addressed in the various subfields of language (e.g. the lexicon, phonology, morphosyntax)?

(2) What kind of approach do the authors take with respect to the presentation of vocabulary? Do they choose a dialectally neutral lexicon or do they instead select lexical items from different dialects at random?

(3) Is the question of sociolinguistic (particularly register) differences, including lexical, phonological and morphological, explained to students in a clear and meaningful manner?

(4) Does the textbook provide exercises that incorporate variation in addition to giving an explanation of the dialectal and sociolinguistic traits of Spanish as it is spoken today?

(5) Does the text refer to historical facts of Spanish where appropriate?

(6) Does the textbook take into account the special needs of heritage speakers in our introductory Spanish language classes?

It is important to note that in our evaluation, we did not consider ancillary materials. There are several reasons for this. First, instructors are often left to their own discretion regarding the use of such materials. Second, at times, the materials are not written for a specific book. For example, McGraw-Hill use the same video for *Puntos de partida* as they do for *Dos Mundos*. Third, instructors do not usually have time to incorporate all of these materials into the curriculum. Finally, relegating the discussion of variation to ancillary materials indicates both to the instructor and to the student that it is not an important aspect of Spanish as it is spoken today. Given this caveat, the following three sections present a point-by-point analysis of these three first-year college-level textbooks, in alphabetical order. The upshot of our review is that each book has different strengths.

6.16.2 *Impresiones*

In our view, of the three books that we are considering, *Impresiones* is the one that makes dialectal variation the most meaningful. When explaining the conceptual basis for the text (Preface: xv), its authors make reference to the three lines along which it has been created: (i) the teaching and learning of culture, (ii) the development of sociolinguistic skills, and (iii) the teaching and learning of grammar. The text has a language-in-culture orientation, and cultural similarities and differences are contrasted and analyzed. This is done not only to bring students to understand the cultures of Spanish-speaking countries, but also to comprehend the way in which language reflects cultural norms in many instances.

With respect to the first question given in (31), *Impresiones* excels. Popularly, the cover-term 'Hispanic' is erroneously thought to represent all cultures where Spanish is spoken. *Impresiones* dispels this notion by focusing on the variety of the Spanish-speaking world. The authors dedicate the *Enfoque cultural* section of each chapter to a specific Spanish-speaking country (or countries, grouped together in a way that represents the macro-dialectal divisions of Spanish). Even the sequence in the presentation of the countries in question is not random, for it starts with those countries with more direct contact and influence in the United States, given its intended audience of North American students learning Spanish as an L2 in this country.

As we have argued before, our students live in a multicultural society, where the presence of Hispanics, from varying origins, is increasing every day. Their language is not uniform, but rather represents the variety of dialects of the Spanish language. Acknowledging this fact, *Impresiones* explicitly focuses on the appropriateness of a language form in a given region. The activities designed for students include all sorts of contexts, and are on a variety of topics. More importantly (from the perspective that we have adopted in this book), *Impresiones* addresses key dialectal differences explicitly, having the students actively manipulate the linguistic characteristics of different regions. In other words, they are not merely exposed to language variation, say, in a footnote or Appendix, but rather actively acquire a great deal of linguistic knowledge of the pluricentrism of Spanish.

An introductory overview of Hispanic dialectology, therefore, is one of the cornerstones of this textbook. The first chapter provides a brief explanation in English about the meaning of dialectal variation. It further gives a practice exercise related to lexical variation specifically, both in English and in the Spanish-speaking world. In the exercise related to the Spanish language, students work in pairs. Each pair of students is assigned ten countries, and is responsible for discussing in Spanish the lexical variants that are common in those areas for three words ('boy,' 'bus' and 'blond'), Impresiones (32, 522):

(32)   *Lexical variation in Spanish*
       Student A
       1-30 ¿Cómo se dice 'bus' en tu región?

       Student A

       Paso 1. AB. With your partner, find out as many variations as you can for the Spanish equivalents of the following words: Little boy, bus and blond.

       MODELO: E1 ¿Cómo se dice 'bus' en México?
       E2 Se dice camión.

       Student B
       ¿Cómo se dice 'bus' en tu region?
       Paso 1. Estudiante B. Busca información sobre Cuba, Guatemala, El Salvador, México y Panamá.

The exercise is visually enhanced by the maps on page (32) and page (522), which provide information on which lexical variants are found in the above countries. Although the exercise is given to students very early in their learning process of L2 Spanish, they can nonetheless do the activity in Spanish, exchanging the relevant dialectal information as directed.

In our view, this manner of presentation is very logical and accessible, since it starts with something that the students know and leads them to explore what they do not know. The design of the exercise is to have students work in a collaborative manner, manipulating diverse forms of the target language from the first chapter of the text. While we believe that the exercise in (32) above is excellent, we have a suggestion for a follow-up exercise. Students could also be instructed to create a chart similar to the one we presented in Chapter 4, borrowed from Azevedo (1992). This table, once completed, could look like (33) below:

(33)   Regional variants for 'little boy,' 'bus' and 'blond' in 10 Spanish-speaking countries

	little boy	*bus*	*blond*
México	chamaco	camión	güero
Guatemala	patojo	camioneta	canche
El salvador	cipote	camioneta	chele
Panamá	chico	chiva	fulo
Cuba	chico	guagua	rubio
Colombia	pelado	autobús	mono
Chile	cabro	micro	rubio
Argentina	pibe	colectivo	rubio
Uruguay	niño	ómnibus	rubio
España	niño	autobús	rubio

It is clear that the involvement of the students in the activity is the most important aspect of the introductory exercise in (32). By actively using the regional terms themselves, presented to them in the context of the whole Spanish-speaking world, textually enhanced with maps, students are more likely to become aware of how extensive dialectal variation is in the Spanish-speaking world. This kind of exercise is far more effective, in our opinion, than if students were passively presented with the dry facts, for example, with a table like (33) above already completed for them.

Phonological and morphosyntactic dialectal differences are also presented to students. After the introduction that we have mentioned, every chapter contains a sub-section *Diferencias dialectales*, included within the *Comparaciones culturales* section of the chapter. The dialectal differences addressed are of all kinds, and are always related to the geographical area that is the protagonist of the *Enfoque cultural* section of the chapter.

For example, when Spain is the focus, *distinción/ceceo* is presented, as is the term of address for second person plural *vosotros*. When Argentina and Uruguay, in turn, are at the center of the *Enfoque cultural*, the use of *vos* and the pronunciation of /j/ and /ʒ/ are discussed and practiced. The use of *vos* is revisited when Costa Rica and Nicaragua are addressed. When Cuba and the Dominican Republic are the cultural focus, the lack of inversion in questions is the topic treated and practiced. Lexical and pragmatic information/variation is often addressed, both within this specific section and throughout the text.

Now let us consider what the presentation of the lexicon is in *Impresiones*, specifically considering our second question, which asks if dialect-neutral lexicon forms are given. Again, *Impresiones* is largely successful in this regard. The choice of words that should become active vocabulary, presented at the end of every chapter, seems to reflect an unmarked variety. In some occasions, the lexical forms seem to favor Latin American usage. Some examples are the choice of the words *videocasetera* 'VCR,' *enojado* 'angry,' *lindo* 'pretty,' *contador* 'accountant,' *pachanga* 'fun,' *durazno* 'peach,' *cola* 'buttocks' and *licencia* 'license.' For these terms, the Peninsular counterparts would be *vídeo, enfadado, guapo, contable, jarana, melocotón, culo* and *carnet*.

Quite often, however, *Impresiones* offers several options, from different standards, for some common words. For example, it lists *marrón* or *café* for 'brown,' *fontanero* or *plomero* for 'plumber,' *camiseta, playera* or *remera* for 't-shirt,' *campera, chaqueta* or *saco* for 'jacket,' *vaqueros, jeans* or *pantalones mezclillas* for 'jeans,' *la piyama* or *el pijama* for 'pajamas,' and *mamá* or *mami* for 'mom.' Other examples include *papá* or *papi* for 'dad,' *esposa* or *mujer* for 'wife,' *camarones* or *gambas* for 'shrimp,' *champiñones* or *hongos* for 'mushrooms,' *habas, frijoles, habichuelas* or *porotos* for 'beans,' and *legumbres* or *vegetales* for 'vegetables.'

The text does not commit the error of using a 'cafeteria approach,' by which we mean randomly selecting vocabulary words from widely divergent dialects for active presentation.[157] Books following such a method present students, for example, a vocabulary word such as *lentes* 'glasses,' a term used in Latin America (Peninsular *gafas*), while presenting the lexical item *piscina* 'swimming pool,' from Spain (Latin American *alberca*). Unfortunately, the presentation of dialectal variation with respect to the lexicon is not entirely satisfactory in *Impresiones*. The text gives more than one option for widely used terms, as mentioned above. Yet no mention is made of the regions in which a given term is used. How to work with them is left to the instructor's discretion.

In summary, the dialectal coverage in *Impresiones* is excellent. Yet with few exceptions, there is little discussion of sociolinguistic variation. There are a few isolated notes to the instructor, such as the following (34):

(34)   Point out that – as is the case in English – the use of formal–informal language is not necessarily reciprocal. This is most obvious in relations such as that of a boss with an employee, in which the latter may use *usted* to address his/her boss but the former may prefer to use *tú* to address the employee. The same rule applies to English, although the formal–informal dimension is represented by the contrast between titles and first names. For example, your boss may address you by your name (e.g. Robert), whereas you may address your boss as Mr Smith or Dr Smith.

In the student text, no mention is made of the difference of formal/ informal on this page. One problem with the note itself, in our view, is that it has little or no relation to the students' lives. A better example would have been the relationship between a professor and a student. After all, the likelihood that they are going to be an employee in a Spanish-speaking country is quite low. Moreover, the note itself is simplistic. There are sharp dialectal differences regarding the non-reciprocal use of *tú* and *usted*. Mexico, for example, tends to use the formal in many settings where Spain would use the informal. Finally, raising the question of the non-reciprocal forms of address on page six of the student text is not ideal. In our opinion, what needs to be stressed at this point is how not to insult native speakers by choosing the wrong register (i.e. use *tú* instead of *usted* in a formal exchange).

With respect to our fourth question, whether or not the text provides exercises that incorporate variation, the answer with respect to *Impresiones* is unequivocally 'yes,' at least where dialectal (not sociolinguistic) variation is concerned. Indeed, as far as *Impresiones* and dialectal variation go, the key word might be 'practice.' Students are never simply passive recipients of dialectal information; rather, they always have the opportunity to manipulate the language. The activities have the ultimate goal of increasing the students' awareness about dialectal variation, and we believe that this goal is achieved. Below we offer two concrete examples taken from this text, one morphological/pragmatic (the use of *vosotros* as the informal plural way of address in Peninsular Spanish) and one regarding syntactic variation (the formation of questions in some Caribbean dialects).

As mentioned above, when Spain is the cultural focus of the chapter, the terms of address in Peninsular Spanish are discussed. As (35) shows, students work actively with the forms that correspond to the present, and they are exposed, passively, to the imperative forms. It is an inductive presentation, and we see how in step 2 students have to predict what the verb endings for the three verb conjugations are likely to be:

(35)   Introducción a *vosotros* (*Impresiones* 214)

Diferencias dialectales

In most regions of Spain the pronoun **vosotros/as** is used to convey familiarity and informality in place of the pronouns **ustedes** (*you all, you guys*). Like the **nosotros/as** forms, the **vosotros/as** forms of verbs do not change stem either.

¿Cuánto sabéis vosotros sobre vosotros?

2. **Paso 1. 2.** Emparejad las preguntas con las respuestas y prestad atención al contenido.

(1) ___ ¿Tenéis planes para esta noche?
(2) ___ ¿Servís paella de naranja con frecuencia?
(3) ___ ¿Tomáis zumo de naranja con frecuencia?
(4) ___ ¿Estudiáis mucho?
(5) ___ ¿Conocéis al famoso autor Camilo José Cela?
(6) ___ ¿Os gusta la comida española?
(7) ___ ¿Oué vais a pedir para comenzar? o ¿Qué pedís para comenzar?
(8) ___ ¿Sabéis el nombre del restaurante?
    (a) No, no nos gusta mucho el zumo
    (b) Sí la servimos todos los días; la paella es nuestra especialidad.
    (c) Vamos a pedir una tortilla española, unas aceitunas y una sopa de pescado para comenzar.
    (d) ¡Por supuesto que lo sabemos! El nombre del restaurante es *El Molino*.
    (e) No, no tenemos planes para esta noche.
    (f) Sí, estudiamos todos los días.

(g) Sí, nos encanta. Las tapas de este bar son deliciosas.
(h) Sí, lo conocemos.

Paso 2. Analizad las formas verbales que se utlizan en las preguntas del Paso anterior. ¿A qué pronombre corresponden? Con esa información, completad la siguiente tabla.

PRONOMBRE SUJETO	AR-TOMAR	ER-TENER	IR-SERVIR
Nosotros/as	————	————	
Uds.	toman	tienen	————
Vosotros/as	————	————	————
Ellos/as	toman	————	sirven

In turn, when the cultural focus is Cuba and the Dominican Republic, syntactic variation is addressed, and the typical lack of inversion in question making is presented and practiced, as shown in (36) below (*Impresiones* 144):

(36)   Asking questions in the Caribbean
Diferencias dialectales
4–26 ¿Qué tú quieres?

Paso 1. Usually when Cubans and Domicans form questions, they do not change the order of subject and verb, but rather maintain the same order as in an affirmative sentence. According to this statement, select the questions they usually make (*Impresiones* 144).

MODELO: Quiero ir al parque.
(a) ¿Qu tú quieres hacer?
(b) ¿Que quieres hacer?
(1) Me llamo Roberto Albornoz Pérez.
(a) ¿Cómo usted se llama?
(b) ¿Cómo se llama usted?
(2) Quiero encontrar un trabajo con un buen sueldo.
(a) ¿Qué quieres tú?
(b) ¿Qué tu quieres?
(3) Vamos a las 9 menos cuarto.
(a) ¿Cuándo ustedes van al cine?
(b) ¿Cuándo van al cine ustedes?
(4) Te recomiendo usar tu traje negro.
(a) ¿Qué me recomiendas usar para la entrevista?
(b) ¿Qué tú me recomiendas usar para la entrevista?

Paso 2. Dominicans tend to use subject pronouns that in other varieties of Spanish are usually dropped. Rewrite the following sentences as if they were used by non-Dominican speakers of Spanish. **MODELO**: Cuando tú tienes una entrevista, tú tienes que vestirte bien. Cuando tienes una entrevista tienes que vestirte bien.

(1) Si tú trabajas mucho tú vas a tener éxito.
(2) Tú tienes un trabajo que tú disfrutas.
(3) Ustedes van al cine porque ustedes no tienen que trabajar.

As we have repeatedly noted, the treatment of the regional variation in this text goes beyond the simple passive reception of information on the part of the student. Students work with the language, contrasting the forms. They are led toward recognition of the regional form. In some cases, students also 'produce' sentences based on these dialectal characteristics.

Our fifth question, given in (31), concerns whether diachronic explanations are given. In *Impresiones*, little reference to earlier forms in the history of the Spanish language is made in this textbook, although some minor points, such as *ojalá*, are covered in notes to the students called *consejitos* 'pieces of advice.' This is a bit surprising, given its generally excellent integration of variation into both the student textbook and instructor's manual. It would not be difficult for the authors to add at least a few footnotes regarding the diachronic evolution of Spanish and how it has contributed to the current variability evinced by the language.

Finally, *Impresiones* does not address heritage speakers in our classrooms, either in the student text or in the instructor's manual. There is a brief reference to 'Spanglish' in the student text (69). The note tells students that it is a combination of the two languages and that it exists because these speakers 'still prefer to say some things in Spanish,' although they are English dominant. They conclude the note with a statement that many Hispanics in the United States use Spanish as a sign of their 'linguistic identity.' Clearly, such a note does not accurately describe heritage speakers, who have a range of levels of competence in Spanish and English. We next turn to a review of *Plazas*.

6.16.3 *Plazas*

This textbook also addresses the topic of dialectal variation in a systematic way. In the presentation of their work, the authors state:

Plazas is comprehensive in its treatment of the Spanish speaking world, yet also recognizes the growing presence and importance of

Spanish in the U.S. Furthermore, *Plazas* (3rd edition) does not gloss over regional differences in accent, diction or modes of address, but rather emphasizes them as subjects of study that further accentuate the cultural richness of the Spanish language. (*Plazas* IAE 9)

Three sections, found in every chapter, are important from our point of view. The first is *Encuentro cultural* 'cultural encounter,' a section that is country specific and focuses on subtopics, such as famous people, history, geographic features, industries, art, and music (IAE 11). The second is *¿Nos entendemos?*, 'Do we understand each other?', sociolinguistic notes that are interspersed throughout each chapter. Finally, the third is *Cultura* 'culture,' cultural notes that are, again, distributed throughout the chapters.

The *Encuentro cultural* section in the preliminary chapter of the text offers the student information on the extensive territories where Spanish is spoken. It focuses mostly on the geographical characteristics of these areas, but also on the composition of their population, and their background. Very current information is included (e.g. the recent immigration patterns in Spain and the United States). After working with this reading, students will have no doubt about the importance of the Spanish language in the world and about the increasing number of Spanish speakers.

We again consider the questions given above in (31). With respect to dialectal variation, our first question, *Plazas* succeeds in addressing it systematically. The *¿Nos entendemos?* notes, present in every chapter, address all types of variation including dialectal. These notes are written in English, small in size, but colored, to attract the attention of the students. They are examples of what Sharwood Smith (1993) has termed positive input enhancement. As an example, the note in (37) deals with morphological variation; the student learns about the different endings used for present tense with the pronoun *vos* (*Plazas* 236):

(37)   When *vos* is used with present tense verbs, it is conjugated differently: for *ar* verbs, add *ás*: *Vos hablás español como un argentino(a)*; for *er* verbs, add *és*:

Vos comés parrillada argentina todos los fines de semana; and for *ir* verbs, add *ís*: *¿Vos decidís estudiar en Buenos Aires o en Córdoba?* The irregular verb *ser* has an irregular form for *vos* also: *Vos sós muy inteligente.* (*Plazas*, 226)

This note is related to a previous *Comentario cultural* (a section that, as stated above, is at times devoted to sociolinguistic information). *Plazas* introduces the concept of *voseo* very briefly: 'In Argentina, and on a limited basis in southern Mexico, Central America, and northwestern South

America, *vos* is used in lieu of *tú'* (*Plazas* 236). This information about *vos* is pertinent, because the chapter where it appears is devoted to Argentina. The concept of *voseo* is revisited when the geographical area featured in the chapter is Uruguay.

Typically, the *¿Nos entendemos?* notes have content that is relevant to the specific geographical area to which the chapter in question is devoted. The note in (38) appears in the chapter related to the Caribbean islands and discusses the different lexical variants for *bus* in this area (*Plazas* 309):

(38)   Note in *Plazas* with lexical information

> In Puerto Rico, buses are called *las guaguas*; in Argentina and El Salvador *los colectivos*; in Mexico, *los camiones*; and in other countries like Cuba, the terms *el omnibus* and *el microbus* are common. In some countries, the terms *el trolebús* and *el tranvía* are still used. *Un camello* ('camel') is what Cubans call a bus that is mounted on the bed of a truck and used as public transportation.

This approach, linking regional variation with the geographical focus of the chapter, although very well presented, is not always consistent. For example, this chapter also includes other *¿Nos entendemos?* notes addressing lexical variants for other concepts in other areas of the Spanish-speaking world (Latin American usage vs. Peninsular usage, mostly) rather than just the Caribbean. In other words, dialectal information does not only focus on the region under discussion.

With respect to phonology, we did not find any mention of dialectal characteristics. This could be added easily in the text, given its emphasis of various regions in the Hispanic world. Again, in our view, a neutral pronunciation must be chosen and actively taught to students. However, by presenting specific characteristics of different dialects, their comprehension will be improved.

In terms of the presentation of vocabulary (Question 2), *Plazas* strives to offer dialectally neutral terms in its section *Vocabulario esencial*, the section in each chapter listing the lexical items that the students should actively master. For the most part, these vocabulary items represent an undetermined Latin American standard, which we agree with given the intended audience (i.e., U.S. students learning Spanish as an L2) of the text.

Sometimes, however, there is no consistency in the terms offered, and a mixture of dialects is found, which we have referred to above as a 'cafeteria approach.' For example, the vocabulary about clothing suggests *vaqueros* for 'jeans,' a term that is characteristic of the Peninsular norm, together with other terms clearly belonging to Latin American usage (e.g. *aretes* 'ear rings,' where a Spaniard would use the word *pendientes*). Another example is related to the vocabulary about traveling. Most terms listed represent a Latin American norm, but the words *reserva* 'reservation' and *ascensor* 'elevator,' characteristic of Spain, are the ones presented, instead of *reservación* or *elevador*, more commonly used in Latin America. For the most part, however, as we have said above, the vocabulary in *Plazas* represents a neutral Latin American standard.

Sociolinguistic variation, addressed in (31), Question 3, is also incorporated in a consistent manner into *Plazas*. For example, the note in (39) contains pragmatic information, emphasizing what native speakers would say in a very common daily life situation (*Plazas* 194):

(39)   Note in *Plazas* with pragmatic content

In several Latin American countries, it is quite common to use the diminutive form when requesting common beverages such as *un cafecito* ('little coffee') or *una cervecita* ('little beer'). Also, note that in Latin America it is more appropriate to use *yo quisiera ...* ('I would like,' the past subjunctive of the verb *querer*) when ordering food. In Spain, it is more common to use the more direct present tense form *(yo) quiero ...* ('I want').

As we can see, this information concerns daily, colloquial usage, but also contrasts regions in the Spanish-speaking world. It is commonly accepted that Spaniards are more straightforward and less polite in their ways than other Spanish speakers. The development of the pragmatic competence of students is clearly a goal of the authors of *Plazas*. This can be illustrated by another *¿Nos entendemos?* note that introduces students to some rules of 'proper' linguistic behavior, regarding commands and requests, as in (40) (*Plazas* 315):

(40)   You can soften commands to make them sound more like requests than demands, by using *usted* or *ustedes* after the command form or by adding *por favor*: *Pasen ustedes por aquí* or *Pasen por aquí, por favor* ('Come this way, please'). *No hable usted tan rápido* or *No hable tan rápido, por favor* ('Don't speak so fast, please').

When you want people to do something, but you wish to say so tactfully, ask a question or make a simple statement with reference to your wish rather than using a direct command. For example, suppose that you are a dinner guest at a friend's house. The dining room is uncomfortably hot, and you want a window opened or the air conditioning turned on. You might say: *Hace un poco de calor ¿no?*

As was the case in *Impresiones*, the role of phonology in register differences is not addressed in *Plazas*.

It is evident, then, that *Plazas* addresses all sorts of regional and sociolinguistic variation in the student textbooks themselves. While these notes are certainly very informative, and present students with the issue of regional variants, their usefulness is not always clear to us. Indeed, one shortcoming of this text is that students are not provided with the opportunity to practice the information that they receive about regional variation. What is lacking in *Plazas* with respect to dialectal variation, in our view, are practice exercises (Question 4).

For example, with regard to the lexicon, students are simply exposed to a set of alternative words. They do not actively manipulate these dialectal forms, and the idea that lexical variation is not arbitrary is not highlighted at any point. With respect to information about other aspects of regional variation, its value would depend on the students' dedication and on the teacher's approach to these texts in the classroom. The instructor's edition offers helpful teaching tips, but not with respect to regional or sociolinguistic variation. In this regard, instructors would have to rely on their own resources. Given the varied linguistic training of Spanish instructors, this approach is not ideal. We believe that the presentation of variation in *Plazas* could be greatly improved by adding exercises that involve practice of the regional and sociolinguistic characteristics under discussion.

Question 5 above concerns whether the textbook in question, in this case *Plazas*, makes mention of the evolution or earlier forms of the Spanish language. Such information is lacking in *Plazas*, even in the instructor's manual, although it could easily be added. Finally, *Plazas* does not address heritage speakers in our classroom. As we have seen repeatedly throughout this book, many of these speakers have special linguistic needs and characteristics. In today's Spanish classroom in the United States, it is essential that heritage speakers are mentioned repeatedly throughout the text. Additional information could then be given in the instructor's manual. Overall, *Plazas'* greatest strength is its presentation of sociolinguistic variation. Its weaknesses include the fact that it does not have practice exercises for variation. It further lacks diachronic information and notes regarding heritage speakers. We next consider *Puntos de partida*.

6.16.4   *Puntos de partida*

Puntos de partida introduces students to the notion of dialectal variation immediately, in the preliminary chapter, by means of a reading, in English, entitled 'Spanish around the world' (*Puntos* 10–11). Their brief introduction reviews the notion of dialects, by making students reflect on their own language, and emphasizes the extension of the territories where Spanish is spoken. It makes students aware of the existence of different regional varieties of Spanish, but also emphasizes the idea that, beyond differences, there is an essential unity in the language (*Puntos* 10).

> Although these differences are most noticeable in pronunciation ('accent'), they are also found in vocabulary and special expressions used in different geographical areas. Despite these differences, misunderstandings among native speakers are rare, since the majority of structures and vocabulary are common to the many varieties of each language.

With this passage, students are also invited to reflect on the situation of Hispanics in their country, their many origins and their many backgrounds.

In terms of regional differences in morphology, this textbook gives limited information. It always presents *vosotros* in the verb paradigms, and it also includes the possessive form *vuestro(a)(os)(as)* associated with this personal pronoun. When discussing subject pronouns, a note to the instructors encourages them to point out to the students the use of *vos* in some parts of Latin America, but it is a form that is not presented in the student text of *Puntos de partida*.

However, brief notes are sometimes included in the students' textbook. For example, the idea of *leísmo*, as discussed in depth in Chapter 3, is also mentioned in the following footnote in the students' text (*Puntos* 209):

(41)   Note on the use of *leísmo*
       In Spain and in some other parts of the Spanish-speaking world, *le* is frequently used instead of *lo* for the direct object pronoun *him*. This usage, called *el leísmo*, will not be used in *Puntos*.

Such notes notwithstanding, the only systematic references to dialects that students have in their textbooks have to do with the lexicon. For example, every chapter contains one or more *Así se dice* 'That's how it's said' sections. Similarly to *Plazas*, *Puntos* provides textual enhancement of these notes. They consist of small, colored boxes that introduce regional variations on theme vocabulary from around the Spanish-speaking world. In some instances, the origin of those alternative lexical items is stated, but quite frequently it is not. For example, in Chapter 7, students are introduced to different terms that would translate English 'truck.' The list of lexical variants for 'truck' is as follows (*Puntos* 237):

(42)   *la camioneta = la ranchera, la rubia, el coche rural, el coche familiar, el monovolumen (Sp.)*

In (42), five lexical variants are provided as alternatives to *la camioneta*, but no information is given to students regarding where they are used (with the exception of *el monovolumen*). It is not obvious to us what students will do with these boxes that contain alternative lexical items. It is true that they are not intended for active knowledge. Yet considering the way in which these regional terms are presented, it would be easy for students to simply skip them, unless their instructors make a point to address the issue. To be fair, this is something that teachers are systematically encouraged to do in the notes that appear in the margins of the instructor's edition.

Phonetic regional variation, another consideration of Question 1, is not regularly presented or recycled in *Puntos*, in either the instructor's manual or the student text. Yet there are isolated examples in which dialectal variation in phonology is touched upon in the instructor's manual. For example, when introducing the alphabet, in the *Ante todo* (preliminary) chapter, instructors are encouraged in the instructor's manual to teach the pronunciation of their own dialect and to allow for variation. The manual further recommends that they point out dialectal pronunciations, such as the lateral pronunciation of *ll* [ʒ] in northern Peninsular Spanish or the strong palatal fricative [ʎ] from Argentina. While this is a good start, we question the presentation of these variants so early in the semester.

We have argued in this chapter that the best method for presenting vocabulary, given the pluricentrism of Spanish, is to actively teach a neutral variety (Question 2 above). By this we mean a lexicon that is understood by speakers of different dialects. The vocabulary that *Puntos de partida* presents for active use and learning strives for this neutral character like *Impresiones* and *Plazas*. Indeed, *Puntos* generally succeeds in representing a non-specific Latin American standard in vocabulary.

There are exceptions, however, such as *computación* 'computing' (clearly a Latin American term) and *bolígrafo* 'pen' (common in Peninsular Spanish), which appear in the same thematic unit. Similarly, *alquiler* (a lexical item from Peninsular Spanish) is the word used for 'rent' in the unit regarding the house. At the same time, however, many other terms that obviously hail from Latin America, such as *refrigerador* 'refrigerator' and *estufa* 'stove,' are given as active vocabulary in this chapter. However, for the most part, the vocabulary, as stated above, represents an undetermined Latin American norm.

As far as pragmatic variation is concerned, our third question, the *Así se dice* notes that we have previously mentioned, sometimes contain this kind of information. This is in agreement with the goal that the authors state in the preface: '[provide] content that aims to raise awareness of the interaction of language, culture and society.' (*Puntos de partida* xxvi) An example of this kind of note is the following (*Puntos* 61):

(43)   Terms of endearment for family members in *Puntos de partida*
       The terms *mami* and *papi* are used to speak to one's parents. To speak to your grandparents, use the terms *abuelito* or *tata*, and *abuelita* or *nana*.

Our fourth question was whether there was any kind of practice exercises regarding the regional variants that might be present in the student textbook. This is not the case in *Puntos de partida*, neither with the lexicon nor with the other instances of regional variation that we have mentioned. In Chapter 1, we argue that sometimes instructors, due to different academic preparation, do not always possess the necessary linguistic background to address regional variation in the classroom. The instructor's edition of *Puntos de partida* excels at helping teachers in this area. There is a plethora of notes in the margins of the text, providing hints as to how to approach a given grammar point or the presentation of the vocabulary.

For our purposes, however, it is important to mention that many of these also 'remind' instructors of aspects related to variation (lexical, morphological or pragmatic) of which they may or may not be aware. Generally speaking, the information is accessible to the untrained reader. For example, related to an *Así se dice* note in the student book, where alternative lexical items are mentioned in the area of food, the instructor is given the following advice (*Puntos* 227):

(44)   Note to the instructor with lexical content
       The following information will be useful if you choose to explore the topic of variation in food words with your students in more depth. The list contains both variations for words that are introduced in the text and optional vocabulary with variations.
       la banana = el banano, el guineo, el plátano
       la barbacoa = el asado, la parrillada
       el bistec = el biftec, el bisté
       el bróculi = el brócoli
       el cerdo = el cochino, el chancho, el guarro, el marrano, el puerco
       (Note: *la carne de cerdo* is a relatively generalized term)
       los champiñones = los hongos
       la chuleta = la costilla
       la dona = el buñuelo (Sp)
       las espinacas = la espinaca
       las fresas = las frutillas (Arg. Uru.)

los frijoles = los porotos (Arg. Uru.)
las habichuelas = las judías verdes (Sp) = los ejotes (Mex.)
= las chauchas (Mex.)
la naranja = la china
el pastel = el queque = la torta
la piña = el ananá
el sándwich = el emparedado, el bocadillo (Sp) = la torta (Mex.)

What are the instructors to do with such a variety of terms? One problem with this note is that, with few exceptions, no mention is made regarding the source dialects of these lexical items. Yet this note can serve to remind instructors of the extensive lexical variety that exists in the Spanish-speaking world. It is not reasonable to expect instructors to recognize all the variants that they come across so that additional information in the instructor's manual could be quite helpful.

Another example of this kind of note where pragmatic content is instead the focus concerns the use of terms of address. In this regard, the following are two important pieces of information of which instructors are reminded:

(45)   Notes for the instructor with pragmatic content
        tú vs. *usted* (*Plazas* 39)

Emphasize the difference between *tú* and *Ud.*, explaining that the nature of the relationship between two people determines the form they will use. Point out that the contexts for *tú* and *Ud.* are very different throughout the Spanish-speaking world, and they vary from country to country, and from one generation to another. In some countries (e.g. Spain, Puerto Rico and Cuba), people are much more liberal in the use of *tú* than others (e.g. Colombia, Honduras or Costa Rica).

tú vs. *vos* (*Plazas* 82)

Generally, *tú* is used as the familiar form and *Ud.* is used to show respect. As mentioned previously, the form *vos* is similar to *tú*, and is used mainly in Argentina and Uruguay. The use of *tú*, *vos* or *Ud.* depends on a variety of factors: age, social status or socioeconomic status. For example, teachers and parents use *tú* with young adults and children. Nevertheless, an abrupt change from *tú* or *vos* to *Ud.* can indicate a change of tone in a conversation. In Bogotá, Colombia, the use of *tú* is very limited. It is used mainly by parents, grandparents and couples.

As was the case in the other two texts, *Puntos de partida* does not indicate either to students or to instructors what phonological processes characterize informal speech.

Our fifth question concerns the use of diachronic explanations in the text. In *Puntos de partida*, we find a few notes in this instructor's edition that address issues related to the history of the language. Consider the note in (46), (*Puntos* 168):

(46)

> The origin of the word *izquierda* has been the focus of much debate by linguists. The Latin word for *left* [*sinister, sinistra, sinistrum*] was not adopted in Spanish due to the negative context that was associated with *sinister*. Despite the existence of a Latinate word for *left*, the Basque word for *left, izquierda,* was adopted instead.

As seen in (46) above, the origin of the words *izquierda* ('left') and *ojalá* ('God willing') is explained briefly, in a manner that even a teacher who is not trained in linguistics can easily follow.

Finally, *Puntos de partida* is one of the few elementary Spanish textbooks that acknowledge the fact that we will likely have heritage speakers in our lower-level classes. This is, in our view, a highly important feature of this text *vis à vis* the other two. Thus, the instructor's edition, once more, provides helpful information aimed at the inexperienced instructor regarding some of the features of the language of these speakers. These notes are written in Spanish to facilitate an exchange with native speakers (given the fact that the teacher himself/herself might not be a native speaker). The authors further encourage the instructor to be respectful of non-standard forms, while pointing out the preferred variants. An example of this kind of note appears below (*Puntos* 218):

(47)

> En algunos dialectos del español que se hablan tanto en los países de habla española como en los EE.UU., a veces se oye decir *siéntensen, acuéstensen, o vístansen* para la tercera persona del plural (Uds.). Aunque haya personas que usen estas formas en el habla popular, las formas preferidas son *siéntense, acuéstense, vístanse.*

In summary, we truly believe that the instructor's edition of this textbook can be of tremendous help for the inexperienced language teacher who lacks training in the areas of linguistic terminology and the processes that characterize regional and sociolinguistic variation in Spanish. As was the case for *Plazas*, our recommendation is that exercises be created for students so that they can better understand Spanish sociocultural differences. Finally, *Puntos de partida* is clearly superior to *Impresiones* and *Plazas* with respect to addressing the special needs and characteristics of heritage speakers in our classrooms.

6.17   Conclusion

In this chapter, we have given a series of specific tips to integrate variation, both regional and sociolinguistic, into the Spanish language classroom from beginning levels. We began our discussion by variation in general, advocating an approach that first raises students' metalinguistic awareness by completing exercises in English. We then considered phonological, morphosyntactic, and lexical variation and the Spanish language student. We argued for an approach that actively teaches a neutral form but passively exposes students to the rich variety found in Spanish today.

We then turned to three popular first-year textbooks used widely in the United States, *Impresiones, Plazas,* and *Puntos de partida.* We found that dialectal variation is addressed in all of them, to varying degrees. In our opinion, *Impresiones* is the text where dialectal variation is presented in the most meaningful manner. Indeed, the fact that students are allowed to practice with alternative forms makes it more likely that they will come to understand and accept the pluricentrism of Spanish.

Despite their lack of exercises, both *Plazas* and *Puntos de partida* contain abundant references to lexical regional variation in the students' textbook. The *¿Nos entendemos?* notes of *Plazas* and the *Así se dice* notes of *Puntos de partida* are both instances of textual enhancement. *Plazas* uses these remarks to inform students about lexical and morphosyntactic regional variation, whereas *Puntos de partida* explains only lexical variants in their notes. In our short discussion of these texts, we have expressed doubts, however, as to how engaged students might be by this type of enhanced input. Again, the shortcoming, in our view, is that no additional tasks integrating this information are given.

With respect to sociolinguistic variation, we found that the presentation in *Plazas* is the most consistent. We must again emphasize, however, that with regard to *Puntos de partida,* one of its most outstanding features is its instructor's edition, written for teachers who might lack a background in linguistics. It provides helpful information regarding dialectal variation and gives suggestions regarding heritage speakers in our classrooms, the only textbook to do so.

Finally, we have two general recommendations for each of the three textbooks. Our first recommendation is that they at least briefly explain the phonological processes involved in sociolinguistic variation. This is needed, as we have argued above, for students to develop communicative competence. In other words, such knowledge will improve students' comprehension of native speech in both formal and informal contexts. The second recommendation is that the texts include more systematic reference to earlier forms of the Spanish language. Naturally, this must be done in less detail in first-year introductory Spanish texts than would be the case, say, at the third year. These limitations notwithstanding, we believe that *Impresiones*, *Plazas* and *Puntos de partida* all acknowledge the importance of variation in Spanish today.

Chapter 7

Putting it All Together: Linguistics and Variation in the Spanish Language

7.1 Introduction

In this book, we have presented Spanish as a pluricentric language. This means that variation is not only tolerated in the Spanish language, but also recognized and almost universally accepted. We have emphasized the importance of Spanish, both to the world at large and to the United States. With some 28 million speakers in the United States currently, the significance of Spanish as a world language cannot be understated. Businesses in the United States have risen to the challenge, typically giving clients the choice of completing their transactions in either English or Spanish.

The wide dissemination of Spanish in the United States affects our educational system in many ways. As mentioned in Chapter 1, at least 5.5 million students currently in our schools are not native speakers of English. Of these, more than 80% consider Spanish to be their L1. At the university level, the impact of Spanish cannot be overemphasized. The latest MLA enrollment report found that 52.2% of students had enrolled in Spanish, many of them heritage speakers.

This high enrollment in Spanish presents both opportunities and challenges. Opportunities, because in this era of budget difficulties, reaping the income from high student enrollment is of extreme importance. However, the number of students who seek to learn Spanish also creates challenges. For example, it is not always easy to staff the multitude of Spanish sections required to meet student enrollment. Oftentimes, as there are so many instructors, it is not always possible to give them linguistic training. Such information is especially important, in our view, for L2 teachers of Spanish, given its pluricentrism and broad sociolinguistic variation to which students will be exposed.

7.2 Towards a Standard of Spanish

In this book, we have consistently adopted a descriptive view of language, which presents language as it exists, not as it should be in some idealized notion. We have done this so as not to pass a value judgment on varieties of Spanish considered by prescriptivists to be substandard. In the view espoused in this book, it does a disservice to our students to fail to recognize the existence of other varieties of Spanish, especially since they will come into contact with many dialects and sociolects of Spanish outside of the classroom. In the case of heritage speakers, this is of particular importance. If the instructor brands their Spanish as substandard, it can affect their view of Spanish and even of themselves and their family members.

[handwritten margin notes: did place some judgement]

We have also recognized the importance of teaching students a standard variety of Spanish, which we have labeled 'academic.' In short, we have acknowledged variety while understanding that at university settings students are taught to be hyperliterate. Therefore, academic Spanish will continue to be taught in the classroom. We believe that teaching standard Spanish while acknowledging the variation that exists in the language is not only possible, it is essential.

7.3 Dialects of Spanish

Throughout this book, we have emphasized a descriptive view of dialects, which we defined as regional variation, a neutral term. We believe that we must stress the fact that dialects vary from one another in systematic ways. By looking at dialectal variation through a linguistic lens, students can come to appreciate the rich diversity of Spanish. To view dialects as merely a different set of phonological, morphological or lexical characteristics frees both instructors and students from prescriptivism. We must acknowledge dialectal variation, in our classrooms and in our daily lives, if we are to take into account the reality of Spanish as it is spoken today. The challenge is to raise linguistic awareness in our students without overwhelming them. The solution is to gradually present students with characteristics of other dialects throughout their years of Spanish instruction (Cook, 2001: 87).

In our discussion, we have incorporated the most basic tenets of linguistics. We have argued in every chapter that these aspects of linguistics are necessary for students and instructors of Spanish. For example, in order to teach or learn the sound system of Spanish, one must have a grounding in Spanish phonology, including articulatory phonetics. To understand L2 morphological acquisition, we must understand the concept of morpheme. Finally, in order to appreciate the variation in Spanish vocabulary, we must first understand the lexicon.

7.4 Variation in Spanish Phonology

How is variation manifested in phonology? We considered this question in Chapter 2, after giving students a grounding in the IPA, articulatory phonetics and basic phonology. Following Arteaga (2000), we argued that phonetics is important for L2 learners for many reasons, including the fact that L2 learners care about pronunciation, the importance of pronunciation for bilateral communication, and its effect on impaired short-term memory in the L2. We noted that regional variation includes several phonological processes. We discussed several of these in Chapter 2, including the following from the *tierras altas*: *distinción/seseo* (1), *consonantism* (2) and *debilitamiento vocálico* (3). We also presented the following from the *tierras bajas*: žeísmo (4), and the aspiration or deletion of syllable-final consonants (5):

(1) *zapato* 'shoe' [θa pá to] or [sa pá to]
     circo 'circus' [θír ko] or [sír ko]
(2) *verdad* 'truth' [ber ðáθ]
(3) *los muchachos* 'the boys' [lᵒs mu čá čᵒs]
(4) *llorar* 'to cry' [ʒo rár]
(5) *los niños* 'the children' [loh ní ɲoh] or [lo ní ɲo]

For students in the United States, we have advocated actively teaching them to produce a basic pronunciation from the *tierras altas*, while gradually teaching them to understand speech from other regional varieties. A common-sense approach is needed here, however, because if classes are taught in Spain, Castilian pronunciation would generally be appropriate.

In Chapter 2, we explained some of the processes seen in rapid speech, including syneresis and synalephy. We emphasized that our students should be taught to understand natural speech. We then turned to register variation, which is also seen in phonology. For example, consider the following, which illustrate the processes of metathesis and syneresis:

(6) *probe* [pró βe] 'poor' (cf. standard [pó βre])
(7) *teatro* [tjá tro] 'theater' (cf. standard [te átro])

In contrast to the natural processes in rapid speech, we do not propose actively presenting register differences in Spanish phonology, because these are not always neutrally received by the listener. Instead, we did not recommend that these processes be taught actively at beginning levels. In beginning language courses, the goal is for students to understand informal speech, without necessarily producing it. We instead argued that production of informal speech be left for more advanced courses or even linguistic courses at the upper-division levels.

Finally, in Chapter 2, we presented an overview of L2 acquisition of phonology. It is important for instructors to realize that most students who begin their study of Spanish after puberty will not achieve native-like pronunciation. Rather, the goal, in our view, should be intelligibility. As Bongaerts (1999) notes in his studies, the only way for students to reach native-like pronunciation with an age of acquisition beyond puberty were those who had explicit phonetics training. Yet even so, most L2 students will never reach ultimate attainment with respect to phonology.

7.5 Morphosyntactic Variation in Spanish

In Chapter 3, we turned our attention to morphosyntax. We began our discussion with a general overview of the topic to provide readers with the necessary grounding to follow our discussion regarding morphosyntactic variation in Spanish. While variation in this area of the grammar is less common among dialects (and less generally accepted from a sociolinguistic point of view), we nonetheless emphasized areas where variation may be found. One way in which dialects vary in morphosyntax is with gender variation, as in the following:

(8)   *la/el moto* 'the motorcycle'
(9)   *la/el problema* 'the problem'

The reason for the variation in examples such as (8) and (9), we have argued, is the disconnect between the grammatical gender and the form. This is because masculine nouns in Spanish typically end in *o*, whereas feminine nouns often end in *a*. We further noted that in Latin America, as opposed to Spain, there are many innovative forms regarding professions not associated with women in the past, as in (10):

(10)   *el médico/la médica* 'the doctor (m.)/the doctor (f.)'

Such forms have had broad acceptance in Latin America for decades.

We then turned our discussion to diminutives, which also show dialectal variation. We noted that the following forms are typically found: *ito*, *ico*, *illo*, *ino*, *ejo*, *zuelo*, and *uca*. Some of these diminutive endings and their affective meaning are illustrated in (11)–(13):

(11)   *niñito* 'little boy'
(12)   *casica* 'little house'
(13)   *actorzuelo* 'poor actor'

With respect to verb conjugations, fewer variants are found across Spanish dialects. However, forms like *dijistes* are not uncommon. Another way in which dialects vary systematically in this regard is whether or not the verb is singular or plural in examples like the following:

(14)   *Había/n muchas personas en la calle.* 'There were many people in the street.'

The difference in plurality in constructions like (14) appears to stem from native speaker analysis of the phrase. If the subject is considered to be an impersonal 'one', the singular is used, and the subject is unexpressed in Spanish. This is to be expected, as it is a null-subject language and is the form typically found in Peninsular Spanish. On the other hand, if *personas* is considered to be the subject, the verb is necessarily plural, and this is the interpretation found in many Latin American dialects.

To continue our summary of Chapter 3, we noted that another way in which dialects vary is in terms of verb tense. For recent events, Spain prefers the present perfect (15), whereas Latin America uses the preterit extensively (16):

(15)   *He comprado el libro.* 'I have bought the book.'
(16)   *Compré el libro.* 'I bought the book.'

This is in notable contrast to the general Latin American preference for periphrastic expressions, such as the future; in other words, speakers from this region show a preference for (17) over (18):

(17)   *Voy a hablar.* 'I am going to speak.'
(18)   *Hablaré.* 'I will speak.'

One significant way in which dialects vary throughout the Spanish-speaking world is in terms of address. Indeed, Peninsular Spanish uses *vosotros* for the plural of *tú*, a form that never took root in Latin America:

(19)   *(Vosotros) habláis inglés.* 'You (informal, plural) speak English.'

In Latin America, *ustedes* does double duty, as the only plural form of both *tú* and *usted* (20)–(21):

(20)   *(Tú) llegas tarde.* 'You (informal, singular) arrive late.'
(21)   *(Ustedes) llegan tarde.* 'You (formal/informal, plural) arrive late.'

Chapter 3 presents a detailed overview of forms of address, including their sociolinguistic nuances and history. Here again we see regional variation concerning forms of address whether or not dialects use *vos* instead of, or in addition to, *tú*. In other words, is (22) (whatever the verbal ending, which varies across dialects) typically used?

(22)   (Vos) hablás mucho. 'You (informal, singular) talk a lot.'

Voseo is found exclusively (and extensively) in Latin America as opposed to Spain. Dialects also vary a great deal with respect to the third person object pronouns, most likely because of their ambiguity. In other words, the *uso etimológico* of the pronouns in question reflects either case at the expense of gender (e.g. *le*) or gender at the expense of case (*lo*). It is not surprising, therefore, for dialects to have chosen one form over another. The various possibilities are illustrated in (23)–(25):

(23)   *Le veo.* 'I see him.'
(24)   *La/lo veo.* 'I see her/him/it.'
(25)   *Le hablé.* 'I talked to him.'

Other variants, such as *loísmo* (26) and *laísmo* (27), found in some dialects of Peninsular Spanish, were presented. It was pointed out, however, that these forms are not widely accepted and should therefore not be adopted:

(26)   *Lo regalé un libro.* 'I gave him a book.'
(27)   *La dije la verdad.* 'I told her the truth.'

In (26) and (27) above, the corresponding academic form of the third person pronoun would be *le*. One reason that we gave in Chapter 3 for the regional variation of object pronouns in Spanish is the existence of 'personal *a*.' This particle marks an animate direct object, as in *Quiero a mi hija*. 'I love (to) my daughter' (literally 'I love to my daughter'). We have argued that this free morpheme has been misinterpreted, by native speakers, as the dative *a*, *Le hablo a mi hija* 'I speak to my daughter.'

Dialects of Spanish vary little with respect to syntax. Yet, as mentioned in Chapter 3, regional syntactic differences do exist. For example, conditional sentences using the imperfect or pluperfect subjunctive (instead of the conditional or conditional perfect) are also common, particularly in Latin America (28):

(28)   *Si me hicieras este favor, estuviera muy agradecido.* 'If you did me this favor, I would be very thankful.'

In (28), speakers of Peninsular Spanish generally prefer the conditional (e.g. *estaría* 'I would' in the prótasis).

We also discussed, under the rubric of syntax, *dequeísmo and queísmo*, such as in (29) and (30) below:

(29)   *Creo **de** que van a llegar pronto.* 'I believe that they are going to arrive soon.'
(30)   *Estamos seguros **que** todo va a salir bien.* 'We are sure that everything is going to turn out well.'

In (29), *de* is unnecessary in academic Spanish, while it should be expressed in (30).

As a final example of syntactic variation discussed in Chapter 3, we present again below question formation in Caribbean Spanish, which takes the following form:

(31)   *¿Qué tú quieres?* 'What do you want?'

Such utterances stand in contrast to the syntax of most other dialects (32):

(32)   *¿Qué quieres (tú)?* 'What do you want?'

With regard to register variation in morphosyntax, we noted that this can be a difficult issue for instructors. In our university-level classes, our goal is typically to teach academic Spanish. Therefore we most likely should not accept analogical formations, such as *freído* for *frito*. One challenge that we face is that in the Spanish spoken by many heritage speakers, such forms are prevalent. Our goal should be to correct these forms in the students' formal oral and written production, without being judgmental. This can be accomplished by explaining the logic behind such analogical forms (perhaps using forms like *he gone* in English as a starting point), while stressing that academic forms will be required (as recommended by Hidalgo, 1990).

We ended our discussion in Chapter 3 with an overview of L2 acquisition of morphology. We noted that current debate revolves around the issue of whether it is indeed possible for L2 learners to successfully acquire L2 morphology. L1 learners invariably acquire the morphology of their language, often by a very young age. Among the researchers who hold the view that L2 acquisition of morphology is necessarily imperfect, Hawkins (1997, 2001, 2004) is undoubtedly the most influential. However, other schools of thought, including Flynn (1986) and Lardiere (2000), take the opposite view, noting that advanced L2 speakers often master L2 morphology, with few mistakes overall.

It was noted that Trahey and White (1993), among other scholars, argue for the necessity of input flooding, if students are to successfully acquire L2 morphology. Finally, the most effective means of correction was also presented. Lyster and Ranta (1995) show that metalinguistic explanations are ineffective, as are recasts. They therefore recommend negotiation.

7.6 Variation in the Lexicon in Spanish

Chapter 4 addressed the lexicon of Spanish, again adopting a highly descriptive approach. We began the chapter with a discussion of regional lexical variation, which is quite extensive. One reason for this variation is the fact that Latin American Spanish evinces forms that stem from the indigenous languages of the area, as in (33):

(33)   *guajolote* (Aztec) vs. *chompipe* (Quechua) vs. *pavo* (neutral) 'turkey.'

Languages in contact are another source of lexical variation. In Spain, the language in question may be Basque, as in (34):

(34)   *lehendakari* vs. *presidente* 'president'

In the dialect of Spanish spoken in the Southwest, we may hear terms like (35), which are borrowed from English:

(35)   *bluyines* vs. *pantalón de mezclilla* vs. *vaqueros* 'blue jeans'

Another source of lexical variation is words stemming from Portuguese (36):

(36)   *facón* (Colombian Spanish) vs. *cuchillo grande* 'big knife'

French has given many words to Spanish, as it was a language of extreme influence in the past (37):

(37)   *adición* (Rioplatense Spanish) vs. *cuenta* 'bill'

Finally, Italian has greatly influenced the lexicon of Argentinean Spanish, given the immigration patterns in that country. An example of this influence can be seen in (38):

(38)   *Chao* (from *ciao*) vs. *adiós* 'bye'

Another systematic difference between the Spanish of Latin America vs. Peninsular Spanish is the use of archaisms. Indeed, Latin American Spanish (39) uses many forms that ceased to be used in Spain decades or centuries ago, and are, therefore, synchronic archaisms in Peninsular Spanish (40):

(39)   Latin American: *lindo* 'pretty'
(40)   Spain: *bonito* 'pretty'

The sources of other lexical variation in Spanish, while quite extensive, are not so easy to pigeonhole. However, it is a reality that must be accepted.

In Chapter 4 we presented a table contrasting several dialects of Spanish. One example of variation for a simple word like *jacket* is illustrated in (41):

(41)   Spain: *cazadora* Argentina: *campera* Mexico: *chamarra* El Salvador: *chumpa*

We proposed that instructors actively teach a neutral dialect of Spanish, by which we mean dialectal terms that have the greatest currency in the Spanish-speaking world. We returned to this notion in Chapter 6.We stressed the need for effective dictionary use, as dictionaries can be a valuable resource for both dialectal and register variation (Gu & Johnson, 1996; Hulstijn, 1996; Underhill, 1980), although not all scholars agree (Paribakht & Wesche, 1999).

In Chapter 4, we also addressed the notion of register variation in the Spanish lexicon, in such words as *panza* vs. *estómago*. We noted that often-times, in informal speech, idiomatic expressions like the following are found:

(42)   *Me vale un cacahuate* vs. *Me importa muy poco.* 'It's not at all important to me.'

We further discussed the use of euphemisms to describe taboo or topics that are generally avoided, like sexual relations or death (e.g. *fallecer* 'to pass away' for *morir* 'to die'). We have argued that students must be taught to understand register variation, as least for passive recognition, in the lexicon of Spanish. This is necessary because they will most likely come into contact with the informal register given their young ages and its wide diffusion among US Hispanics.

7.7   Diachronic Linguistics and Variation in the Spanish Language

We began Chapter 5 by linking to varying pedagogical trends the importance (or lack thereof) of diachronic linguistics in the curriculum of Spanish language programs. Within the Grammar-Translation method, widely used until WWII, historical information about language was considered *de rigeur* (Bronk, 1921). During World War II, however, emphasis was placed only on using a language, particularly in combat situations. The kind of academic knowledge previously taught was not positively regarded (Kurz, 1938). In the 1950s, there was a return to a general acceptance of linguistics, including historical information, given the influence of linguistics in general during that period (Giduz, 1952).

In the 1960s, the Audio-lingual approach was quite common, due in part to the availability of new technologies, such as language laboratories. This method, unlike the Grammar-Translation method of the pre-WWII era, placed an emphasis on listening and speaking. It routinely used pattern drills, typical of a behavioral approach to language learning (cf. Skinner, 1957). There was no place for historical information in such a method.

Linguistics as a field continued to have greater currency over the next several decades. Therefore, in the 1970s many scholars began to propose that students take a general linguistics class as preparation for their study of an L2. This did not mean, however, that they recommended that historical information be integrated into language classes. Indeed, as we note in Chapter 5, since the 1960s, diachronic information has been considered to be an archaism in the curriculum of the Spanish language (MacAllister, 1964). A few scholars (e.g. Rini, 1990; Arteaga & Herschensohn, 1995) have nonetheless recently argued for its importance if students are to appreciate synchronic variation.

In virtually all cases today, courses on the History of Spanish are relegated to the MA or PhD level, where they are invariably an option rather than a requirement. In Chapter 5, we argued against this trend, because there are many facts about Spanish that cannot be explained, in any real sense, without reference to diachronic information. Specifically, we proposed that if a linguistics course is required at the undergraduate level, it should take the form of a History of Spanish language course that emphasizes the evolution of the language (rather than a philology course).

As an example of the importance of diachronic information, we argued in Chapter 5 that many regional phonological variants, such as *distinción*, have their roots in historical change, which did not happen in Latin America (or vice versa, as in the case of *žeísmo*). Even the pronunciation of entire dialect regions, such as the *tierras altas*, can be attributed to the fact that Lima and Mexico City were the locations of the *virreinatos* of Spain. *Voseo* has a historical evolution as well, in that it originally stemmed directly from Latin.

Latin did not distinguish formal vs. informal. This system arose during the Golden Age in Spain, and eventually *vos* ceased to be used in Spain. Its spread in Latin America is because it was used as a pejorative term for the indigenous peoples of Latin America, long after it ceased to be used in Spain. Linking synchronic variation to earlier stages of the language gives students a global view of their own Spanish or that spoken by others. For example, the fact that forms such as *haiga* and *dijistes* existed in Old Spanish can legitimize them as informal forms in the minds of both instructors and students.

Similarly, the explanation for the forms *se lo* 'it to him/her/you' (as opposed, for example, to the 'expected' form **le lo*) is historical. Although its development is complex, it may very well lead at least advanced students (or instructors) to appreciate that most synchronic variation is not arbitrary. Stem changing verbs, similarly, can be linked to sound change in the Spanish language. Where the stem vowel is stressed, diphthongization occurred (43). Conversely, where the vowel is unstressed, it remained unchanged (44):

(43)   *quiero* 'I want' [kjé ro].
(44)   *queremos* 'We want' [ke ré mos].

We noted that the dialectal variation with respect to the gender of nouns beginning with a stressed *a* similarly has a historical explanation. Indeed, in Old Spanish, there were two forms of the definite feminine article, *la* and *el*, the latter used as it is today. Since the article *el* is homophonous with the masculine article *el*, it is unsurprising from a linguistic point of view that some dialects have reanalyzed these stressed nouns as masculine.

Another example given in Chapter 5 concerned the historical facts behind the formation of an adverb. We attach *mente* to the feminine form of an adjective, today, as this noun was feminine in Latin. We also noted that the neuter (45) is inherited directly from Latin:

(45)   *Sí, yo también lo creo.* 'Yes, I also think so.'

We have emphasized repeatedly that the greatest dialectal difference between Latin American Spanish and Peninsular Spanish is lexical. One factor that contributes to this variation is that many terms widely used in Latin America are archaisms. This means that they were used in an earlier form of the language in Peninsular Spanish, but have ceased to be used in that dialect.

Arteaga and Llorente (2003), following Arteaga and Herschensohn (1995), stress the fact that by integrating historical explanations where relevant, students can come to appreciate the fact that much synchronic variation stems directly from Old Spanish (and oftentimes, from spoken Latin). This gives them an understanding that language is 'organic and constantly evolving' (Arteaga & Herschensohn, 1995: 219).

7.8   Variation in Spanish and the Spanish L2 Classroom

Chapter 6 is directed toward current and future Spanish instructors. Our goal was twofold: first, to provide instructors with concrete tips for integrating variation in the Spanish language classroom, and second, to evaluate three popular first-year texts widely used in the United States,

Impresiones, Plazas and *Puntos de partida*. We chose these three texts as they generally integrate well the notion of variation.

Currently, most classrooms seek to integrate a communicative, eclectic approach, in which grammar presentations are interspersed with communicative activities that develop speaking and listening skills. It can be overwhelming, however, to meet the goals of helping students acquire proficiency in speaking, listening, reading and writing skills, while addressing variation and historical information. With an understanding of L2 acquisition, also presented in this book, instructors are better armed with techniques to address the complexity of language as it exists.

We began the chapter by stressing the importance of dialectal and register variation in the L2 classroom. With respect to regional variation, we advocated a broad, macrodialectal approach so as not to overwhelm the student. We recommended that instructors begin by using exercises in English. We provided a sample exercise that included utterances like the following:

(46)   *Have you parked the car?* [hǽv ju pákt ðə ká]

We noted that addressing register variation in the L2 classroom is a more complex issue, because informal speech can sometimes be highly inappropriate. This is the case when addressing highly educated speakers or in an academic setting. Again, we proposed the use of exercises in English, like the one we presented, in which register variation is highly marked (e.g. *Dude* vs. *Dr. Martínez*).

In Chapter 6, we also addressed the integration of linguistics in general in the Spanish L2 classroom. We noted that within methodological approaches throughout the years, greater (in the case of the Audio-lingual approach) or lesser (in the case of the Academic/Translation approach) importance has been accorded to pronunciation. We followed Arteaga (2000) by arguing against this trend. Assuming our focus on variation, we noted that students cannot come to appreciate dialectal variation in Spanish phonology without a background in Spanish phonology in general.

In our discussion, we followed Flege (1995) and Rochet (1995), among many others, in assuming that perception of differences in speech sounds necessarily precedes production. We gave sample exercises for the former, such as (47)–(48), which illustrate the stop-fricative alternation common in Spanish:

(47)   *dar* [dár] 'give'
(48)   *lado* [lá ðo] 'side'

Once students can perceive the differences in sounds, we argue, they can proceed to production exercises. We agreed with Terrell (1989), who recommends that exercises be meaningful to the student. At more advanced levels, proverbs can be integrated (Teschner, 2000). The ultimate goal, however, will be for students to generally master the phonology of Spanish even in free conversation (Barrutia & Schwegler, 1994). We also emphasize the need for the recycling of sounds, as it is not reasonable to expect students to correctly produce [8], for example, upon a single exposure.

We noted that instructors may not welcome additional material, given the typically packed syllabus of Spanish language courses. However, ten to fifteen minutes twice or thrice a week can make an enormous difference in students' pronunciation. For heritage speakers, explicit phonological instruction can help them not only to expand their bilingual range (Valdés, 2000), but also to master the orthography of Spanish and improve their ability to read aloud (Nash, 1973).

With respect to which dialect of pronunciation we should emphasize in our classrooms, we recommended teaching the phonology of the *tierras altas*. However, in our view, students should be taught to understand speakers of other dialects frequently encountered. One way to do this is to present them with basic phonological characteristics of other dialects, which include the aspiration of syllable-final consonants, *distinción*, and *lleísmo*. Regarding register variation as manifested in phonology, we proposed presenting the phonological process characteristic of rapid speech in Spanish (e.g. synalephy as in *lo obtuvo* [loβ tú βo] or [lop tú βo]), while eschewing processes that may be negatively received by the listener (e.g., metathesis as in *probe* [pró βe] for [pó βre]).

Following our recommendations regarding phonology and its manifestations in the Spanish-speaking world, we turned to morphosyntactic variation in the L2 classroom. We noted that according to Van Patten, as discussed in more detail in Chapter 3, we must teach morphosyntactic forms without semantic clues, which is not often done in L2 classrooms. In such an approach, for example, only the *que* clause would be pronounced (49). Alternatively, the main clause would have a verb, such as *creer* 'to think,' which can take either the indicative or the subjunctive (50):

(49) *(Creo) que **vienes** mañana.* '(I think) that you are coming tomorrow.'
(50) *(No creo) que **vengas** mañana.* '(I don't think) that you are coming tomorrow.'

We advocated teaching the characteristics of the dominant dialect in the area, so, for example, *vosotros* would be actively taught in Spain, but not in Latin America. *Voseo* should be addressed in Latin America, given its frequency. We recommended against teaching (or accepting) variants such as *ponido* (standard 'puesto'). In our opinion, a common-sense approach is needed when addressing topics such as third person pronouns. The *uso etimológico* should be taught in an academic setting, although *leísmo*, accepted even by prescriptivists for animate nouns, should not be considered an error.

We noted that the lexical variety found in Spanish is quite extensive. Instructors themselves speak different dialects, and often Anglicisms are used widely among Spanish speakers in the United States. We recommended against adopting a 'cafeteria' approach, by which we mean a seemingly arbitrary mixing of words of different dialects. We proposed the active instruction of a neutral vocabulary, by which we mean a vocabulary understood across dialects. Regional lexical variants should then be presented for passive knowledge. However, even if students use vocabulary that has little currency in the Spanish-speaking world, such lexical choices should not be considered to be errors, in our view.

Instead, our solution was to provide students with a more neutral term to facilitate communication across dialects, while recognizing that the word in question may be the most commonly used in the dialect of Spanish that they speak. Finally, we presented arguments for explicitly teaching students to effectively use a dictionary as a tool for lexical acquisition. As we noted, dictionaries also contain a great deal of information regarding variation (dialectal, sociolinguistic), which can be tapped by students provided that they have been instructed how to consult them.

We ended Chapter 6 by considering the presentation of variation in three popular first-year Spanish textbooks widely in use in the United States, *Impresiones*, *Plazas* and *Puntos de partida*. Our selection of these textbooks was not arbitrary, but represented what we considered to be the textbooks that integrate well the notions of dialectal and sociolinguistic variation. Through our review, we concluded that these three textbooks have differing strengths and weaknesses.

Of the three textbooks under consideration in Chapter 6, we decided that the best in presenting the regional variation found in Spanish today was without doubt *Impresiones*. In its *Enfoque cultural* sections, dialectal information, including morphosyntactic information, is clearly presented. One major difference between this text and the other two considered is that students actively manipulate the forms presented in exercises. For example, where question formation in Caribbean Spanish is introduced (tied directly to the countries discussed in the chapter), students are directed to form questions in this way.

One weakness of *Impresiones*, as in the other two textbooks, is its lexical presentation. *Impresiones* does not so much present a 'cafeteria' approach as a 'smorgasbord' approach. In other words, a variety of terms for a vocabulary item, such as *marrón* and *café*, are given as alternates in short notes to the student and also in the vocabulary presented during the chapter. Yet mention is not always made of where the terms are used.

Plazas also presents dialectal variation systematically in the sections for the student entitled *¿Nos entendemos?* and *Notas culturales*. However, phonological dialectal variation is not addressed in the text. With respect to the lexicon, *Plazas* strives to present a neutral dialect, but is not always successful. For example, it presents for active knowledge the Peninsular word *vaqueros* while also teaching Latin American *aretes*.

Plazas does provide an extensive overview of *voseo*, including verbal endings, in its *Comentario cultural*. Other sociolinguistic topics, including how to soften commands, are also included in these sections, as is the use of diminutives. Indeed, of the three textbooks, *Plazas* provides the most sociolinguistic information. The information in *Plazas* is directed exclusively to the student. In our view, this material should be supplemented by more extensive information in the instructor's edition. Finally, *Plazas* does not present any activities for students to actively use regional or sociolinguistic variants, nor does it present diachronic information.

Puntos de partida includes most of its dialectal variation in notes to the instructor, who is free to introduce them to students as he or she deems fit. Register variation is also addressed only in the instructor's notes. These notes are excellent, but do presuppose at least basic training in linguistics. Only lexical differences are emphasized in the student text, in sections entitled *Así se dice*. Pronunciation is only addressed in Chapters 1–3, with regional phonological variation only discussed in the presentation of the alphabet. With respect to the vocabulary taught, *Puntos de partida* unfortunately adopts the 'cafeteria approach,' which we have recommended against. For example, while Latin American terms are generally used (e.g. *computación*), Peninsular terms are also presented actively (e.g. *bolígrafo*).

Morphological variation is barely discussed in *Puntos de partida*, even in the instructor's edition. One exception is *vosotros*, which is actively taught in this text, despite the fact that its intended audience is students in the United States. However, at the instructor's discretion, this form could be presented only for passive academic knowledge. Little sociolinguistic or diachronic information (almost none) is presented to the instructor, although this could be added to the text in footnotes, as well as to the instructor's manual. Like *Plazas*, one shortcoming of this text is that it provides no exercises for students in which they can actively use forms representing regional variation.

However, one valuable characteristic of *Puntos de partida*, lacking in both *Impresiones* and *Plazas*, is its repeated reference to the Spanish spoken by heritage speakers. This is the book's greatest strength, in our view. For example, *Puntos de partida* gives the form often used by this group of Spanish speakers, *siéntensen* for *siéntense*, although it does not explain the logic behind it (i.e. that native speakers want to add an *n* to make the verb 'sound' plural).

In summary, the three textbooks under consideration have different strong points. *Impresiones* excels in its presentation of dialectal character-istics. Indeed, it is the only text that gives students exercises in which they actively manipulate regional forms. *Plazas*, on the other hand, provides the best overview of sociolinguistic variation of the three. Finally, *Puntos de partida* stands alone in addressing heritage speakers throughout the instructor's manual.

7.9 Conclusion

The central theme of this book has been the pluricentricity of Spanish today, especially that spoken in the United States. We have argued that this pluricentricity greatly impacts instructors and students (both heritage speakers and L2 learners) of Spanish. In our view, a descriptive view of the reality of regional variation is necessary for all speakers of Spanish, and must be integrated into Spanish classes from the earliest levels. Moreover, register variation plays an important role in Spanish, perhaps even more so than in other languages. This is because of the wide variety of contexts in which Spanish is spoken in the United States. Most impor-tantly, throughout our book, we have also repeatedly emphasized that while this regional and sociolinguistic variety complicates the teaching and learning of Spanish, it also adds greatly to the richness of the Spanish language today.

Notes

1. This number excludes Latin and Ancient Greek, which drew roughly 55,000 combined (Furman *et al.*, 2007: 11).
2. Terms shaded in gray are defined when first presented. The reader is directed to consult the glossary if more information is needed. The Spanish equivalent of the term in question is also given in the glossary.
3. We will alternate in this book between the terms *standard* and *academic*, with the understanding that they are largely interchangeable.
4. For a recent discussion of these topics, see Edwards (2008).
5. Not all researchers consider Spanish to be pluricentric. For example, Figueroa (2004) argues that Peninsular Spanish, Mexican Spanish and Colombian Spanish are 'high-prestige' dialects, whereas the Spanish spoken in Guatemala, Cuba and Peru would be of 'low' prestige.
6. By *standard* we are referring to a formal variety of language that has wide social acceptance.
7. By *dialect* we simply mean regional variation, without sociolinguistic judgment. In the view we espouse in this book, all are speakers of a dialect.
8. The percentages represented in (4) above are approximate; (4) is adapted from a similar chart from www.npr.org. See also Population Resource Center (2004).
9. See Chapter 5 for a detailed view of RAE as a historical artifact.
10. See Figueroa (2000) for a detailed discussion of native Spanish speaker (including heritage speakers) attitudes toward the RAE.
11. We do not take into account native speakers who have attended high school in a Spanish-speaking country, as they typically do not attend beginning language classes.
12. See especially Teschner (2000) for a detailed description; he uses the terms *zona bajeña, alteña* and *castellana*.
13. Regional variation in phonology is discussed in more detail in Chapter 2.
14. The symbols in parentheses are part of the International Phonetic Alphabet, which is used to represent sounds cross-linguistically. See Chapter 2 for more information. In the words in (5), [ʒ] represents the medial sound in the English word *pleasure*; [ʃ], on the other hand, is an example of the sound commonly spelled *sh* in English, as in the word *shoe*.
15. In fact, *žeísmo* is not the homogeneous phenomenon described above. There are dialects within River Plate Spanish in which *ll* is pronounced [ʒ] but *y* is pronounced [j]. See Canfield (1981) for discussion.
16. The symbol [j] is similar, although not identical, to the sound *y* in English, as in the word *yes*.
17. The symbol [ʎ] is roughly equivalent to the medial sound in the English word *million*.

18. The symbol [θ] corresponds roughly to the initial sound in the English word *think*.

19. The abbreviations that we use in this text are the following: *you-pl-inf* or you plural informal; and *you-pl-form* or 'you plural formal.'

20. (7) 'Do you (singular, formal) speak Spanish?' (8) 'Do you (plural, formal) speak Spanish?'

21. In the dialect of Spanish under discussion here, *os* is used as a direct or indirect object pronoun; *vosotros* is used as the object of a preposition; examples are given in (12) and (13). (12a) 'I see you (plural, informal)' (12b) 'I see you/ them (plural, formal/informal)' (13a) 'The dog is afraid of you (plural, informal)' (13b) 'The dog is afraid of you (plural, formal)'; (14a) 'Do you have your (informal, plural) book?' (14b) 'Do you have your (formal/informal) book?' 'Do you have his/her/their book?'

22. There is in fact another pronoun used in two-thirds of Latin America, namely *vos* (=*tú*). A complete discussion of all forms of address in Spanish is found in Chapter 3.

23. *What do you want?* (13a) literally, 'What you want?' It would, moreover, be typical in this dialectal region to pronounce the final *s* either as *h* or as a mute sound.

24. The expression of *vos*, however, discussed in Chapter 3, Section 3.6.1, seems to be obligatory in those dialects that have *voseo*.

25. Interestingly, this view was equally held by Spanish speakers educated abroad and US Spanish speakers.

26. The example in (19b) is not from Fromkin *et al.* (2007), but is rather our example.

27. 'People promise many things they do not do.'

28. See Pinto (2002) for a discussion on English vs. Spanish pragmatic norms as well as interlanguage difficulty in acquiring pragmatic strategies.

29. (22) 'Here is a size 8 for you to try.' (23) 'No, to be made to order.'

30. 'I don't agree that you should have arrived late.'

31. See Chapter 2 for a detailed discussion on the symbols of the International Phonetic Alphabet.

32. The symbol [β] refers to the fricative /b/, as in *haba*. In the articulation of this sound, the lips are very close to one another but do not touch.

33. (25a) 'stomach'; (25b) 'belly.'

34. Sánchez-Muñoz (2007) argues that while heritage speakers do not have a great range of registers, they do, indeed, show some register variation, so that they are not completely monostylistic.

35. (28a) 'Have you seen conflicts between Blacks and Hispanics?' (28b) 'Yes, like, "Oh, don't talk to them."' (28c) "She told me that she asked, she asked something and they were like 'what are you talking about?'"

36. For a detailed discussion of Spanish phonetics and phonology, including regional and social variants, the reader is referred to Barrutia and Schwegler (1994), Dalbor (1996) and Teschner (2000).

37. Our discussion of the inadequacies of orthography in favor of the IPA mirrors almost completely that given by Fromkin *et al.* (2007, but also all previous editions) regarding the IPA and English orthography.

38. In some dialects, particularly the *tierras bajas*, the group [ks] reduces to [s].

39. The spelling *ll* varies cross-dialectally; it can represent [j], [ʎ] or [ʒ]. See Section 2.4 for discussion.

40. The major difference between Spanish [d] and English [d] is that the former is dental, meaning that the tip of the tongue touches the back of the upper teeth, whereas the latter is alveolar, a sound in which the speaker places the very front of the tongue against the ridge behind the upper teeth, the alveolar ridge.

41. Another advantage of the IPA is that it allows speakers of various languages to pronounce a word in a language they do not speak.

42. In keeping with Arteaga's (2000) suggestion that phonetics should be taught with words known to students at a given level, we are using very simple words to illustrate sounds. With regard to the transcription of Spanish vowels, our presentation is an oversimplification, as other vowels are articulated in Spanish, such as [ɛ], equivalent to the *e* in the English word *bed*. However, we believe that such a narrow transcription is unnecessary for our purposes of a first presentation of the IPA in Spanish.

43. The strong vowels in Spanish are [a], [e] and [o].

44. The representation of Spanish diphthongs is highly controversial. For example, Teschner (2000) distinguishes between rising (glide + vowel) and falling (vowel + glide) diphthongs, whereas Dalbor (1996) does not. Here we follow Whitley (2002) in transcribing both rising and falling diphthongs with the same symbols, for simplicity's sake. We do not believe that such a topic should be broached outside of a Spanish Phonetics/Phonology class.

45. By absolute initial position, we refer here to the first sound in a spoken stream. So, for example, the 'b' in the command *¡Baje!* ('Come down!') is in absolute initial position, whereas it is intervocalic (between vowels) in the following sequence *¡No baje!* ('Don't come down!').

46. In most dialects of Spanish with the exception of parts of Columbia (cf. Cotton & Sharp, 1988), there is no corresponding voiced labiodental fricative, in other words [v], despite the fact that the word in question may be spelled with a v, such as *Victor* [bík tor].

47. Some of the information illustrated in (19)–(21) may not be necessary for a beginning Spanish language class, as discussed below in Chapter 6 and in Arteaga (2000). However, Spanish instructors and advanced students should be aware of these details in Spanish, normally transcribed in a narrow (vs. broad) transcription.

48. There is some dialectal variation with respect to syllabification. Unlike other dialects of Spanish, the dialects of the central plains of Mexico do not divide the sequence *tl*, as in *atlas* [át las] 'atlas,' pronouncing instead [á tlas] which has been attributed to the Náhuatl influence in that area.

49. See Section 2.7 below for a discussion of syneresis across word boundaries in informal speech.

50. The symbol * refers to, in linguistics, a sequence of sounds/morphosyntax/ words that are not uttered by a native speaker of a given language, regardless of the formality of speech.

51. Our discussion of rhythm follows very closely the presentation by Barrutia and Schwegler (1994).

52. The schwa [ə] is equivalent to the *a* in the word *sofa*.

53. Our discussion of Spanish stress mirrors that of Barrutia and Schwegler (1994).

54. Here we follow Teschner (2000: 122–127) in his discussion of Spanish intonation.

55. The numbers 1, 2 and 3 refer to low, medium and high pitch, respectively.
56. In Spanish, the order is *manner of articulation, place of articulation, voicing*, as in *una fricative bilabial sonora*, 'a voiced bilabial fricative.'
57. In some dialects of Spanish, [s] can be dental; see Dalbor (1981), Cotton and Sharp (1988) and Barrutia and Schwegler (1994).
58. In Spanish the word order in the articulatory description of consonants is different, namely manner of articulation + point of articulation + voicing (e.g. *una fricativa bilabial sonora* 'a voiced bilabial fricative').
59. In Spanish, the order of the parameters is different (vowel + height of vowel + position of tongue + rounding of lips), so that [i], for example, is described as *una vocal alta anterior estirada* 'a high front unrounded vowel'.
60. See especially Teschner (2000) for a detailed description; he uses the *terms zona bajeña, alteña* and *castellana*.
61. This phonological process is not to be confused with the vowel reduction to schwa that characterizes many Anglophones learning Spanish; see Section 2.10 below for discussion.
62. In the dialect of Castile, the spelling 'j' is articulated with even more friction and is therefore oftentimes transcribed with a different symbol, such as [χ].
63. The aspiration of 's' also has register connotations; see Section 2.4 below for discussion.
64. The process of pronouncing a [p] before the [s] is a strengthening of the consonant. Strictly speaking, the strongest consonants are voiceless stops. Castile and the *tierras altas*, when possible, strengthen consonants.
65. Another characteristic of the Caribbean dialect, particularly that of Puerto Rico, is the velarization of initial [r̄], so that the resulting sound is articulated like the French 'r' [ʁ], as in *rico* 'rich' [ʁí ko].
66. A related process, known as rhotacism (rotacismo), is found in Andalucía. In rhotacism, syllable-final [l] is replaced by [r], so that *falda* 'skirt,' for example, is realized as *farda* [fár ða].
67. Compare [ʎó ras] of *Castile* and the Andes and [jó ras] of the rest of the *tierras altas* region, as well as the *tierras bajas*.
68. There is in fact a third possibility, namely *ceceo*, which is characteristic of parts of Southern Spain. In dialects with *ceceo*, the graphemes *s*, *ce*, *ci* and *z* are represented by a sole phoneme, [θ]. We would recommend against exposing students to this dialectal possibility because of its low prestige within Spain.
69. Synalephy is a broader term than we have indicated, as it also refers to vowel linking in general, such as between e and a in [re̯a li ðáð]. See Teschner (2000: 113–116) for discussion.
70. We do not completely agree with Hidalgo (1990), because, as we have noted, heritage speakers may show L1 English transfer, so that pronunciation should be presented in SNS courses. Moreover, as we have discussed, overt pronunciation training also facilitates the heritage speaker's acquisition of orthography. Finally, as discussed below, heritage speakers may be unaware of the pronunciation of the formal register in Spanish.
71. This is not a new idea. Stockwell and Bowen (1969) also ranked suprasegmentals first in their preferred pedagogical sequence of Spanish pronunciation.
72. He refers here to the phonetic manifestation of Spanish vowels based on Delattre (1965).

73. Recall that there are dialects of Spanish, specifically the _tierras altas_, that do pronounce 'll' as [ʎ]; however, that pronunciation corresponds to the digraph 'll' not (necessarily) to a syllable-final segment. See (76) above for discussion.

74. Cf. Dalbor (1981: 113) and Barrutia and Schwegler (1994: 109).

75. A caveat is in order, as Arteaga (1999) notes: the sample group was very small, so that the results cannot be viewed as conclusive regarding student attitudes toward pronunciation in general.

76. Although forms such as _guapa-guapita_ 'attractive' might appear to support the analysis of _it_ as a suffix rather than a circumfix, Bermúdez-Otero and Borjars (2006) provide compelling evidence that even in such cases, _it_ is a circumfix, due to the fact that suffixation cannot occur when nouns end in _e_, such as *_cochito_ for _coche_ 'small car' (correct form _cochecito_) or *cafito for café '(little) cup of coffee' (correct form _cafecito_). In his analysis, this is due to the fact that -_it_ selects for noun stems that end in –_o_ and –_a_.

77. The prefix _im_ is an _allomorph_ (different forms of the same morpheme) of the prefix _in_.

78. 'In Latin American Spanish, the innovation of creating feminine nouns and adjectives on the basis of words without gender distinction is more obvious.'

79. While this form can be ungrammatical, there are exceptions, as described below. For this reason, we have put * between parentheses.

80. See Lázaro (1999) for a detailed presentation of this topic.

81. There are also sociolinguistic aspects to diminutive use in Spanish; we return to this in Section 3.8.5 below.

82. We have used Penny (1991) as a basis of our presentation of this topic, especially as far as what values are associated with the different diminutive infixes we treat.

83. The subject in (42b) follows the verb, because it is an ergative verb; in the case of such verbs, the subject is not the agent (e.g., _doer_ of the action). In English, the verbs _arrive_, _break_, _drop_ and _move_ are ergative verbs.

84. For a detailed discussion of this topic, see Zagona (2002: 24–26), among others.

85. This non-expression of the subject pronoun is due to the fact that as mentioned above, Spanish, a null-subject language, lacks the words _it_ and _there_.

86. Also see Lope Blanch (1995) for further explanation.

87. Other verb conjugations are possible with _vos_; see the discussion below.

88. See Cotton and Sharp (1988), Carreira (2000) and McKenzie (2001) for a discussion of dialectal differences in verb forms.

89. See Akmajian _et al._ (2001: 250) for discussion.

90. This statement might not be totally true. Silva-Corvalán (1989) presents some examples where the subjects of her study hinted at nuances in meaning that one choice offered over the other (imperfect subjunctive denotes greater probability, for example).

91. An example of hypercorrection in English would be the use of _I_ instead of _me_ in the phrase _for Paul and I._

92. For a detailed presentation of the characteristics of a variety of communities, see Fontanella de Weinberg (1999).

93. This example and reference are cited in Cotton and Sharp (1988: 147).

94. The Critical Period, according to researchers such as Lenneberg (1967), refers to the inability to learn an L1 as a native language after puberty. Lenneberg attributes this to lateralization of the brain. The Critical Period Hypothesis is controversial in linguistics, as no general consensus can be currently found.
95. See Fromkin *et al.* (2007) and Bergmann *et al.* (2007) for a more detailed, introductory presentation of L1 morphological acquisition.
96. These studies are cited and explained in detail in Montrul (2004).
97. See Mueller Gathercole *et al.* (1999), who cite, and provide a detailed description of, the following studies: Hernández-Pina (1994), Jacobsen (1986), Cortés (1989), Eisenberg (1985), Fernández-Martínez (1994) and Ezeizaberrena (1997).
98. This statement is generally, but not always, true for accomplishments.
99. There are other differences between achievement verbs and the other classes. The former, but not the latter, can be used with a phrase indicating a specific point in time (cf. Vendler, 1967), like *a las tres* 'at 3:00': *Llegaste al mercado a las tres* 'You arrived at the market at three o'clock', but not, for example, **Tienes razón a las tres* 'you are right at three o'clock'.
100. A revised version of the Lexical Aspect Hypothesis is presented in Andersen (2002: 79), which incorporates the following: '(1) verb semantics, developing from achievements through accomplishments and activities to states; (2) unitary events before habitual and iterative events; (3) real events before hypothetical and counterfactual ones; (4) direct assertions before pragmatic softeners; (5) foreground before background; and (6) an essential discourse structure dimension that interacts with (1)–(5).'
101. Ayoun and Salaberry (2005) report that according to the results of their study, while the Lexical Aspect Hypothesis is generally supported, learners marked tense on stative verbs with a higher rate of accuracy than on other verb classes.
102. See Fromkin *et al.* (2007) and Bergmann *et al.* (2007) for a complete general linguistic introduction to the lexicon. In this section, we follow their general presentation.
103. That is, all of the words of the spoken and written language from all centuries, from all places, from all specialties, jobs, professions, etc.
104. Unity and lexical variety of the Spanish language.
105. Top to bottom: 'sidewalk', 'bus', 'sports coat', 'swimsuit', 'drawer', 'socks', 'coat', 'raincoat', 'glasses', 'block', 'swimming pool' and 'apartment'.
106. We will not discuss the polemical issue of whether this approach is Eurocentric or not. For a detailed account of what an *Americanism* is, see Rona (1969).
107. See Zamora Munné and Guitart (1982: 148–149) for a much more detailed list of lexical items.
108. For a full discussion of these topics, see Cotton and Sharp (1988). As is the case with most languages, there are also superstratum effects on Spanish; see below for discussion.
109. See Fontanella de Weinberg (1995: 170–175) for a detailed discussion.
110. 'chocolate,' 'tomato,' 'llama,' 'alpaca,' 'canoe,' 'hammock,' 'jaguar,' 'tapioca.'
111. 'banana palm,' 'swamp,' 'mangrove.'
112. 'a corn ear,' 'turkey,' 'a sauce.'
113. 'farm,' 'corn,' 'an inefficient or masculine woman.'
114. Zamora Munné and Guitart (1982: 150–153) and López Morales (2005: 63–85).

115. Moreno de Alba (1992: 51) has an interesting discussion of this concept. He highlights the fact that most of these terms, considered to be archaic, may be so from the Peninsular perspective, because they are terms that stopped being used in Spain a long time ago. However, they would not be archaic when the Spanish language is considered as a whole, for they are used in extensive American areas.
116. 'pretty,' 'cakes,' 'stand up,' 'dark,' 'promise.'
117. 'car/cart,' 'town square/base,' 'street,' 'tear.'
118. 'tempt/incite,' 'delay/increase the volume of a body.'
119. Granda (1976, 1978) expands on this topic.
120. For a more detailed account of this topic, including the different kinds of *fronterizo* varieties, see López Morales (2005: 163–164).
121. Such forms are often considered 'mistakes' by speakers, including instructors, of other regional varieties, because of their lack of linguistic training. We address this in detail in Chapter 6.
122. 'Let me see your little paw'/'Let me see your foot.'
123. 'That boy is crazier than a goat. That boy is very crazy.'
124. 'I don't care at all about it' (literally, 'It is as important as a peanut to me'). 'They are very poor' (literally, 'They don't have (even) a place to drop dead in'). 'They are very poor.'
125. Our presentation of the theoretical background regarding L2 lexical acquisition is necessarily brief. However, we must acknowledge the central role that the definition of 'word' occupies in this field. Citing Nation (1990) and Nation and Waring (1997), Lafford *et al.* (2003: 134) state that 'knowing a word requires an understanding of its spoken and written form, frequency, grammatical patterns and collocations, semantic, pragmatic, stylistic and register constraints, sociolinguistic aspects, and connotations as well as its associations with other related words.' In our opinion, presenting this kind of knowledge is far too ambitious at the initial stages of language acquisition, an area that we are focusing on.
126. See Cook (2001) for an in-depth discussion of this and other teaching methods.
127. See Cook (2001: 201–205) for a complete description of the Grammar-Translation method.
128. However, see Doughty and Williams (1988), who argue that students taught in the Grammar-Translation method are unable to provide the metalinguistic explanations that they have been taught.
129. See Cook (2001: 205–211) for an in-depth discussion of the Audio-lingual teaching method.
130. Source:http://www.rae.es/rae/gestores/gespub000001.nsf/voTodosporId/ CEDF300E8D943D3FC12571360037CC94?OpenDocument&i=0: The institution has always adapted its functions to the times in which it has existed. At present, according to the first article of the Statutes, the Academy has as its principal mission to ensure that the changes that 'the Spanish language is currently undergoing as it adapts to meet the needs of its speakers do not sever the essential unity of the entire Hispanic world.'
131. A detailed discussion of these macrodialectal characteristics can also be found in Chapter 2.
132. We have purposely simplified the evolution of Spanish affricates, as a detailed explanation would only be appropriate in a graduate-level seminar on the history of Spanish in our view. The phonological changes that date from this

century include the devoicing and velarization of [ʒ] (spelled *j*) to [ʃ] and then [x]. See also Lapesa (2008) and Penny (1991) for further discussion.
133. These processes are discussed in detail in Chapter 2.
134. The opposite of opaque is transparent.
135. This issue was also touched upon in Chapter 1 .
136. Here we follow Penny's (1991: 123–125) presentation of this topic, enhanced by the information provided by Bentivoglio (2002).
137. 'With *vos*, we address servants and workers and persons of a similar nature; also friends who take neither insult nor compliment from being addressed with *vos*.'
138. See Chapter 4 for an in-depth discussion of the variation, both regional and sociolinguistic, of the Spanish lexicon.
139. There are other languages that have contributed terms to Spanish, such as Arahuaq, the Caribe languages, Aymara, Chinche and Mapuche. Their lexical influence on Spanish is considered in Chapter 4.
140. Similarly, a Spanish language course is not a course in sociolinguistics, although we will argue below in Section 6.3 that some sociolinguistic information, carefully targeted to the linguistic needs of the student, is also essential in the Spanish language classroom.
141. 'What's up?' 'How are things?'
142. More complex topics of vowel linking such as diphthong formation between words (e.g., *estudió historia* [es tu ɖjójs tó rja] 'he studied history') should be left for more advanced classes.
143. See Barrutia and Schwegler (1994) for more examples.
144. Dalbor (1981, 1997) has a series of listening comprehension exercises that can serve as a model for perception exercises.
145. 'Phonetics as a strategy at the reading level to develop comprehension in an authentic form.'
146. 'The normal variation so that s/he is successful in using language in a way so as to communicate with others of Spanish-speaking origin without tainting the language the student already uses.'
147. While these exercises have been traditionally featured in some phonetics textbooks, they are rarely incorporated into Spanish textbooks for bilinguals.
148. The suggested topics here represent a minimum of relevant dialectal processes. Students should be presented with any other process that characterizes the speech of native speakers in their area (e.g. rhotacism/lamdacism, velarization of syllable-final nasals, the deaffrication of [č], etc.). For an overview of dialectal processes in Spanish, see Teschner (2000).
149. This point is also made by Pienemann (1998).
150. (1) 'I have fried the fish' (a is the academic alternative); (2) 'Have you set the table?' (c is the grammatical alternative); (3) 'Did you tell the truth? (d is the grammatical alternative); (4) 'The bank was not open' (c is the grammatical alternative).
151. López Morales (2005: 174) speaks of a 'subconjunto léxico común a todas las variedades hispánicas,' 'a lexical subset common to all of the Hispanic varieties,' and uses the adjective 'neutro,' but acknowledges the difficulty of establishing such a general repertoire.
152. See, among others, Gutiérrez and Fairclough (2006: 174), who follow Kachru (1988) in arguing that 'when creating a pedagogical norm, not only student

needs but also the local or regional sociolinguistic contexts need to be taken into account.'

153. See Table 4.2 in Chapter 4 for further discussion of lexical varieties spoken in Spanish.

154. We do not provide translations in this exercise or in those that follow in this chapter, as they are designed to be used by instructors of Spanish in a Spanish language classroom. We therefore presuppose an advanced level of Spanish.

155. Wieczorek (1991) argues in favor of the inclusion of dialect variation in the L2 classroom, but raises the question about the right place to do so, taking into account the fact that not all teachers might have the necessary linguistic background. He proposes that textbooks should be the source of information regarding dialectal variants, perhaps in the appendix, as suggested by Terrell *et al.* (1990). The upshot of including linguistic explanations in the text, in his view, is (Wieczorek, 1991: 179) 'that a greater amount of time would be spent reinforcing variation within the framework of skill and knowledge that the L2 student already possesses. One other implication is that teachers/curricula would have to confront the hybrid speech of the individual class members, in addition to the IL speech common to all L2 classrooms.'

156. We must emphasize that the explanations should be simple and very general at the beginning stages. More complex discussion must be left to upper-division Spanish classes or Spanish linguistics classes.

157. We have also used this term in reference to students adopting phonological characteristics of a variety of dialects. See Chapter 1 for discussion.

Glossary of Terms

absolute antonyms – (antónimos absolutos) refers to a pair of words in which the meaning of one is the direct opposite of the meaning of the other, as in *vivo* 'living' and *muerto* 'dead.'

accomplishments – (verbos de consecución) verbs that describe a completed action, indicating a process, such as *escribir una carta* 'write a letter.'

achievements – (logros) verbs whose action is true for a given point in time:*Vio a Ana* 'S/he saw Anna'.

activities – (actividades) verbs that describe an action that progresses through time: *cocinar* 'to cook.'

ACTFL – (Consejo Americano sobre la Enseñanza de las Lenguas Extranjeras) – American Council on the Teaching of Foreign Languages. In 1986, this organization first produced the various proficiency guidelines (from low to native). The council has been highly influential with respect to L2 teaching methodology ever since.

adstratum – (adstrato) a language spoken alongside another, such as Basque in Northern Spain and Southwestern France.

affix – (afijo) an affix is an inflectional morpheme; it can be a prefix, suffix or circumfix (interfix). In Spanish, an example of a prefix is *re* in *rehacer* 'to do again.' An example of a suffix is *o* in *hablo* 'I speak,' and an example of a circumfix is *it* as in *chiquito*.

affricate – (africado) the combination of a stop plus a fricative, as in the initial sound in *chico* 'boy'; such sounds can either be transcribed with a single symbol (e.g. [č]) or two separate symbols ([tš]).

allophone – (alófono) a variant of a phoneme. It can be the physical manifestation of a sound. For example, the sound [ð] is an allophone of the phoneme [d].

alveolar – (alveolar) a sound produced with the tip of the tongue against the alveolar ridge, such as [l] in Spanish.

analogy – (analogía) a process by which a speaker adapts a form to the dominant pattern in the language, such as *la telegrama* 'the telegram' for *el telegrama* because most Spanish feminine nouns end in *a*.

213

analytic constructions – (construcción analítica) structures in which grammatical function, is expressed by separate words instead of affixes, such as *Iría a trabajar* 'I would go to work' for *Trabajaría* 'I would work.'

Andalusia – (Andalucía) region in Southern Spain.

aphaeresis – (aféresis) loss of the initial syllable of a word, such as Latin *illa* 'that,' which gave *la* in Spanish.

apocope – (apócope) loss of the final syllable of a word, such as *illum*, which gave *el* in Spanish.

apodosis – (apódosis) the main clause in a conditional sentence, such as *Si lo hubiera sabido, **no habría contestado así** *'If I had known, I would never have answered thusly.'

archaism – (arcaísmo) a form from an earlier stage of the language, such as Spanish *haiga* 'there is/are' for *'haya.'*

articulatory phonetics – (fonética articulatoria) physical description of the production of speech sounds.

aspect – (aspecto) indicates the beginning or end of an action, as opposed to the duration. The difference between the preterit (*habló* 'he spoke') and the imperfect (*hablaba* 'he used to speak') is aspectual in Spanish.

Audio-lingual method – (método audio-lingual) a teaching method that was developed with the advent of language laboratory technology in the 1970s. The method was largely behavioristic in focus, and involved patterned drills.

auxiliary verb – (verbo auxiliar), a helping verb such as *estás* 'you are' in *estás trabajando* 'You are working.'

back – (posterior) as in back vowel. It refers to a vowel articulated with the tongue in the back of the mouth, as in Spanish [u].

base level – (palabra a nivel básico) a word that is a member of a category, such as *perro* 'dog' for *animales* 'animals.'

bilabial – (bilabial) a point of articulation in consonants involving both the upper and lower lips, as in Spanish [β].

bottom-up processing – (procesamiento de abajo a arriba) arriving at the meaning of a sentence by going from the individual words and morphemes to the utterance itself.

bound – (ligado) referring to morphemes that cannot stand alone, such as the derivational morpheme *able* in Spanish *viable* 'viable.'

Castile – (Castilla) region in North Central Spain.

central – (central) as in central vowel. It refers to a vowel articulated with the tongue in the center of the mouth, as in Spanish [a].

ceceo – (ceceo) characteristic of the Spanish spoken in Southern Spain, this pronunciation involves the total replacement of [s] by [θ]. It should not be taught, in our view, because of its marked sociolinguistic status.

circumfix – (circumfijo) a derivational morpheme found in the middle of a word, such as *it chiquito*.

class level (superordinate level) – (palabra a nivel superior) a word referring to all of the members of a semantic group, such as *legumbres* 'vegetables.'

clitic-climbing – (preposición del pronombre objeto) the optional preposition of an object clitic in Spanish, as in *lo voy a comprar* 'I'm going to buy it,' vs. *voy a comprarlo* 'I'm going to buy it.'

closed-syllable – (sílaba trabada) a syllable ending in a consonant, such as the first syllable in *alto* 'tall' [ál-to].

Communicative Approach – (el método comunicativo) Developed in the 1990s as a response in part to the ACFTL guidelines, this approach placed primacy on the production of language.

competence – (competencia) the speaker's innate knowledge of his/her language system.

content level – (nivel del contenido) in the lexicon, this level refers to the meanings of the words. It is in contrast to the form level. The question of whether or not it is separate or joint in the L2 lexicon is a controversial point.

coreferential – (correferencial) referring to the same noun phrase as in *Yo tengo mi libro* 'I have my book'; *yo* and *mi* are coreferential.

Critical Period Hypothesis (CPH) – (la hipótesis del periodo crítico) First proposed by Lenneberg (1963), this hypothesis claimed that after puberty, the acquisition of a second language could no longer mirror the first, due to a loss of plasticity of the brain.

debilitamiento vocálico – (debilitamiento) the tendency found in the tierras altas whereby certain vowels are articulated with less prominence.

deictic pronoun – (pronombres deícticos) a pronoun that takes its reference from discourse context, such as *usted* in *Usted vive ahora en Barcelona* 'You live in Barcelona now.' The reference of *usted* will be a function of whom the speaker is addressing.

dental – (dental) a sound articulated with the tip of the tongue against the upper teeth.

dequeísmo – (dequeísmo) the ubiquitous use of *de* before *que* introducing an embedded clause, as in *Estoy seguro de que tienes razón* 'I am sure that you are right.'

derivational – (derivacional) a type of morpheme used to form new words, such as *ear* in *mopear* 'to mop.'

descriptive – (descriptivo) the view of language espoused in this book, which acknowledges natural L1 speech.

diachronic – (diacrónico) related to the evolution of a language.

dialect – (dialecto) a regional variety of a language, such as the dialect of Madrid.

diminutive – (diminutivo) a derivational morpheme that indicates affection or small size such as *manita* for 'little hand,' used with children.

diphthong – (diptongo) combination of glide + vowel or vowel + glide together in a single syllable, such as in the first syllable of *diapositiva* 'slide.' [**dja** po si tí βa] 'slide' or the first syllable in *Deusto* 'district in the city of Bilbao' [**déws** to].

distinción – (distinción) Characteristic of the Spanish spoken in North Central Spain, this pronunciation makes a phonemic distinction between [s] and [θ], as in *asar* 'to roast' vs. *azar* 'destiny.'

elision – (elisión) the fusion of two identical vowels; for example, final and initial [e] in *un nombre elegante* [u nom bre le án te] 'an elegant man'.

etymology – (etimología) the origin of a word, such as Latin *acqua* yielding Spanish *agua* 'water.'

euphemisms – (eufemismo) words used to express those viewed as taboo in a language, such as *estar ebrio* 'to be inebriated' for estar *borracho/pedo* 'to be drunk (as a skunk).'

Failed Features Hypothesis (FFH) – (la hipótesis de los rasgos fallados) in this view of L2 acquisition, the Critical Period Hypothesis holds. See Hawkins and Chan (1997), Hawkins and Liszka (2003), Hawkins and Franceschina (2004), Franceschina (2001), and Tsimpli and Dimitrakopoulou (2007).

field dependent learners – (aprendices que necesitan un contexto para aprender) those who need a concrete context in order to learn.

field independent learners – (aprendices que no necesitan contexto para aprender) those who can learn without reference to a specific context.

focus on form – (enfoque en la forma) a teaching method which emphasizes grammatical points using the target language.

form level – (el nivel de la forma) refers to the organization of the lexicon; it indicates the words themselves. The question of whether this level is separate from the content level in the L2 is controversial.

fossilize (fosilizar) – the tendency for ungrammatical forms to become fixed in our L2, for example, **él hablaba el año pasado* 'he was speaking last year' (for the correct *él habló* 'he spoke').

free – (libre) refers to morphemes that can stand alone, such as the word *árbol* 'tree.'

fricative – (fricativa) a sound in whose articulation two articulatory organs get close to each other, but do not touch, as in the Spanish sound [β].

front – (anterior) as in front vowel. It refers to a vowel articulated with the tongue in the front of the mouth, as in Spanish [i].

Full Transfer Full Access (FTFA) – (transferencia y acceso completos) An opposing view to the FFH, which argues against the existence of the Critical Period Hypothesis.

glide – (semivocal o semiconsonante) refers to a sound in whose articulation the articulatory organs are quite far apart, such as in the Spanish sound [w].

gradable pairs – (par de palabras graduables) Also known as scalar antonyms, these words have a range of meaning, as in *mojado* 'wet' *and seco* 'dry.'

Grammar-Translation Method – (método de la gramática y de la traducción) the dominant teaching method until WWII. The emphasis was on a metalinguistic, as opposed to a communicative, practical understanding of language.

Guaraní – indigenous language of Paraguay.

heritage speakers – (los hablantes de herencia) speakers who grow up speaking two languages.

high – (alto) as in high vowel. It refers to a vowel articulated with the tongue high up in the mouth, as in Spanish [i].

homonyms – (homónimos) two words that have the same meaning but a different form, such as *chamaco* 'boy' and *niño* 'boy.'

homophones – (homófonos) two words that are pronounced the same although they have a different meaning, such as *son* 'sound' and *son* 'are.'

homorganic – (homorgánico) two sounds that have the same place of articulation, as in Spanish [ŋ] and [g].

hypercorrection – (hipercorrección) when a native speaker incorrectly applies a prescriptive rule such as the use of the imperfect subjunctive *comprara* for the conditional *compraría* in the apodosis in *Si tuviera dinero,* **comprara** *un carro* 'If I had money, I would buy a car.'

idiolect – (idiolecto) the speech characteristic of an individual; for example, the literary style of Gabriel García Márquez.

idiomatic expressions – (las expresiones idiomáticas) also known as idioms, in these expressions, the meaning cannot be gleaned from an understanding of the meaning of the individual units. A Spanish example is *se me fue la onda* 'I lost the plot,' literally 'the wave left me.'

indigenism – (indigenismo) a word whose source is that of a local language, such as *cacao* 'cocoa' from Náhuatl.

Indo-European language – (lengua indo-europea) the largest language family of Europe.

inflectional – (infleccional) refers to a grammatical morpheme indicating tense, aspect, number and gender, as in the final *a* of *niña*, 'girl.'

input flooding – (inundación del ínput) the use of several targeted forms in context, such as *bonita*, 'pretty,' *fea*, 'ugly,' *alta*, 'tall,' *baja* 'short,' illustrating the fact that the feminine gender in Spanish typically ends in *a*.

intervocalic – (intervocálico) a sound between two vowels, as *t* in *chato* 'stubby-nosed.'

intonation – (entonación) rising and falling of pitch, which is, in turn, is a function of the relative speed of vibration of the vocal cords.

labiodental – (labiodental) a point of articulation in consonants involving the upper teeth and lower lip, as in Spanish [f].

labiovelar – (labiovelar) a point of articulation in consonants in which the back part of the tongue raises toward the soft palate; the lips are also rounded, as in Spanish [w].

laísmo – (laísmo) use of the feminine direct object in both accusative and dative functions, such as *La regalé flores* 'I gave flowers her,' instead of *Le regalé flores* 'I gave flowers to her.'

lamdbacism – (lambdacismo) a regional pronunciation found in Puerto Rico in which syllable-final [r] is replaced by [l], as in *arte* 'art' [ál ţe].

lateral – (lateral) a point of articulation in consonants in which the tip of the tongue makes solid contact with another articulatory organ, while the sides of the tongue do not, allowing air flow, as in Spanish [l].

lexicon – (lexicón) all of the words of a given language.

lleísmo – (lleísmo) a regional pronunciation in which there is a phonemic distinction between [j] and [ʎ], as in *haya* 'subjunctive of have,' [á ja'] and *halla* 'finds' [á ʎa].

loísmo – (loísmo) use of the masculine direct object in both accusative and dative functions, such as *Lo trajeron un regalo* 'they brought him a gift' instead of *Le trajeron un regalo* 'They brought a gift to him.'

low – (bajo) as in low vowel. It refers to a vowel articulated with the tongue low in the mouth, as in Spanish [a].

manner of articulation – (modo de articulación) the way in which two articulatory organs are involved in the production of a speech sound, such as total closure, as in Spanish [d], a stop.

Mapuche – indigenous language of Chile.

marked – (marcado) a grammatical form that is not neutrally received from a sociolinguistic perspective, such as *loísmo* in Spanish.

Maya – indigenous language of Belize, Guatemala, and Southern Mexico.

metalinguistic – (metalingüístico) knowledge *about* language, as opposed to knowledge *of* a language. For example, bilingual children show awareness, from a young age, that many languages exist in the world. This is evidence of metalinguistic ability not seen in monolingual children.

metaphony – (metafonía) diachronic raising of a vowel due to the presence of another, higher vowel in a word, such as *hoja* 'leaf' [ó xa] derived from Latin *fŏlia*. In this case, the presence of [i] ([j])prevented the diphthongization of [o].

mid – (medio alto) as in mid vowel. It refers to a vowel articulated with the tongue raised half-way in the mouth, as in Spanish [e].

minimal pairs – (pares mínimos) two words that vary by one sound in the same order in the string, such as *pata* 'paw,' *lata* 'can.'

monomorphemic – (monomorfemático) a word composed of a single, free morpheme, such as *día* 'day.'

morpheme – (morfema) the smallest unit of meaning, such as *o* indicating masculine gender in *feo* 'ugly.'

morphology –(morfología) the study of how morphemes are combined to make words.

morpho-syntax – (morfosintaxis) the intersection of morphology and syntax.

Náhuatl – (Náhuatl) an indigenous language of Mexico spoken by the Aztecs.

nasal – (nasal) a sound in whose articulation the soft palate lowers, allowing air flow from both the oral cavity and the nasal cavity, as in Spanish [n].

nasal assimilation – (asimilación nasal) a process in which a nasal becomes homorganic such as [n] (alveolar) that becomes [m] (bilabial) before [p] (bilabial) in the expression *un puerto* 'a port' [úm pwér to].

neologism – (neologismo) new word formations such as *faxear* 'to fax.'

nominal – (nominal) related to nouns.

normative – (normativo) prescriptive.

null subject language – (lengua de sujeto nulo) language such as Spanish in which the expression of subject pronouns is optional.

opaque – (opaco) the relationship between two forms is not clear (transparent), as in *vaya* 'that s/he/you/go' from the verb *ir* 'to go.'

open-syllable – (sílaba abierta) a syllable ending in a vowel, such as the first syllable in *hacer* 'to do' [a-sér]. Spanish, unlike English, shows a preference for open-syllables.

palatal – (palatal) a sound in whose articulation the blade of the tongue approaches the hard palate, such as Spanish [j].

paradigmatic response – (respuesta paradigmática) responding to an utterance by a related word, such as *hablar* 'to speak,' when the trigger is *hablo* 'I speak.'

perception – (percepción) hearing the difference between two sounds.

performance – (actuación) the actual use of language by a speaker.

periphrastic – (perifrástico) expressions made up of individual words, such as *voy a hacer* 'I'm going to do' for *haré* 'I will do.'

philology – (filología) the traditional descriptive approach to diachronic linguistics.

phoneme – (fonema) an abstract manifestation of a sound, such as /b/, representing both [b] and [β].

phonemic – (fonémico) having a meaning contrast, such as /p/ and /t/ in *papa* 'potato' and *tapa* 'lid.'

phonology – (fonología) the study of the sound system of a language.

phonotactic constraints – (restricciones fonotácticas) limitations on the sequence of sounds in a language. For example, in Spanish, words cannot begin with *s* followed by a consonant.

pitch – (tono fonológico) relative height of a sound created by the rapidity of the vibration of the vocal cords. For example, the speech of a pre-pubescent boy is of a higher pitch than that of a man.

place of articulation – (lugar de articulación) refers to the area in the oral cavity in which a sound is produced. For example, [k] is a velar consonant because the back of the tongue comes into contact with the velum (soft palate).

pluricentricity – (pluricentrismo) refers to several dialects of a language having equal prestige, such as is the case for Spanish.

personal *a* – In Spanish the free morpheme a precedes a person or personalized direct object, such as in *Saludé a la profesora* 'I greeted the (female) professor.'

prefix – (prefijo) a bound morpheme found at the beginning of a word, such as *pre* in *precocinar* 'to cook before.'

prescriptive – (prescriptivo) a view of a language that says that one form is superior to another, regardless of whether it occurs in natural speech. An example of a form that a prescriptive view of language would not recognize, even in speech, is Mexican *se los di* 'I gave it to him,' *for se lo di* 'I gave it to them.'

protasis – (prótasis) in a conditional sentence, the subordinate clause, such as *Si me dieras tu número, te hablaría* 'If you gave me your number, I'd call you.'

Quechua – (Quechua) language spoken by the Incas.

recast – (reformulación de una forma incorrecta) when an instructor produces the correct form of a student error without drawing attention to the correct one, such as saying *sé* 'I know,' after the student utters **sabo*.

regional variability – (variabilidad regional) differences in speech in different geographical areas.

register – (registro) level of formality of speech such as a conversation among good friends (a very informal register) *vis à vis* a class lecture (a formal register).

rhotacism – (rotacismo) systematic substitution of syllable-final [r] for [l] found in Southern Spain, such as *farda* [fár ða] for *falda* [fál ða] 'skirt.'

rhythm – (ritmo) the relative prominence of syllables in a language.

Río de la Plata – Argentina, Paraguay and Uruguay.

Romance language – (lengua románica) language deriving from Latin, such as Spanish.

rounded – (redondeado) refers to the position of the lips in the articulation of a vowel, such as the Spanish vowel [o].

scalar antonyms – (antónimos graduables); see also gradable antonyms. Pairs of words on two ends of a spectrum, with possible values in between. For example, *jóven* 'young' and *viejo* 'old.'

semantics – (semántica) the meaning of words and sentences.

seseo – (seseo) the regional pronunciation, dominant in Andalucía and Latin America, in which the sounds represented by *s, ce, ci,* and *z* are homophonous.

sibilant (sibilante) a sound produced with a whistling noise, such as Spanish [s] or [č] and in River Plate Spanish, also [š] and [ž].

sociolinguistic variability – (variabilidad sociolingüística) differences in speech in different social contexts.

spirantization – (espirantización) when a stop becomes fricative (spirant).

statives – (estados) verbs that describe existence or a state, for example, *tener* 'to have.'

stop – (oclusiva) a consonant in whose articulation two articulatory organs touch, such as Spanish [t].

stress-timed – (un ritmo acentual) the rhythm of a language, such as English, in which duration of an utterance is a function of the number of stressed syllables.

style-shifting – (cambio de registro) adapting one's speak to the context, be it formal or informal.

substratum – (sustrato) a language superimposed by another, such as Quechua, which has been largely replaced by Spanish in South America.

suffix – (sufijo) a derivational or inflectional morpheme at the end of a word, such as *o* in *hablo* 'I speak.'

superstratum – (superestrato) a language superimposed on another; it does not supplant the original language, as Arabic in Spain.

suprasegmentals – (rasgos suprasegmentales) include intonation, rhythm and stress.

syllabification – (silabeo) division of words into syllables such as *lápiz* 'pencil' [lá pis].

syllabify – (silabear) divide words into syllables, such as *taza* 'cup' [tá sa].

syllable-timed – (un ritmo silábico) the rhythm in a language such as Spanish, in which duration of an utterance is directly tied to its number of syllables.

synchronic – (sincrónico) refers to a snapshot of a language at a given point in time.

synalephy – (sinalefa) the elimination of one of two identical vowels, as in lo odio [ló:ðjo] 'I hate him.'

syncretism – (sincretismo) one form having two functions, such as *ó* in *habló* 'he spoke' (i.e., indicates both third person singular and preterit tense).

syneresis – (sinéresis) vowel linking in a word, such as *le hablo* [le_á_ βlo] 'I speak.'

synonyms – (sinónimos) words whose meaning is similar, if not identical, such as *ardor* 'ardor' and *pasión* 'passion.'

syntax – (sintaxis) the structure of sentences.

synthetic – (sintético) structures in which grammatical function is communicated by the use of affixes, such as *ía* which indicates the conditional mood in *haría* 'I would do.'

Taino – (Taíno) indigenous language of the Caribbean.

tap – (vibrante simple) also known as flap; the striking of one articulatory organ against another, as in Spanish [r].

tierras altas – the highlands, including the *altiplano* of Mexico, the mountains of Central America and South America.

tierras bajas – the lowlands, including the coasts of Andalusia, the Caribbean, Central America and South America.

top down processing – (el procesamiento de arriba a abajo) understanding the gist of an utterance.

translation priming – (repetición anterior de un par de palabras) repetition of a word pair, such as *orange/naranja*, thought to speed up processing.

trill – (vibrante multiple) a sound in whose articulation one articulatory organ strikes another from three to seven times, as in Spanish [r̄].

triphthong – (triptongo) a combination of glide, vowel, and glide in one syllable, such as in Spanish *buey* [bwéj] 'ox.'

unrounded – (no redondeado) refers to the position of the lips in the articulation of vowels. In the articulation of an unrounded vowel, the lips are in a neutral position, as in Spanish [a].

uptake – (notar e incorporar una corrección) when a learner notices a correction and incorporates it into his/her speech.

uso etimológico – (uso etimológico) the use of dative and direct object pronouns such as *le escribí* 'I wrote to him,' and *lo vi* 'I saw him.'

variability – (variabilidad) differences in speech.

velar – (velar) a sound in whose articulation the back of the tongue raises toward the soft palate, as in Spanish [g].

velarization of [r̄] – (velarización de la [r̄]) a process found in Puerto Rico, in which the sound [r̄] is supplanted by velar [x].

voiced – (sonoro) a sound produced with vibration of the vocal cords, such as Spanish [b].

voiceless – (sordo) a sound produced without vibration of the vocal cords, such as Spanish [p].

yeísmo – (yeísmo) a regional pronunciation, found in Andalucía and most of Latin America, in which both *ll* and *y* are pronounced [j].

žeísmo – (žeísmo) a regional pronunciation, found in the Río de la Plata area, in which *ll* and *y* are pronounced [ž].

Bibliography

Abbott, M. and Davis, S. (1996) Hyperreality and the study of Latin: Living in a fairy tale world. *The Modern Language Journal* 80, 85–86.

Ahern, A. and Leonetti, N. (2004) The Spanish subjunctive and pragmatic interference. In R. Márquez Reiter and M. Placencia (eds) *Current Trends in the Pragmatics of Spanish* (pp. 35–56). Amsterdam/Philadelphia: Benjamins.

Akmajian, A., Demers, R.A., Farmen, A.K. and Harnish, R.M. (2001) *Linguistics: An Introduction to Language and Communication*. Boston MA: MIT Press.

Alarcos, E. (1947) Perfecto simple y compuesto en español. *Revista de Filología Española* 31, 108–139.

Alonso, A. (1947) Trueques de sibilantes en antiguo español. *Nueva Revista de Filología Hispánica* 1(1), 1–12.

Alonso, A. (1948) Lecture. University of Chicago, Chicago.

Alonso, A. (1967) *De la pronunciación medieval a la moderna en español*. Madrid: Gredos.

Alonso, A. (1982) *Estudios lingüísticos. Temas hispanoamericanos*. Madrid: Gredos.

Álvarez de Miranda, F. (1993) El alomorfo y sus consecuencias. *Lingüística española* 15.5, 42.

American Council for the Teaching of Foreign Languages (1983, Revised 1985) *ACTFL Proficiency Guidelines*. Hastings-on-Hudson, NY: ACTFL Materials Center.

Andersen, R. (1986) El desarrollo de la morfología verbal en el español como segundo idioma. In J. Meisel (ed.) *Adquisición del lenguaje/Aquisiçao da linguagem* (pp. 115–138). Frankfurt: Vervuert.

Andersen, R. (1991) Developmental sequences: The emergence of aspect marking in second language acquisition. In T. Huebner and C.A. Ferguson (eds) *Crosscurrents in Second Language Acquisition and Linguistic Theories* (pp. 305–324). Amsterdam/Philadelphia: John Benjamins.

Andersen, R. and Shirai, Y. (1994) Discourse motivations for some cognitive acquisition principles. *Studies in 2nd Language Acquisition* 16 (2), 113–156.

Andersen, R.W. (2002) The dimensions of pastness. In R. Salaberry and Y. Shirai (eds) *L2 Acquisition of Tense-Aspect Morphology* (pp. 79–106). Amsterdam/Philadelphia: John Benjamins.

Anderson, J. (1981) Considerations in phonological assessment. In J. Good Erickson and D. Omark (eds) *Communication Assessment of the Bilingual Bicultural Child* (pp. 77–98). San Diego: College Hill Press.

Aron, A. (1922) The linguistic background of the modern language teacher. *The Modern Language Journal* 7, 75–83.

Arteaga, D. (1999) On the importance of phonetics in the Spanish for native speakers. *Paper presented at the 5th Annual Conference Teaching Spanish to Native Speakers*. New Mexico State University, Las Cruces, New Mexico, 14 August.

Arteaga, D. (2000) Articulatory phonetics in the first-year Spanish classroom. *The Modern Language Journal* 84, 339–354.

Arteaga, D. (2005) *On the Importance of Register Variation in the Spanish Language Classroom. Paper presented at the 62nd Annual Meeting of the South Central Modern Language Association (SCMLA).* Houston, TX, 28 October.

Arteaga, D. and Herschensohn, J. (1995) Using diachronic linguistics in the language classroom. *The Modern Language Journal* 79, 212–222.

Arteaga, D. and Herschensohn, J. (2007) Parameters and processing: Gender agreement in L2 French. *Paper presented (with co-author Julia Herschensohn of the University of Washington) at the 17th Conference of the European Second Language Association,* Newcastle upon Tyne, UK, 13 September.

Arteaga, D. and Llorente, L. (2003) On the importance of dialectology in the first-year Spanish classroom. *Paper presented at the 60th Annual Meeting of the South Central Modern Language Association (SCMLA),* Hot Springs, 30 October–1 November.

Arteaga, D. and Llorente, L. (2004) Undergraduate curriculum in Spanish: Should history of the Spanish language courses be history? *Paper presented at the 61st Annual Meeting of the South Central Modern Language Association (SCMLA), Undergraduate curriculum in Spanish: Should history of the Spanish language courses be history?* New Orleans, LA, 29 October.

Arteaga, D. and Llorente, L. (2005) Los cursos de historia del español ¿son cosa del pasado? *Paper presented at the Congreso Internacional de FIAPE (Federación Internacional de Profesores de Español), El español, lengua del futuro,* Toledo, Spain, 21–24 March.

Arteaga-Capen, D. and Llorente, L. (2007a) Vocabulary in the Spanish language classroom: Which variety to teach? *Paper presented at the X Encuentros de Lingüística Aplicada,* Sevilla (Spain), 14–16 March.

Arteaga-Capen, D. and Llorente, L. (2007b) On teaching Spanish vocabulary in a pluricentric society. *Paper presented at the 60th Kentucky Foreign Language Conference,* Lexington, 19–21 April.

Arteaga-Capen, D. and Llorente, L. (2007c) La enseñanza de ELE y la variación morfosintáctica: Retos y posibilidades. *Paper presented at the II Congreso Internacional de FIAPE (Federación Internacional de Asociaciones de Profesores de Español), El español: una lengua, muchas culturas,* Granada (Spain), 26–29 September.

Arteaga-Capen, D. and Llorente, L. (2007d) Regional and sociolinguistic variation in Spanish morpho-syntax: Classroom implications. *Paper presented at the 64th Annual Meeting of the South Central Modern Language Association.* Memphis (TN), 1–3 November.

Asher, J. and García, R. (1969) The optimal age to learn a foreign language. *The Modern Language Journal* 53, 343–341.

Asher, J. and García, R. (1992) The optimal age to learn a foreign language. In S. Krashen and R. Scarcella (eds) *Differences in Second Language Acquisition* (pp. 3–12). Rowley, MA: Newbury House.

Aspinwall, W. (1937) The preparation of teachers of French for junior and senior high schools. *The Modern Language Journal* 21, 556–562.

Ayoun, D. and Salaberry, R. (2005) *Tense and Aspect in Romance Languages: Theoretical and Applied Perspectives.* Amsterdam: Benjamins.

Azevedo, M. (1992) *Introducción a la lingüística española.* Upper Saddle River, NJ: Prentice-Hall.

Azurdia, E. (1998) Integrando la fonética en el proceso de la lectura en español. In A. Carrasquillo and P. Segan (eds) *The Teaching of Reading in Spanish to the Bilingual Student* (pp. 87–100). Mahwah: Lawrence Erlbaum.

Bahrick, H. (1984) Semantic memory content in permastore: Fifty years of memory for Spanish learned in school. *Journal of Experimental Psychology: General* 113, 1–30.

Ball, R. and Ellsworth, J.D. (1996) The emperor's new clothes: Hyperreality and the study of Latin. *The Modern Language Journal* 80, 77–84.

Banathy, B.H. (1968) The design of foreign language teacher education. *The Modern Language Journal* 52, 490–500.

Barrutia, R. and Schwegler, A. (1994) *Fonética y fonología españolas: teoría y práctica.* New York: Wiley.

Bentivoglio, P. (2002) Spanish forms of address in the sixteenth century. In I. Taavitsainem and A.H. Jucker (eds) *Diachronic Perspectives on Address Term Systems* (pp. 177–191). Amsterdam/Philadelphia: John Benjamins.

Bergen, J. (1974) A practical framework for teaching pronunciation in beginning Spanish courses. *Hispania* 57, 479–483.

Bergmann, A., Currie Hall, K. and Miriam Ross, S. (2007) *Language Files: Materials for an Introduction to Language and Linguistics.* Columbus: The Ohio State University Press.

Bermúdez-Otero, R. and Borjars, K. (2006) Markedness in phonology and in syntax: The problem of grounding. *Lingua* 116, 710–756.

Best, C. (1995) A direct realist view of cross-language speech perception. In W. Strange (ed.) *Speech Perception and Linguistic Experience: Theoretical and Methodological Issues* (pp. 1–24). Baltimore: York Press.

Bever, T. (1981) Normal acquisition processes explain the critical period for language learning. In K. Diller (ed.) *Individual Differences and Universals in Language Learning Aptitude* (pp. 176–198). Rowley, MA: Newbury House.

Biber, D. (1995) *Dimensions of Register Variation: A Cross-linguistic Comparison.* Cambridge: Cambridge University Press.

Bieler, A. (1964) A case for the teaching of the history of the French language. *The Modern Language Journal* 48, 134–136.

Birdsong, D. (1999) *Second Language Acquisition and the Critical Period Hypothesis.* Boston: Lawrence Erlbaum Associates.

Bjarkman, P. (1986) Natural phonology and strategies for teaching English/Spanish pronunciation. In P. Binkman and V. Raskin (eds) *The Real World Linguist* (pp. 77–115). Norwood, NJ: Abley.

Bongaerts, T. (1999) Ultimate attainment in L2 pronunciation: The case of very advanced late L2 learners. In D. Birdsong (ed.) *Second Language Acquisition and the Critical Period Hypothesis* (pp. 133–160). Mahwah: Lawrence Erlbaum Associates.

Bosque, I. and Demonte, V. (1999) *Gramática descriptiva de la lengua española.* Madrid: Espasa.

Boyd, P.A. (1975) The development of grammar categories in Spanish by Anglo children learning a second language. *TESOL Quarterly* 8 (2), 125–135.

Bronk, I. (1921) Attainable aims in modern language teaching in colleges, or what may we safely hope to accomplish in modern languages courses in colleges. *The Modern Language Journal* 5, 179–185.

Brooks, N. (1966) The ideal preparation of foreign language teachers. *The Modern Language Journal* 50, 71–78.

Brown, R. (1973) *A First Language: The Early Stages*. Cambridge, MA: Harvard University Press.

Brown R. and Gilman, A. (1972) The pronouns of power and solidarity. In P.P. Giglioli (ed.) *Language and Social Context* (pp. 253–277). Harmondsworth: Penguin.

Brown, A. (1991) *Teaching English Pronunciation: A Book of Readings*. London/New York: Routledge.

Brysbaert, M., Van Dyck, G. and Van de Poel, M. (1999) Visual word recognition in bilinguals: Evidence from masked phonological priming. *Journal of Experimental Psychology: Human Perception and Performance* 25, 137–148.

Canfield, D. (1981) *Spanish Pronunciation in the Americas*. Chicago: University of Chicago Press.

Carreira, M. (2000) Validating and promoting Spanish in the United States: Lessons from linguistic science. *Bilingual Research Journal* 24, 333–352.

Chen, Y. (1982) Principles and methods of the teaching of pronunciation. *Language Learning and Communication* 2, 75–76.

Chodorowska-Pilch, M. (2004) The conditional: A grammaticalised marker of politeness in Spanish. In R. Márquez Reiter and M. Placencia (eds) *Current Trends in the Pragmatics of Spanish* (pp. 57–78). Amsterdam/Philadelphia: John Benjamins.

Churchland, P.S. (1986) *Neurophilosophy*. Cambridge, MA: MIT Press.

Collins, L. (2002) The roles of L1 influence and lexical aspect in the acquisition of temporal morphology. *Language Learning* 52, 43–94.

Colomé, À. (2001) Lexical activation in bilinguals' speech production: Language-specifice or language independent? *Journal of Memory and Language* 45, 721–736.

Comajoan, L. (2006) The aspect hypothesis: Development of morphology and appropriateness of use. *Language Learning* 56, 201–268.

Contreras, H. (1991) On the *position* of subjects. In S. Rothstein (ed.) *Perspectives on Phrase Structure: Heads and Licensing* (pp. 63–79). New York: Academic Press.

Cook, V. (2001) *Second Language Learning and Language Teaching*. London: Arnold.

Cortés, M. (1989) Temps I aspecte: mo els infants aprenen a parler del passat. Unpublished PhD dissertation, University of Barcelona.

Costa, A. and Caramazza, A. (1999) Is lexical selection language specific? Further evidence from Spanish–English bilinguals. *Bilingualism: Language and Cognition* 2, 231–244.

Costa, A., Miozzo, M. and Caramazza, A. (1999) Lexical selection in bilinguals: Do words in the bilingual's two lexicons compete for selection? *Journal of Memory and Language* 41, 365–397

Cotton, E. and Sharp, J. (1988) *Spanish in the Americas*. Washington, DC: Georgetown University Press.

Crawford, J.W. (1925) Progress of the modern foreign language study. *Hispania* 8, 184–189.

Crawford, W. (1987) The pronunciation monitor: L2 acquisition considerations and pedagogical priorities. In J. Morley (ed.) *Current Perspectives on Pronunciation: Practices Anchored in Theory* (pp. 103–121). Washington, DC: TESOL.

Criado Costa, J. and Criado Costa, M. (1992) *Estudios de dialectología andaluza: el habla de San Sebastián de los Caballeros*. Córdoba: Diputación Provincial de Córdoba.

Crystal, D. (1980) *A Dictionary of Linguistics and Phonetics* (3rd edn). London: Blackwell.

D'Ambrosio, H. (2004) Pragmática, sociolingüística y pedagogía de los pronombres de tratamiento en lengua española. *Estudios de lingüística aplicada* 39, 37–52.

Dalbor, J. (1981) *Spanish Pronunciation: Theory & Practice*. Fort Worth: Holt, Rinehart & Winston.

Dalbor, J. (1996) *Spanish Pronunciation: Theory and Practice*. Fort Worth: Holt, Rinehart & Winston.

Dansereau, D. (1995) Phonetics in the beginning and intermediate oral proficiency-oriented French classroom. *French Review* 68, 638–651.

De Groot, A.M.B. and Barry, C. (eds) (1992) The multilingual community: A special issue on bilingualism of the *European Journal of Cognitive Psychology*. 4, 241–365.

De Groot, A. and Kejzer, R. (2000) What is hard to learn is easy to forget: the roles of word concreteness, cognate status, and word frequency in foreign-language vocabulary learning and forgetting. *Language Learning* 50, 1–56. (Also published as a book by Lawrence Erlbaum in 1992.)

Delattre, P. (1965) *Comparing the Phonetic Features of English, German, Spanish, and French*. Heidelberg/Philadelphia, PA: Julius Groos, Chilton.

DeStefano, J. and Rentel, V. (1975) Theory into practice. *Language Variation: Perspectives for Teachers* 14, 328–337.

Dietrich, R., Klein, W. and Noyau, C. (eds) (1995) *The Acquisition of Temporality in a Second Language*. Amsterdam & Philadelphia: John Benjamin.

Di Pietro, R., Lantolf, J. and Labarca, A. (1983) The graduate foreign language curriculum. *The Modern Language Journal* 67, 365–373.

Dijkstra, A.F.J. (1998) From tag to task: Coming to grips with bilingual control issues. *Bilingualism: Language and Cognition* 1 (1), 88–89.

Dijkstra, A. and Van Heuven, W. (1998) The BIA model and bilingual word recognition. In J. Grainger and A. Jacobs (eds) *Localist Connectionist Approaches to Human Cognition* (pp. 189–225). Hillsdale, NJ: Lawrence Erlbaum Associates.

Doughty, C. and Williams, J. (eds) (1998) *Focus on Form in Classroom Second Language Acquisition*. Cambridge, UK: Cambridge University Press.

Dressler, W.U. (1982) Acceleration, retardation, and reversal in language decay? In R.L. Cooper (ed.) *Language Spread* (pp. 321–336). Bloomington, IN: Indiana University Press.

Dressler, W.U. (1988) Language death. In *Linguistics: The Cambridge Survey* (Vol. 4) (*Language: The Socio-cultural Context*) (pp. 184–191). Cambridge: Cambridge University Press.

Dressler, W.U. (1991) N.C. Dorian (ed.) Investigating obsolescence: Studies in language contraction and death. *Studies in language* 15(2), 501–503.

Duggan, S. (1944) Teaching foreign languages. *The Modern Language Journal* 28, 552–554.

Edelman, G. (1989) *The Remembered Present: A Biological Theory of Consciousness*. New York: Basic Books.

Edwards, V. (2008) *Learning to be Literate in Multilingual Settings*. Bristol: Multilingual Matters.

Eisenberg, A. (1985) Learning to describe past experiences in conversation. *Discourse Processes* 8, 177–204.

Elliot, A. (1997) On the teaching and acquisition of pronunciation within a communicative approach. *Hispania* 80, 95–108.

Elliot, A. (1995) Foreign language phonology: Field independence, attitude, and success of formal instruction in Spanish pronunciation. *Modern Language Journal* 79, 530–542.

Ellis, N. (1993) Rules and instances in foreign language learning: Interactions of explicit and implicit knowledge. *European Journal of Cognitive Psychology* 5, 289–318.

Elman, J.L. (1993) Learning and development in neural networks: The importance of starting small. *Cognition* 48, 71–99.

Estarellas, J. (1972) Problems in teaching Spanish pronunciation and writing by the audio-lingual method: A case study. *Hispania* 55, 96–98.

Ezeizabarrena, M.J. (1997) Morfemas de concordancia con el sujeto y con los objetos en el castellano infantil. In W. Glass and A.T. Pérez Leroux (eds) *Contemporary Perspectives on the Acquisition of Spanish* (pp. 21–36). Sommerville: Cascadilla Press.

Fernández Martínez, A. (1994) El aprendizaje de los morfemas verbales: Datos de un estudio longitudinal. In S. López Ornat, A. Fernández Martínez, P. Gallo and S. Mariscal (eds) *La adquisición de la lengua española* (pp. 29–46). Madrid: Siglo XXI de España Editores.

Ferrara, K. and Bell, B. (1995) Sociolinguistic variation and discourse function of constructed dialogue introducers: The case of Be+Like. *American Speech* 70, 265–290.

Figueroa, N. (2000) Us and them: A study of the language attitudes of speakers of high and low prestige varieties toward world Spanishes. Unpublished PhD dissertation, Purdue University.

Flege, J.E. (1995) Second-language speech learning: Findings, and problems. In W. Strange (ed.) *Speech Perception and Linguistic Experience: Theoretical and Methodological Issues* (pp. 233–273). Timonium, MD: York Press.

Flege, J.E., Bohn, O.S. and Jang, S. (1997) The production and perception of English vowels by native speakers of German, Korean, Mandarin, and Spanish. *Journal of Phonetics* 25, 437–470.

Flynn, S. (1986) *A Parameter-Setting Model of L2 Acquisition: Experimental Studies in Anaphora.* Holland: Dordrecht.

Flynn, S. and O'Neil, W. (1988) Introduction. In S. Flynn and W. O'Neil (eds) *Linguistic Theory in Second Language Acquisition* (pp. 1–24). Dordrecht: Kluwer.

Fontanella de Weinberg, M.B. (1976) *La lengua española fuera de España.* Madrid: Paidós.

Fontanella de Weinberg, M.B. (1995) *El español de América.* Madrid: Mapfre.

Fontanella de Weinberg, M.B. (1999) Sistemas pronominales de tratamiento usados en el mundo hispánico. In I. Bosque and V. Delmonte (eds) *Gramática descriptiva de la lengua española* (pp. 1399–1425). Madrid: Espasa.

Franceschina, F. (2001) Morphological or syntactic deficits in near-native speakers? An assessment of some current proposals. *Second Language Research* 17, 213–247.

Franceschina, F. (2003) Parameterized functional features and SLA. In J. Liceras, H. Zobl and H. Goodluck (eds) *Proceedings of the 6th Generative Approaches to Second Language Acquisition Conference (GASLA 2002)* (pp. 97–105). Somerville, MA: Cascadilla Proceedings Project.

Freeman, S. (1941) What constitutes a well-trained modern language teacher? *The Modern Language Journal* 25, 293–305.

Freeman, S. (1949) What about the teacher? *The Modern Language Journal* 33, 255–267.

Fromkin, V., Rodman, R. and Hyams, N. (2007) *An Introduction to Language.* Boston: Heinle & Heinle.

Furman, N., Goldberg, D. and Lusin, N. (2006) *Enrollments in languages other than English in United States institutions of higher education,* Fall 2006. Web publication 13.

Gairns, R. and Redman, S. (1986) *Working with Words: A Guide to Teaching and Learning Vocabulary.* New York: Cambridge University Press.

Galmés de Fuentes, Á. (1983) *Dialectología mozárabe.* Madrid, Gredos.

García, C. (2004a) Coercion and cooperation: A case study of Argentinean reprimands and response to reprimands. In R. Márquez Reiter and M. Placencia (eds) *Current Trends in Pragmatics of Spanish* (pp. 231–265). Amsterdam/Philadelphia: John Benjamins.

García, C. (2004b) Reprendiendo y respondiendo a una reprimenda: similitudes y diferencias entre peruanos y venezolanos. *Spanish in Context* 1(1), 113–147.

Garcia, G., McCardle, P. and Nixon, S. (2007) Prologue: Development of English literacy in Spanish-speaking children: Transforming research into practice. *Language, Speech, and Hearing Services in Schools* 38, 213.

Gardner, R. and Lambert, W.E. (1972) *Attitudes and Motivation in Second Language Learning.* Rowley, MA: Newbury House.

Gass, S. (1988) Second language vocabulary acquisition. *Annual Review of Applied Linguistics* 9, 92–106.

Gass, S. and Selinker, L. (2001) *Second Language Acquisition: An Introductory Course.* Mahjaw, NJ: Laurence Erlbaum.

Gathercole, S. and Baddeley, A. (1993) *Working Memory and Language.* Hove: Erlbaum.

Gerard, L. and Scarborough, D. (1989) Language-specific lexical access of homographs by bilinguals. *Journal of Experimental Psychology. Learning, Memory, and Cognition* 15, 305–315.

Giduz, H. (1952) Teaching modern foreign languages. *The Modern Language Journal* 36, 65–67.

Gil Narro Garcia, G., McCardle, P. and Nixon, S.M. (2007) *Prologue: Development of English Literacy in Spanish-speaking Children: Transforming Research into Practice.* Washington, DC: Institute of Education Sciences, U.S. Department of Education.

Gómez Molina, J. (1995) La variación lingüística en el español hablado en Valencia. *Paper given at II Simposio de pragmática y gramática del español hablado.* Universitat de Valencia, 14–16 November.

Gonzalez Pino, B. and Pino, F. (2000) Serving the heritage speaker across a five-year program. *ADLF Bulletin* 32, 27–35.

Granda, G. (1976) Elementos lingüísticos afroamericanos en el área hispánica: nuevos materiales para su estudio. *Thesaurus. Boletín del Instituto Caro y Cuervo* 29 (3), 481–501.

Granda, G. (1978) *Estudios lingüísticos hispánicos, afrohispánicos y criollos.* Madrid: Gredos.

Green, J. (1990) Spanish. In M. Harris and N. Vincent (eds) *The Romance Languages* (pp. 79–130). London: Routledge.

Greiner, O. (1938) The main objective in the study of foreign languages. *The Modern Language Journal* 23, 209–213.

Gu, Y. and Johnson, R. (1996) Vocabulary learning strategies and language learning outcomes. *Language Learning* 46, 643–679.

Guitart, J. (1981) Sobre la posteriorización de las consonantes posnucleares en el español antillano: Reexamen teórico-descriptivo. *Paper presented at the El VI Simposio de Dialectología del Caribe Hispánico*, Universidad Católica Madre y Maestra, Santiago, República Dominicana.

Guitart, J. (1983) On the contribution of Spanish language variation studies to the contemporary linguistic theory? In L. Elías-Olivares (ed.) *Spanish in the U.S. Setting.* Rosslyn, VA: National Clearinghouse for Bilingual Education.

Guzmán, B. (2001) The Hispanic population. *Census 2000 Brief.* Washington, DC: U.S. Department of Commerce/Cenus Bureau.

Haden E.S. (1986) *¿Qué es la lingüística?* Madrid: Editorial Gredos.

Hadley, A.O. (1993) *Teaching Language in Context.* Boston, MA: Heinle and Heinle Publishers.

Hagboldt, P. (1928) *How to Study Languages in High School.* Chicago: University of Chicago Press.

Haile, H.G. (1970) Learning about language: Introduction to the study of foreign language for college freshmen. *The Modern Language Journal* 54, 120–125.

Halliday, M., McIntosh, A. and Strevens, P.D. (1964) *The Linguistic Sciences and Language Teaching.* London: Longmans, Green.

Hammond, R. (1991) Pronunciation proficiency and the affective filter: Attitudes and stereotypes in second language acquisition. In *1990 Mid-America Linguistics Conference Papers* (pp. 138–150). Lawrence: University of Kansas.

Hammond, R. and Flege, J. (1989) The acquisition of second language phonological systems in a communicative framework – The role of attitudes and experience. *Romance Languages Annual* 1, 671–676.

Harley, B. (1998) Focus-on-form tasks in child L2 acquisition. In C. Doughty and J. Williams (eds) *Focus on Form in Classroom Second Language Acquisition* (pp. 156–174). Cambridge: Cambridge University Press.

Hawkins, R. (2001) *Second Language Syntax: A Generative Introduction.* Cambridge: Blackwell.

Hawkins, R. and Chan, C.Y. (1997) The partial availability of Universal Grammar in second language acquisition: The 'Failed Functional Features Hypothesis'. *Second Language Research* 13, 87–226.

Hawkins, R. and Liszka, S. (2003) Locating the source of defective past tense marking in advanced L2 English speakers. In R. Van Hout, R.A. Hulk, F. Kuiken and R. Towell (eds) *The Lexicon-Syntax Interface in Second Language Acquisition* (pp. 21–44). Amsterdam/Philadephia: John Benjamins.

Hawkins, R. and Franceschina, F. (2004) Explaining the acquisition and non-acquisition of determiner-noun gender concord in French and Spanish. In P. Prévost and J. Paradis (eds) *The Acquisition of French in Different Contexts* (pp. 175–206). Amsterdam and Philadelphia: John Benjamins.

Hazen, K. (2001) Teaching about dialects. ED456674—Teaching about Dialects. ERIC Digest.

Herbst, T. and Stein, G. (1987) The dictionary and the language learner. In A. Cowie (ed.) *The Dictionary and the Language Learner* (pp. 115–127). Tübingen: Niemeyer.

Hermans, D., Bongaerts, T., De Bot, K. and Schreduer, R. (1998) Producing words in a foreign language: Can speakers prevent interference from their first language? *Bilingualism: Language and Context* 1, 213–229.

Hernández-Flores, N. (2004) L2 politeness as 'face' enhancement: An analysis of Spanish conversations between friends and family. In R. Márquez Reiter and M. Placencia (eds) *Current Trends in the Pragmatics of Spanish* (pp. 265–286). Amsterdam/Philadelphia: John Benjamins.

Hernández Pina, F. (1985) Adquisición y desarrollo de los términos cuantitativos. Estudio de un caso. *Actas del V Congreso Internacional de la ALFAL,* 310–319.

Hernández Pina, F. (1994) Teorías psicosociolingüísticas y su aplicación a la adquisición del español como lengua materna. In S. López Ornat, A. Férnandez,

P. Gallo, S. Mariscal and X. Mariscal (eds) *La adquisición de la lengua española* (pp. 29–46). Madrid: Siglo XXI de España.

Herron, C. and Tomasello, M. (1992) Acquiring grammatical structures by guided induction. *The French Review* 65, 708–718.

Hershberger, R., Navey-Davis, S. and Borrás Álvarez, G. (2008) *Plazas. Lugar de encuentros* (3rd edn). Boston: Thomson-Heile.

Hidalgo, M. (1990) On the question of 'standard' versus 'dialect': Implications for teaching Hispanic college students. In J. Bergen (ed.) *Spanish in the United States: Sociolinguistic Issues* (pp. 110–126). Washington, DC: Georgetown University Press.

Holman, R. (1996) Problems posed by the teaching of colloquial French in the lower-level classroom. *Paper presented at the 69th Annual Convention of the American Association of Teachers of French.* Lyon, France.

Hout, R. van, Hulk, A., Kuiken, F. and Towell, R. (eds) (2003) *The Lexicon-Syntax Interface in Second Language Acquisition.* Amsterdam: Benjamins.

Hualde, J., Olarrea, A., and Escobar, A. (2001) *Introducción a la lingüística hispánica.* Cambridge: Cambridge University Press.

Hudelson, S. (1981) *Learning to Read in Different Languages.* Washington, DC: Center for Applied Linguistics.

Huebner, T. (1945) What shall the aims of foreign language teaching be in the light of recent experience? *The Modern Language Journal* 29, 411–413.

Hulstijn, J.H. and Greidanus, T. (1996) Incidental vocabulary learning by advanced foreign-language students: The influence of marginal glosses, dictionary use, and reoccurrence of unknown words. *The Modern Language Journal* 80, 327–339.

Hunt, A. (1996) Evaluating bilingual and monolingual dictionaries for L2 learners. *Kansai Gadai University Journal of Inquiry and Research* 65, 15–27.

Hyams, N. (1992) A reanalysis of null subjects in child language. In J. Weissenborn, H. Goodluck and T. Tom Roeper (eds) *Theoretical Issues in Language Acquisition: Continuity and Change in Development* (pp. 249–267). Hillsdale, NJ: Lawrence Erlbaum.

Jacobsen, T. (1986) ¿Aspecto antes que tiempo? Una mirada a la aquisición temprana del español. In J. Meisel (ed.) *Adquisión del lenguaje* (pp. 97–113). Frankfurt: Vervuert.

Janda, R. and Varela-García, F. (1991) On lateral hermaphroditism and other variation in Spanish: 'Feminine'. *CLS* 27, 276–290.

Jordan, E. (1944) Languages for use and the Liberal Arts. *The Modern Language Journal* 28, 342–345.

Kachru, B.B. (1988) Teaching world Englishes. *ERIC/CLL News Bulletin* 12 (1), 1, 3–4, 8.

Keating, G.D. (2006) Processing gender agreement across phrases in Spanish: Eye movements during sentence comprehension. *Dissertation Abstracts International, A: The Humanities and Social Sciences* 66 (7), 2558-A.

Kellerman, E. (1979) Transfer and non-transfer: Where we are now. *Studies in Second Language Acquisition* 2, 37–57.

Keniston, H. (1922) The role of the graduate school in the training of the modern language teacher. *Modern Language Journal* 7, 1–4.

Kirsner, K., Brown, H.L., Abrol, S., Chadha, N.K. and Sharma, N.K. (1980) Bilingualism and lexical representation. *The Quarterly Journal of Experimental Psychology*, 32, 585–594.

Knorre, M., Dorwick, T., Pérez-Gironés, M., Glass, W. and Villarreal, H. (2008) *Puntos de Partida: An Invitation to Spanish* (8th edn). New York: McGraw-Hill.

Krashen, S. (1977) The monitor model of adult second language performance. In M. Burt, H. Dulay and M. Finocchiaro (eds) *Viewpoints on English as a Second Language* (pp. 152–161). New York: Regents.

Krashen, S. (1980) The input hypothesis. In J. Alatis (ed.) *Current Issues in Bilingual Education* (pp. 168–180). Washington DC: Georgetown University Press.

Krashen, S. (1981) *Second Language Acquisition and Language Learning*. Oxford: Pergamon.

Krashen, S. (1982) *Principles and Practices in Second Language Acquisition*. Oxford: Pergamon.

Krashen, S. (1991) The input hypothesis: An update. In J. Alatis (ed.) *Georgetown University Round Table on Languages and Linguistics 1991* (pp. 409–431). Washington, DC: Georgetown University Press.

Kroll, J. (1993) Accessing conceptual representations for words in a second language. In R. Schreuder and B. Weltens (eds) *The Bilingual Lexicon* (pp. 53–82). Amsterdam/Philadelphia: John Benjamins.

Kroll, F., Sumutka, B. and Schwartz, A. (2005) A cognitive view of the bilingual lexicon: Reading and speaking words in two languages. *International Journal of Bilingualism* 9, 27–48.

Kuijpers, C.T.L. (1996) Perception of the voicing contrast by Dutch children and adults. *Journal of Phonetics* 24, 367–382.

Kurinski, E. (2006) Gender attribution by adult native English speakers learning Spanish. Doctoral dissertation, University of Minnesota.

Kurz, H. (1943) The future of modern language teaching. *The Modern Language Journal* 27, 460–469.

Kvaal, J.T., Shipstead-Cox, N., Nevitt, S.G. and Hodson, B.W. (1988) The acquisition of 10 Spanish morphemes by Spanish speaking children. *Language, Speech, and Hearing Services in Schools* 19, 384–394.

Kvaal, J., Shipstead-Cox, N., Nevitt, S., Hodson, B. and Launer, P. (2003) The acquisition of 10 Spanish morphemes by Spanish-speaking children. *Journal of Child Language* 30, 305–331.

Labeau, E. (2005) *Beyond the Aspect Hypothesis: Tense-aspect Development in Advanced L2 French*. Oxford: Peter Lang.

Lafford, B. and Salaberry, R. (eds) (2003) *Spanish Second Language Acquisition*. Washington, DC: Georgetown University Press.

Lapesa, R. (1980) *Historia de la lengua española* (8th edn). Madrid: Gredos.

Lardiere, D. (2000) Mapping features to forms in second language acquisition. In J. Archibald (ed.) *Second Language Acquisition and Linguistic Theory* (pp. 102–120). Malden, MA/Oxford: Blackwell.

Lathrop, T. (1980) *The Evolution of Spanish: An Introductory Historical Grammar*. Newark, DE: Juan de la Cuesta.

Laufer, B. and Paribakht, T. (1998) The relationship between passive and active vocabularies: Effects of language learning context. *Language Learning* 48, 365–391.

Lázaro Mora, M. (1999) La derivación apreciativa. In I. Bosque and V. Delmonte (eds) *Gramática descriptiva de la lengua española* (pp. 4645–4682). Madrid: Espasa.

Lenneberg, E. (1967) *The Biological Foundations of Language*. New York: Wiley.

Leonetti, M. (1999) El artículo. In I. Bosque and V. Delmonte (eds) *Gramática descriptiva de la lengua española* (pp. 787–890). Madrid: Espasa.

Levac, P. (1991) Teaching languages communicatively: An examination of the presentation of phonology to first-year students of French. In J. Alatis (ed.) *Georgetown University Round Table on Languages and Linguistics 1991* (pp. 215–222). Washington, DC: Georgetown University Press.

Lightbown, P. and Spada, N. (2006) *How Languages are Learned.* Oxford: Oxford University Press.

Lipski, J. (1994) *Latin American Spanish.* Harlow: Longman.

Lipski, J. (1997) El lenguaje de los *negros congos* de Panamá y el *lumbalú* palenquero: Función sociolingüística de criptolectos afrohispánicos. *América Negra* 14, 147–165.

Llorente, L. (2005) Language and politics: Lexical borrowing in the Castilian Spanish of the Basque country. *Paper presented at the 62nd Annual Meeting of the South Central Modern Language Association (SCMLA),* Houston, TX, 27–29 October.

Llorente, L. and Parra, M.F. (2006a) Uso del diccionario en la clase de traducción: Algunas reflexiones. *Paper presented at the 88th Annual Conference of the American Association of Teachers of Spanish and Portuguese (AATSP),* Salamanca, Spain, 27 June–2 July.

Llorente, L. and Parra, M.F. (2006b) Can translation be taught? An introduction to translation for the undergraduate language student. *Paper presented at the 63rd Annual Meeting of the South Central Modern Language Association (SCMLA),* Dallas–Fort Worth, TX, 26–28 October.

Lloyd, P. (1987) *From Latin to Spanish.* Philadelphia, PA: Memoirs of the American Philosophical Society.

London, G.H., Mead, R.G. and London, K. (1955) A guide for the Spanish major. *Hispania* 1955, 131–149.

Lope Blanch, J. (1988) *Estudios de lingüística hispanoamericana.* México DF: Publicaciones del Centro de Lingüística Hispánica, UNAM.

López Morales, H. (2005) *La aventura del español en América.* Madrid: Espasa-Calpe.

López Ornat, S. (1997) What lies in between a pre-grammatical and a grammatical representation? Evidence on nominal and verbal form-function mapping in Spanish from 1;7 to 2;1. In A. Pérez-Leroux and W. Glass (eds) *Contemporary Perspectives on the Acquisition of Spanish* (pp. 12–38). Somerville, MA: Cascadilla Press.

Lyster, R. and Ranta, L. (1997) Corrective feedback and learner uptake. Negotiation of form in communicative classrooms. *Studies in Second Language Acquisition* 20, 37–66.

MacAllister, A. (1964) The preparation of college teachers of modern foreign languages. *Hispania* 47, 544–559.

Mackenzie, I. (2001) *A Linguistic Introduction to Spanish.* Munich: Lincolm.

Mapes, E.K. (1943) Teaching modern languages in war time. *The Modern Language Journal* 27, 538–555.

Marchman, V. (1993) Constraints on plasticity in a Connectionist Model of the English past tense. *Journal of Cognitive Neuroscience* 5, 215–234.

Márquez Reiter, R. and Placencia, M. (eds) (2004) *Current Trends in Pragmatics of Spanish.* Amsterdam/Philadelphia: John Benjamins.

Mathis, T. and Yule, G. (1994) Zero quotatives. *Discourse Processor* 18, 63–76.

McCuaig, W.D. (1940) A reconsideration of the teaching of Spanish on the undergraduate level. *The Modern Language Journal* 25, 108–112.

Meador, D., Flege, J.E. and MacKay, I.R.A. (1997) Nonnatives' perception of English sentences presented in noise. *Journal of the Acoustical Society of America* 101 (A), 3129.

Menéndez Pidal, R. (1940) *Manual de gramática histórica española,* (23rd edn). Madrid: Espasa-Calpe.

Mesthrie, R., Swann, J., Deumert, A. and Leap, W. (2002) *Introducing Sociolinguistics.* Edinburgh: Edinburgh University Press.

Michie, S. (1938) A new general language curriculum for the eighth grade. *The Modern Language Journal* 22, 343–347.

Miller, N.A. and Kroll, J.F. (2002) Stroop effects in bilingual translation. *Memory & Cognition* 30, 614–628.

Modern Language Association (1973) *Modern Spanish.* New York: Harcourt Brace Jovanovich.

Modern Language Journal (1955) Qualifications for secondary school teachers of modern foreign languages. *The Modern Language Journal* 39, 290–292.

Modern Language Journal. Part III (1966) Guidelines for teacher education programs in modern foreign languages. *The Modern Language Journal* 50, 342–344.

Montrul, S. (2004) *The Acquisition of Spanish.* Amsterdam: Benjamins.

Moreno de Alba, J. (1992) *Diferencias léxicas entre España y América.* Madrid: Mapfre.

Morgan, B. (1944) After the war. *The Modern Language Journal* 28, 323–324.

Mott, B. (1996) *A Spanish–English, English–Spanish Translation Companion for Spanish Learners of English.* Barcelona: EUB, S.L.

Moulin, A. (1987) The dictionary and encoding tasks. In A. Cowie (ed.) *The Dictionary and the Language Learner* (pp. 105–114). Tübingen: Niemayer.

Mueller Gathercole, V., Sebastián, E. and Soto, P. (1999) The early acquisition of Spanish verbal morphology: Across-the-board or piecemeal knowledge? *International Journal of Bilingualism* 3, 133–182.

Murillo Medrano, J. (2002) Verbal courtesy in Costa Rican Spanish. *Cañiña* 109–118.

Nabholz, J. (1953) Applied philology. *The Modern Language Journal* 37, 347–350.

Nash, R. (1973) Orthographic interference in pronunciation. In R. Nash (ed.) *Readings in Spanish–English Contrastive Linguistics* (pp. 123–135). Puerto Rico: Inter American University Press.

Nation, P. (1990) *Teaching and Learning Vocabulary.* New York: Newbury House/ Harper & Row.

Nation, P. and Waring, R. (1997) Vocabulary size, text coverage and word lists. In N. Schmitt and M. McCarthy (eds) *Vocabulary: Description, Acquisition and Pedagogy* (pp. 6–19). Cambridge: Cambridge University Press.

Odlin, T. (2001) With the dictionaries and beyond. In D. Belcher and Alan Hirvela (eds) *Linkng Literacies: Perspectives on L2 Reading–Writing Connections* (pp. 271–290). Ann Arbor: The University of Michigan Press.

Oliver, R. (1995) Negative feedback in child NS–NNS conversation. *Studies in Second Language Acquisition* 17 (4), 459–481.

Omaggio Hadley, A. (1993) *Teaching for Proficiency* (2nd edn). Boston: Heinle & Heinle.

Ordóñez, F. and Olarrea, A. (2001) Weak subject pronouns in Caribbean Spanish and XP pied-piping. In J. Herschensohn, E. Mallén and K. Karen Zagona (eds) *Features and Interfaces in Romance* (pp. 223–238). Amsterdam/Philadelphia: Benjamins.

Oxford Spanish Dictionary (1998) C. Styles Carvajal and J. Horwood (eds) (2nd edn). Oxford/New York/Madrid: Oxford University Press.

Oyama, S. (1973) *A sensitive period for the acquisition of a second language.* Unpublished doctoral dissertation, Harvard University.

Oyama, S. (1979) The concept of the sensitive period in developmental studies. *Merrill-Palmer Quarterly* 25, 83–103.

Oyama, S. (1982a) A sensitive period for the acquisition of a nonnative phonological system. In S. Krashen, R. Scarcella and M. Long (eds) *Child–Adult Differences in Second Language Acquisition* (pp. 105–109). Rowley, MA: Newbury House.

Oyama, S. (1982b) The sensitive period for the comprehension of speech. In R.S. Krashen, R. Scarcella and M. Long (eds) *Child–Adult Differences in Second Language Acquisition* (pp. 39–51). Rowley, MA: Newbury House.

Papagno, C. and Vallar, G. (1992) Phonological short term memory and the learning of novel words. *Quarterly Journal of Experimental Psychology* 44A, 47–67.

Pargment, M.S. (1945) On learning a foreign language. *The Modern Language Journal* 29, 198–209.

Paribakht, T.S. and Wesche, M. (1999) "Incidental" L2 vocabulary acquisition through reading: An introspective study. In M. Wesche and T.S. Paribakht (guest eds) *Studies in Second Language Acquisition* 21(2), 195–224.

Pennington, M. (1989) Teaching pronunciation from the top down. *RELC Journal* 20, 20–38.

Penny, R. (1991) *A History of the Spanish Language.* Cambridge: Cambridge University Press.

Penny, R. (2000) *Variation and Change in Spanish.* Cambridge: Cambridge University Press.

Pica, T., Young, R. and Doughty, C. (1987) The impact of interaction on comprehension. *TESOL Quarterly* 21(4), 737–758.

Pienemann, M. (1998) Developmental dynamics in L1 and L2 acquisition: Processibility theory and generative entrenchment. *Bilingualism: Language and Cognition* 1, 1–20.

Pinto, D. (2002) Passing greetings and interactional style: A cross-cultural study of American English and Peninsular Spanish. *Multilingual Journal of Cross Cultural and Interlanguage Communication* 27(4), 371–388.

Placencia, M. and García, C. (2007) *Research on Politeness in the Spanish-speaking World.* Mahwah: Erlbaum.

Population Resource Center (2004) *Executive Summary: A Demographic Profile of Hispanics in the U.S.* Washington, DC: Population Resource Center.

Posner, R. (1996) *The Romance Languages.* Cambridge: Cambridge University Press.

Potter, M., So, K., VonEckardt, B. and Feldman, L. (1984) Lexical and conceptual representation in beginning and proficient bilinguals. *Journal of Verbal Learning and Verbal Behavior* 23, 23–38.

Pountain, C. (2001) *A History of the Spanish Language Through Texts.* New York: Routledge.

Prévost, P. and White, L. (2000) Missing surface inflection or impairment in second language acquisition? Evidence from tense and agreement. *Second Language Research* 16 (2), 103–133.

Prince, J. R. (1954) Philology at work. *The Modern Language Journal* 38, 75–79.

Purin, C. (1928) *The Training of Teachers of Modern Foreign Languages.* New York: MacMillan (A.C.C.M.L.).

Quilis, A. and Fernández, J.A. (1992) *Curso de fonética y fonología españolas*. Madrid: Consejo Supperior de Investigaciones Científicas.

Real Academia Española (1973) *Esbozo de una nueva gramática de la lengua española*. Madrid: Espasa-Calpe (decimoquinta reimpresión, 1996).

Real Academia Española (2005) *Diccionario panhispánico de dudas*. Madrid: Editorial Santillana.

Resnick, M. (1981) *Introducción a la historia de la lengua española*. Washington, DC: Georgetown University Press.

Rini, J. (1990) The application of historical linguistic information to the foreign language classroom. *Hispania* 73, 842–844.

Ritchie, W. and Bhatia, T. (1996) *Handbook of Second Language Acquisition*. San Diego: Academic Press.

Rivero, M.L. (1980) On left-dislocation and topicalization in Spanish. *Linguistic Inquiry* 11, 363–393.

Rivers, W. (1992) *Teaching Languages in College: Curriculum and Content*. Lincolnwood, IL: National Textbook Company.

Rivers, W., Azevedo, M. and Heflin, W.H. (1989) *Teaching Spanish: A Practical Guide*. Chicago: National Textbook Company.

Rochet, B. (1995) Perception and production of L2 speech sounds by adults. In W. Strange (ed.) *Speech Perception and Linguistic Experience: Theoretical and Methodological Issues* (pp. 379–410). Timonium, MD: York Press.

Romaine, S. and Lange, D. (1991) The use of *like* as a marker of reported speech and thought: A case of grammaticalization progress in progress. *American Speech* 63 (3), 234–246.

Rona, J. (1969) *Buenas y malas palabras en el castellano de Venezuela*. Madrid: Mediterráneo.

Rosch, E. (1983) Prototype classification and logical classification: The two systems. In E. Scholnick (ed.) *New Trends in Cognitive Representation: Challenges to Piaget's Theory* (pp. 73–86). Mahwah: Erlbaum Associates.

Rosenblat, A. (1958) *El castellano de Venezuela. La influencia indígena*. Caracas: Universidad Central de Venezuela.

Sagarra, N. and Herschensohn, J. (2008) Processing gender and number in L2 Spanish. *Conference presentation, Linguistic Symposium on Romance Languages*. University of Illinois at Urbana-Champaign, April.

Salaberry, R. (2002) Tense and aspect in the selection of past tense verbal morphology. In R. Salaberry and Y. Shirai (eds) *Tense-Aspect Morphology in L2 Acquisition* (pp. 397–415). Amsterdam and Philadelphia: John Benjamins.

Salaberry, R. and Lafford, B. (eds) (2006) *The Art of Teaching Spanish*. Washington, DC: Georgetown University Press.

Salaberry, R., Barrette, C., Elliott, P. and Fernández-García, M. (2004) *Impresiones*. Upper Saddle River: Pearson/Prentice-Hall.

Sánchez-Muñoz, A. (2007a) Style variation in Spanish as a heritage language: A study of discourse particles in academic and non-academic registers. In K. Potowski and R. Cameron (eds) *Spanish in Contact: Policy, Social and Linguistic Inquiries* (pp. 153–171). Amsterdam/Philadelphia: John Benjamins.

Sánchez-Muñoz, A. (2007b) Register and style variation in speakers of Spanish as a heritage and as a second language. Unpublished PhD dissertation, University of Southern California.

Saville-Troike, M. (2006) *Introducing Second Language Acquisition*. Cambridge: Cambridge University Press.

Schrader Knissi, M. (2004) Speaking Spanish with Zapotec meaning: Requests and promises in intercultural communication in Oaxaca, Mexico. In R. Márquez Reiter and M. Placencia (eds) *Current Trends in the Pragmatics of Spanish* (pp. 157–174). Amsterdam: John Benjamins.

Schulz, R. (2000) Foreign language teacher development: MLJ perspectives 1916–1999. *The Modern Language Journal* 84, 495–522.

Schutz, A.H. (1939) About intermediate linguistics. *The Modern Language Journal* 23, 489–499.

Schwartz, A.I., Kroll, J.F. and Diaz, M. (2007) Reading words in Spanish and English: Mapping orthography to phonology in two languages. *Language and Cognitive Processes* 22, 106–129.

Schwenter, S.A. (1993) Diferenciación dialectal por medio de pronombres: una comparación del uso de tú y usted en España y México. *Nueva Revista de Filología Hispánica* 41(1), 127–149.

Selinker, L. (1972) Interlanguage. *International Review of Applied Linguistics* 10, 209–231.

Service, E. (1992) Phonology, working memory, and foreign language learning. *Quarterly Journal of Experimental Psychology* 45A, 21–50.

Shanahan, D. (1997) Articulating the relationship between language, literature, and culture: Toward a new agenda for foreign language teaching and research. *The Modern Language Journal* 81, 164–174.

Sharwood Smith, M. (1993) Input enhancement in instructed SLA: Theoretical bases. *Studies in Second Language Acquisition* 15, 183–203.

Siegel, R. (2007) Hispanics in the U.S.: Breaking down the numbers. On WWW at http://npr.org. Accessed 26 January 2007.

Silva-Corvalán, S. (1989) *Sociolingüística. Teoría y análisis*. Madrid: Editorial Alhambra.

Simões, A. (1996) Phonetics in second language acquisition: An acoustic study of fluency in adult learners of Spanish. *Hispania* 79, 87–95.

Simpson, L. (1945) Linguistic blitz. *The Modern Language Journal* 29, 382–385.

Singer, A. (1946) A reexamination of objectives in teaching Spanish. *The Modern Language Journal* 30, 337–344.

Skinner, B.F. (1957) *Verbal Learning*. New York: Appleton-Century-Crofts.

Smith, P., Nix, A., Davey, N., López Ornat, S. and Messer, D. (2003) A connectionist account of Spanish determiner production. *Journal of Child Language* 30 (2), 305–331.

Stewart, M. (1999) *The Spanish Language Today*. New York: Routledge.

Stockwell, R.P. and Bower, T. (1969) *The Sounds of English and Spanish*. Chicago: The University of Chicago.

Stroop, J. (1935) Studies of interference in serial verbal reactions. *Journal of Experimental Psychology* 18, 643–662.

Strozer, J. (1976) *Clitics in Spanish*. Unpublished PhD dissertation, University of California, Las Vegas.

Suter, R. (1976) Predicators of pronunciation accuracy in second language learning. *Language Learning* 26, 233–533.

Swaffar, J., Arens, K. and Byrnes, H. (1991) *Reading for Meaning: An Integrated Approach to Language Learning*. Englewood Cliffs, NJ: Prentice-Hall.

Teichrow, F.M. (1982) A study of receptive versus productive vocabulary. *Interlanguage Studies Bulletin* 6, 3–33.

Terrell, T. (1982) The natural approach to language teaching. An update. *Modern Language Journal* 66, 121–132.

Terrell, T. (1989) Teaching Spanish pronunciation in a communicative approach. In P. Bjarkman and R. Hammond (eds) *American Spanish Pronunciation* (pp. 196–214). Washington, DC: Georgetown University Press.

Terrell, T., Andrade, M., Egasse, J. and Muñoz, E. (2006) *Dos Mundos*. New York: Random House.

Teschner, R. (2000) *Camino oral. Fonética, fonología y práctica de los sonidos del español*. New York: McGraw-Hill.

Teschner, R., Bills, G. and Craddock, J. (1975) *Spanish and English of United States Hispanos: A Critical, Annotated, Llinguistic Bibliography*. Washington, DC: Center for Applied Linguistics.

Tharp, J. (1946) The training of foreign language teachers for current methods and objectives. *The Modern Language Journal* 30, 413–420.

Toribio, A. (2000) Setting parametric limits on dialectal variation in Spanish. *Lingua* 110, 315–341.

Torrejón, A. (1986) Acerca del *voseo* culto en Chile. *Hispania* 69, 677–683.

Torrejón, A. (1991) Fórmulas de tratamiento de segunda persona singular en el español de Chile. *Hispania* 74, 1068–1079.

Torres Cacoullos, R. (1999) Construction frequency and reductive change: Diachronic and register variation in Spanish clitic climbing. *Language Variation and Change* 11, 143–170.

Trahey, M. and White, L. (1993) Positive evidence and preemption in the second language classroom. *Studies in Second Language Acquisition* 15 (2), 181–203.

Tsimpli, I. and Dimitrakopoulou, M. (2007) The interpretability hypothesis: Evidence from WH-interrogatives in second language acquisition. *Second Language Research* 23 (2), 215–242.

Underhill, A. (1980) *Use Your Dictionary*. London: Oxford University Press.

U.S. Office of Education, Federal Security Agency (1943) Adjustment of the college-curriculum to wartime conditions and needs. *Hispania* 26, 430–438.

U.S. Census Bureau (2003) *Census 2000 Brief: Language Use and English-Language Ability*. Washington, DC: U.S. Census Bureau.

Valdés, G. (1991) *Bilingual Minorities and Language Issues in Writing: Toward Profession-Wide Responses to a New Challenge*. National Center for the Study of Writing and Literacy Technical Report 54.

Valdés, G. (1997) The teaching of Spanish to bilingual Spanish-speaking students: Outstanding issues and unanswered questions. In M. Celilia Colombi and F. Alarcón (eds) *La enseñanza del español a hispanohablantes: Praxis y teoría* (pp. 8–44). Boston, MA: Houghton Mifflin.

Valdés, G. (2000) Introduction. In The American Association of Teachers of Spanish and Portuguese (ed.) *Professional Development Series Handbook for Teacher K-16: Vol. I. Spanish for Native Speakers* (pp. 1–20). Fort Worth, TX: Harcourt College.

Van Heuven, W., Dijkstra, A. and Grainger, J. (1998) Orthographic neighborhood effects in bilingual word recognition. *Journal of Memory and Language* 39, 458–483.

Van Patten, B. (1996) *Input Processing and Grammar Instruction: Theory and Research*. Stamford: Ablex.

Van Patten, B. (2003) *From Input to Output: A Teacher's Guide to Second Language Acquisition*. New York: McGraw-Hill.

Van Patten, B. (2004a) *Form–Meaning Connections in Second Language Acquisition*. Boston, MA: Erlbaum.

Van Patten, B. (2004b) *Processing Instruction: Theory, Research, and Commentary.* Boston: Erlbaum.

Vendler, Z. (1967) *Linguistics in Philosophy.* Ithaca: Cornell University Press.

Walsh, T. (1985) The historical origin of syllable final aspirated /s/ in dialectal Spanish. *Journal of Hispanic Philology* 9, 231–246.

Weinrich, U. (1955) *Languages in Contact.* New York: Linguistic Circle of New York.

White, L., Valenzuela, E. and Kozlowska-MacGregor, M. (2004) Gender and number agreement in nonnative Spanish. *Applied Psycholinguistics* 25 (1), 105–133.

Whitley, M.S. (2002) *Spanish/English Contrasts: A Course in Spanish Linguistics.* Washington DC: Georgetown University Press.

Wieczorek, J. (1991) Spanish dialects and the foreign language textbook: A sound perspective. *Hispania* 74, 174–181.

Wong, R. (1985) Does pronunciation teaching have a place in the communicative classroom? In J. Alatis (ed.) *Georgetown University Round Table on Languages and Linguistics 1991* (pp. 226–236). Washington, DC: Georgetown University Press.

Yeni-Komshian, G., Flege, J. and Lieu, H. (1997) Pronunciation proficiency in L1 and L2 among Korean–English bilinguals: The effect of age of arrival in the U.S. *The Journal of the Acoustical Society of America* 3138.

Zagona, K. (2002) *The Syntax of Spanish.* Cambridge: Cambridge University Press.

Zamora Vicente, A. (1960) *Dialectología española* (2a edición, 1967). Madrid: Gredos.

Zamora Munné, J. and Guitart, J. (1982) *Dialectología hispanoamericana: Teoría-descripción-historia.* Salamanca: Ediciones Alimar, SA.

Zampini, M. (1994) The role of native language transfer and task formality in the acquisition of Spanish spirantization. *Hispania* 77, 470–481.

Websites Cited

http://www.cal.org/resources/diest/0104dialects.html
http://www.cal.org/heritage/sns/sns-fieldrpt.html
http://www.mla.org/auto/stest.pl?/adfl/bulletin/v32n1/321027
www.npr.org
www.sil.org
http://www.prcdc.org/summaries/hispanics/hispanics.html

Suggestions for Future Reading

General Linguistics

Alcaraz Varó, E. and Linares, M. (1977) *Diccionario de lingüística moderna*. Barcelona: Editorial Ariel.

Bergmann, A., Currie Hall, K. and Miriam Ross, S. (2007) *Language Files: Materials for an Introduction to Language and Linguistics*. Columbus: The Ohio State University Press.

Crystal, D. (1980) *A Dictionary of Linguistics and Phonetics* (3rd edn). London: Blackwell.

Fromkin, V., Rodman, R. and Hyams, N. (2007) *An Introduction to Language*. Boston: Heinle & Heinle.

Marcellesi, J. and Gardin, B. (1979) *Introducción a la lingüística*. Madrid: Gredos.

Heritage Language Speakers and Bilingualism

Colombi, C. and Alarcón, F. (eds) (1997) *La enseñanza del español a hispanohablantes*. Boston: Houghton Mifflin.

Dulay, H., Burt, M. and Krashen, S. (1982) *Language Two*. New York: Oxford University Press.

Gonzalez Pino, B. and Pino, F. (2000) Serving the heritage speaker across a five-year program. *ADLF Bulletin* 32, 27–35.

Gonzalez Pino, B. and Pino, F. (2008) A second look at linguistic self-concept of heritage speakers of Spanish in the United States. *Paper presented at the 65th Annual Meeting of the South Central Modern Language Association (SCMLA)*. San Antonio, TX, 8 November.

Makkai, V. (1975) Bilingual phonology: Systematic or autonomous? In P. Reich (ed.) *The Second LACUS Forum* (pp. 596–601). Columbia, MD: Hornbeam Press.

Valdés, G., Anthony, G.L. and Rodolfo, G.-M. (1985) *Teaching Spanish to the Hispanic Bilingual: Issues, Aims, and Methods*. New York: Teachers' College Press.

Hispanic Linguistics

Alarcos, E. (1984) *Estudios de gramática funcional del español*. Madrid: Gredos.

Alvar, M. and Pottier, B. (1983) *Morfología histórica del español*. Madrid: Gredos.

Azevedo, M. (1992) *Introducción a la lingüística española*. Upper Saddle River: Prentice Hall.

Barrutia, R. and Schwegler, A. (1994) *Fonética y fonología españolas: teoría y práctica*. New York: Wiley & Sons, Inc.

Bosque, I. and Demonte, V. (1999) *Gramática descriptiva de la lengua española*. Madrid: Espasa.

Dalbor, J. (1981) *Spanish Pronunciation: Theory and Practice*. Fort Worth: Holt, Rinehart & Winston.

Dalbor, J. (1996) *Spanish Pronunciation: Theory and Practice*. Fort Worth: Holt, Rinehart & Winston.

Hualde, J., Olarrea, A. and Escobar, A. (2001) *Introducción a la lingüística hispánica*. Cambridge: Cambridge University Press.

Laca, B. (1999) Presencia y ausencia de determinante. In I. Bosque and V. Delmonte (eds) *Gramática descriptiva de la lengua española* (pp. 891–928). Madrid: Espasa.

Mackenzie, I. (2001) *A Linguistic Introduction to Spanish*. Munich: Lincoln.

Quilis, A. and Fernández, J.J. (1992) *Curso de fonética y fonología españolas*. Madrid: Consejo Superior de Investigaciones Científicas.

Real Academia Española (1973) *Esbozo de una nueva gramática de la lengua española*. Madrid: Espasa-Calpe (decimoquinta reimpresión, 1996).

Seco, M. (1992) *Gramática esencial del español*. Madrid: Editorial Aguilar.

Stewart, M. (1999) *The Spanish Language Today*. New York: Routledge.

Teschner, R. (2000) *Camino oral. Fonética, fonología y práctica de los sonidos del español*. New York: McGraw-Hill.

Zagona, K. (2002) *The Syntax of Spanish*. Cambridge: Cambridge University Press.

History of Spanish

Cano, R. (2004) *Historia de la lengua española*. Barcelona: Editorial Ariel.

Fontanella de Weinberg, M.B. (1992) *El Español de América*. Madrid: Mapfre.

Lapesa, R. (1980) *Historia de la lengua española*. Madrid: Gredos.

Lathrop, T. (1980) *The Evolution of Spanish: An Introductory Historical Grammar*. Newark, DE: Juan de la Cuesta.

Lloyd, P.M. (1987) *From Latin to Spanish* (Vol. 173). Philadelphia: Memoirs of the American Philosophical Society.

Menéndez Pidal, R. (1940) *Manual de gramática histórica española* (23rd edn). Madrid: Espasa-Calpe.

Penny, R. (1991) *A History of the Spanish Language*. Cambridge: Cambridge University Press.

Pharies, D.S. (2007) *Breve historia de la lengua española*. Chicago: University of Chicago Press.

Posner, R. (1996) *The Romance Languages*. Cambridge: Cambridge University Press.

Resnick, M. (1981) *Introducción a la historia de la lengua española*. Washington, DC: Georgetown University Press.

Urrutia, H. and Álvarez, C. (1988) *Esquema de morfosintaxis histórica del español*. Bilbao: Publicaciones de la Universidad de Deusto.

Woehr, R. (1992) The undergraduate meets Spanish language history. *Hispania* 75(2), 391–397.

L2 Acquisition

Altman, G. (1990) Cognitive models of speech processing: An Introduction. In G. Altman (ed.) *Cognitive Models of Speech Processing: Psycholinguistic and Computational Perspectives* (pp. 1–23). Cambridge, MA: MIT Press.

Archibald, J. (2000) *Second Language Acquisition and Linguistic Theory.* Malden, MA/Oxford: Blackwell.

Brown, D.H. (2000) *Principles of Language Learning and Teaching.* Englewood Cliffs, NJ: Prentice-Hall.

Diehl, R. (1991) The role of phonetics within the study of language. *Phonetica* 48, 120–134.

Duphenthaler, P. (1991) What about pronunciation? *English Today* 27, 32–36.

Ellis, R. (2002) *Second Language Acquisition.* New York: Oxford University Press.

Hecht, B. and Mulford, R. (1987) The acquisition of a second language phonology: Interaction of transfer and developmental factors. In G. Ioup and S. Weinburger (eds) *Interlanguage Phonology* (pp. 213–229). Cambridge, MA: Newbury House.

Krashen, S. (1981) *Second Language Acquisition and Language Learning.* Oxford: Pergamon.

Lafford, B. and Salaberry, R. (eds) (2003) *Spanish Second Language Acquisition.* Washington, DC: Georgetown University Press.

Lenneberg, E. (1967) *The Biological Foundations of Language.* New York: Wiley.

Lightbown, P.M. and Spada, N. (2006) *How Languages are Learned.* Oxford: Oxford University Press.

Macken, M. and Ferguson, C. (1987) Phonological universals in language acquisition. In G. Ioup and S. Weinburger (eds) *Interlanguage Phonology* (pp. 3–22). Cambridge, MA: Newbury House.

McLaughlin, B. (1977) Second language learning in children. *Psychological Bulletin* 84, 438–459.

Mitchell, R. and Myles, F. (2004) *Second Language Learning Theories.* London: Arnold.

Ritchie, W. and Bhatia, T. (1996) *Handbook of Second Language Acquisition.* San Diego: Academic Press.

Saville-Troike, M. (2006) *Introducing Second Language Acquisition.* Cambridge: Cambridge University Press.

Tarone, E. (1987) The phonology of interlanguage. In G. Ioup and S. Weinburger (eds) *Interlanguage Phonology* (pp. 70–85). Cambridge, MA: Newbury House.

Van Patten, B. (1996) *Input Processing and Grammar Instruction: Theory and Research.* Stamford: Ablex.

Van Patten, B. (2003) *From Input to Output: A Teacher's Guide to Second Language Acquisition.* New York: McGraw-Hill.

Van Patten, B. (2004a) *Form-Meaning Connections in Second Language Aacquisition.* Boston: Erlbaum.

Van Patten, B. (2004b) *Processing Instruction: Theory, Research, and Commentary.* Boston: Erlbaum.

Weeren, J. and Theunissen, J.J.M. (1987) Testing pronunciation: An application of generalizability theory. *Language Learning* 37, 109–122.

L2 Pedagogy

Carroll, J.B. (1963) Research on teaching foreign languages. In N. Gage (ed.) *Handbook of Research on Teaching* (pp. 1060–1100). Chicago: Rand McNally.

Celce-Murcia, M. (1987) Teaching pronunciation as communication. In J. Morley (ed.) *Current Perspectives on Pronunciation: Practices Anchored in Theory* (pp. 1–12). Washington, DC: TESOL.

Gutiérrez, M. and Fairclough, M. (2006) Incorporating linguistic variation into the classroom. In R. Salaberry and B. Lafford (eds) *The Art of Teaching Spanish* (pp. 173–191). Washington, DC: Georgetown University Press.

Hadley, A.O. (2003) *Teaching Language in Context: Proficiency-oriented Instruction* (3rd edn). Boston, MA: Heinle & Heinle.

Hammerly, H. (1973) The correction of pronunciation errors. *The Modern Language Journal* 57, 106–110.

Herschensohn, J. (1990) Toward a theoretical basis for current language pedagogy. *The Modern Language Journal* 74, 451–458.

Herschensohn, J. (1993) Applying linguistics to teach morphology: Verb and adjective inflection in French. *International Review of Applied Linguistics in Language Teaching* 32, 97–112.

Leckie-Tarry, H. (1993) The specification of a text: Register, genre and language teaching. In M. Ghadessy (ed.) *Register Analysis: Theory and Practice* (pp. 26–42). London: Frances Pinter.

Lyster, R. and Ranta, L. (1997) Corrective feedback and learner uptake negotiation of form in communicative classrooms. *Studies in Second Language Acquisition* 20, 37–66.

Nation, I.S.P. (1990) *Teaching and Learning Vocabulary*. New York: Newbury House/Harper & Row.

Richard-Amato, P. (1996) *Making it Happen: Interaction in the Second Language Classroom: From Theory to Practice*. White Plains, NY: Longman.

Stevick, E. (1982) *Teaching and Learning Languages*. Cambridge: Cambridge University Press.

Strevens, P. (1988) Language learning and language teaching: Towards an integrated model. In D. Tannen (ed.) *Linguistics in Context: Connecting Observation and Understanding* (pp. 299–312). Norwood, NJ: Ablex.

Tschirner, E. (1996) Scope and sequence: Rethinking beginning foreign language instruction. *The Modern Language Journal* 80, 1–14.

Valdman, A. (1988) Classroom foreign language learning and language variation: The notion of pedagogical norms. *World Englishes* 7, 221–236.

Van Patten, B. and Cardierno, T. (1993) Explicit instruction and input processing. *Studies in Second Language Acquisition* 18, 495–510.

White, L. (1991) Adverb placement in second language acquisition: Some effects of positive and negative evidence in the classroom. *Second Language Research* 7, 133–161.

Wipf, J. (1985) Towards improving second-language pronunciation. *Die Unterrichtspraxis* 18, 54–63.

Yule, G. and MacDonald, D. (1995) The different effects of pronunciation teaching. *International Review of Applied Linguistics in Language Teaching* 33, 345–350.

Spanish Dialectology

Alonso, A. (1982) *Estudios lingüísticos. Temas hispanoamericanos*. Madrid: Gredos.

Alvar, M. (2000) *Manual de dialectología hispánica. El español de América*. Barcelona: Editorial Ariel.

Canfield, D. (1981) *Spanish Pronunciation in the Americas*. Chicago, IL: University of Chicago Press.

Cotton, E. and Sharp, J. (1998) *Spanish in the Americas*. Washington, DC: Georgetown University Press.
Fontanella de Weinberg, M. (1976) *La lengua española fuera de España*. Madrid: Paidós.
Fontanella de Weinberg, M. (1995) *El español de América*. Madrid: Mapfre.
Lipski, J. (1994) *Latin American Spanish*. Harlow: Longman.
Lipski, J. (1989) Beyond the isogloss: Trends in Hispanic dialectology. *Hispania* 72, 801–809.
Lope Blanch, J. (1988) *Estudios de lingüística hispanoamericana*. México DF: Publicaciones del Centro de Lingüística Hispánica, UNAM.
Montes Giraldo, J. (1982) *Dialectología general e hispanoamericana*. Bogotá: Publicaciones del Instituto Caro y Cuervo.
Núñez Cedeño, R.A., Baez, P. and Guitart, J.M. (eds) (1986) *Estudios sobre la fonología del español del Caribe*. Caracas: Fundación Casa de Bello.
Roca, A. and Lipski, J. (eds) (1993) *Spanish in the United States: Linguistic Contact and Diversity*. Berlin/New York: Mouton de Gruyter.
Rosenblat, A. (1958) *El castellano de Venezuela. La influencia indígena*. Caracas: Universidad Central de Venezuela.
Zamora Vicente, A. (1960) *Dialectología española* (2a edición, 1967). Madrid: Gredos.
Zamora Munné, J. and Guitart, J. (1982) *Dialectología hispanoamericana: Teoría-descripción-historia*. Salamanca: Ediciones Alimar, SA.

Spanish Sociolinguistics

Chambers, J. (1995) *Sociolinguistic Theory*. Oxford: Blackwell.
Eckert, P. and Rickford, J. (2001) *Style and Sociolinguistic Variation*. Malden, MA: Blackwell.
Fasold, R. (1990) *The Sociolinguistics of Language*. Oxford: Blackwell.
García, C. (2004a) Coercion and cooperation: A case study of Argentinean reprimands and response to reprimands. In R. Márquez Reiter and M. Placencia (eds) *Current Trends in Pragmatics of Spanish* (pp. 231–265). Amsterdam/Philadelphia: John Benjamins.
García, C. (2004b) Reprendiendo y respondiendo a una reprimenda: Similitudes y diferencias entre peruanos y venezolanos. *Spanish in Context* 1 (1), 113–147.
Gimeno, F. (1990) *Dialectología y sociolingüística españolas*. Alicante: Universidad de Alicante.
Mar-Molinero, C. (1997) *The Spanish-speaking World: A Practical Introduction to Sociolinguistic Issues*. London: Routledge.
Márquez Reiter, R. and Placencia, M. (2004) *Current Trends in the Pragmatics of Spanish*. Amsterdam/Philadelphia: John Benjamins.
Placencia, M. and García, C. (2007) *Research on Politeness in the Spanish-speaking World*. Mahwah: Erlbaum.
Silva-Corvalán, S. (1989) *Sociolingüística: Teoría y análisis*. Madrid: Editorial Alhambra.

Author Index

Subject Index

Josep Ballarín

4 lenguas oficiales
- español
- gallego
- vasco
- catalan

3 tipos de bilinguismos
- individual
- territorial
- social

bilinguismo pasivo
        activo

diversos grados.
    symmetrico
    vr
    asymmetrico

territorio
cada lengua
fijada en un
territorio
no ahi conflicto
se acopla a la lengua
del territorio

Comunidad
2 lenguas.
conflicto linguistico / social.

differencia
en el uso

cataluña
individual
social.
(no reutilizan al 50%
election de lengua

inseguridad linguistica

altero poseensie

lengua inmigrade
menos lengua

catalan 7 dialectos.

10%

Siglo 20

lenguas fluchan.
arma politica.
identidades.

1976
1978 constitución
    4 lenguas
    reconocidos.

poder
contexto
proposito